vabnf   VAL
303.484 NASSA

Nassauer, Anne, 1982- author
Situational breakdowns
33410016688964   07/24/20

DISCARD

DISCARD

D1565479

Valparaiso Public Library
103 Jefferson Street
Valparaiso, IN 46383

Situational Breakdowns

Situational Breakdowns

UNDERSTANDING PROTEST VIOLENCE
AND OTHER SURPRISING OUTCOMES

ANNE NASSAUER

OXFORD
UNIVERSITY PRESS

OXFORD
UNIVERSITY PRESS

Oxford University Press is a department of the University of Oxford. It furthers
the University's objective of excellence in research, scholarship, and education
by publishing worldwide. Oxford is a registered trade mark of Oxford University
Press in the UK and certain other countries.

Published in the United States of America by Oxford University Press
198 Madison Avenue, New York, NY 10016, United States of America.

© Oxford University Press 2019

All rights reserved. No part of this publication may be reproduced, stored in
a retrieval system, or transmitted, in any form or by any means, without the
prior permission in writing of Oxford University Press, or as expressly permitted
by law, by license, or under terms agreed with the appropriate reproduction
rights organization. Inquiries concerning reproduction outside the scope of the
above should be sent to the Rights Department, Oxford University Press, at the
address above.

You must not circulate this work in any other form
and you must impose this same condition on any acquirer.

Library of Congress Cataloging-in-Publication Data
Names: Nassauer, Anne, 1982– author.
Title: Situational breakdowns: understanding protest violence and other
surprising outcomes / Anne Nassauer.
Description: New York, NY : Oxford University Press, [2019] |
Includes bibliographical references.
Identifiers: LCCN 2018054473 | ISBN 9780190922061 (hardcover : alk. paper) |
ISBN 9780190922078 (universal pdf) | ISBN 9780190922085 (electronic publication)
Subjects: LCSH: Protest movements. | Demonstrations. |
Political violence. | Riots.
Classification: LCC HM883 .N37 2019 | DDC 303.48/4—dc23
LC record available at https://lccn.loc.gov/2018054473

9 8 7 6 5 4 3 2 1

Printed by Sheridan Books, Inc., United States of America

to
Lee Ann Fuji

CONTENTS

FIGURES AND TABLES

Figures

Tables

PREFACE

How do peaceful protests end in violent clashes? What prevents people from taking the step from aggression to violence? Why does an unarmed store clerk laugh at an armed robber instead of handing him the money, and why can this cause some robbers to run away in panic?

Going through everyday life, we rely on specific routines that make life easier and provide a sense of order—routines of greeting each other, getting to work, organizing the things we do on the job, at the gym, or during family dinners. Yet we all may have experienced situations where these routines fail and people behave contrary to everyone's expectations (including their own). This book will argue that when routines break down, surprising outcomes emerge.

One example is protest marches turning violent. Every day, somewhere around the globe, protesters assemble—for instance, to protest war, nuclear power, or neo-liberal globalization. They march together to make their claims heard. After the march, they might listen to speeches and disperse. This is the protest routine that we are familiar with in North America and Europe. However, some protests turn into something else: clashes emerge, stones fly, tasers are used, tear gas fills the air. Protesters and police engage in physical fights, and people are injured or even killed.

Why do unlikely outcomes—such as violence in protests—occur? In contrast to common assumptions, this book will show that it is not due to actors' motivations, strategies, or background factors. In the case of protest violence, it is not structural factors, the police's strategy, protesters' grievances, protesters' or officers' culture, or violent motivations. These factors are too commonly present in protests that stay peaceful as well. Instead, surprise outcomes occur because of situational breakdowns: moments of chaos, confusion, and fear in which people are overwhelmed because the organizational routines they usually rely on have collapsed. This book argues that by systematically looking at the micro-level, at what happens in particular situations, clear patterns can be identified as to how and why routine interactions break down, not only during large-scale protest marches but in many other situations with surprising outcomes as well, from violent uprisings after police shootings in the United States to offenders failing to rob a store at gunpoint.

I came to conduct this research through personal experience, as well as through an intriguing empirical observation of protests turning violent. Growing up in the Kreuzberg district of Berlin, Germany, May 1 protests took place in our neighborhood once a year. Parties, unions, and other groups celebrated International Workers' Day with various marches and events. My parents—a steelworker unionist and a social worker—were regulars in the late morning marches for decades. In 1987, things took a different turn when massive violence erupted during the evening protests. Outside the window, the wind blew thick smoke through the streets from burning trashcans and cars. We could hear protesters and officers chasing each other, running down the street yelling and screaming. Barricades were built and supermarkets looted. The next morning my mother and I were on our way to my daycare, we could not take the subway because our nearest station had been trashed and was closed. Walking by the station, we passed debris, looted stores, and a two-story supermarket that had burned to the ground and partially collapsed. National news that day reported that the neighborhood looked like it had been in a civil war. Yet my mother told me everything was fine and this would not happen again any time soon. I believed her, but I remember being baffled by how everything went back to normal so soon. It seemed everyone had all of a sudden gone crazy, and the next day, those who weren't hospitalized went back to work, police continued their job, and protesters got on with their lives. Everyone interacted "normally" again, in a setting that had witnessed pure mayhem the night before.

Twelve years later, residents of Seattle must have felt a similar sensation, after the November 1999 "Battle of Seattle" left their inner city shattered and burned. What started as peaceful protests ended in broken store windows, chaos, beatings, and injuries. The next day, most protesters went to work, and debris was cleared from the streets.

While outbreaks of violence at May 1 protests in Berlin became routine in the 1990s, such flare-ups during marches completely break the routine we know and expect of protests. Not surprisingly, the world was shocked by the events in Berlin in 1987 and Seattle in 1999. Yet such surprise outcomes have occurred before and since. How and why do they happen? Considering moderate as well as radical protests, only about 2 percent of all protests turn violent. If protesters or police are merely motivated to use violence and this is why violence breaks out, why do these events occur so rarely and not every time these groups meet?

Later, during my undergraduate studies, I made an intriguing observation that led me to conduct this study: protests that turned violent—by violence, I mean physical interpersonal violence in the sense of actions injuring or killing another person—seemed to show similar patterns in the way they unfolded. Reading on a demonstration in solidarity with the 1968 student movement in Paris on May 10, 1968, and, around the same time but in an entirely different context, learning about a demonstration against the G8 summit in Genoa on July 20, 2001, it struck me how both protests seemed to have evolved in a very similar way. The similarities were all the more surprising to me because these two protests took place in different countries, decades, and social movements. There seemed to be a situational pattern that did not appear in protest marches that had stayed peaceful. This observation sparked my interest in studying the situational dynamics of these outcomes.

Beginning this project, it seemed that most existing approaches to studying protest violence lacked a systematic and detailed comparative analysis of situational patterns—of the things that happen between the start of a protest and the outbreak of violence—to determine whether these aspects matter. Fortunately, in 2008, shortly after I started this project, Randall Collins published his groundbreaking title, *Violence: A Micro-Sociological Theory*, challenging what we believed to be true about violence. In his work, Collins shows that humans have an inhibition threshold for violence and that this threshold is not easily overcome. Only very particular emotional dynamics can lead people to use violence, and these dynamics only occur in specific situations. Hence, according to Collins, something distinct needs to happen in a situation for violence to occur. This was exactly the hunch that I wanted to explore.

Yet, while Collins's focus is on the emotions in the minutes and seconds before violent confrontation, I also wanted to know more about the interactional patterns in the hours that lead up to violence. Inspired by Charles Tilly and Sidney Tarrow's contentious politics approach and Herbert Blumer's symbolic interactionism, I wanted to explore the relational mechanisms and processes to protest violence, as well as the role of people's expectations and interpretations in these situations. Did they matter in whatever it was that caused violence to erupt? If not, what caused the emotional dynamics Collins described? I wanted to gain a better understanding of how context factors (such as police and protester cultures and motivations) and situational factors interact. Further, I wanted to know if situational dynamics might be key to understanding the breakdown of other routine behaviors as well. Can we find similar situational patterns leading to other surprising outcomes?

To examine protests in detail, I made use of recent technological advancements: the surge in the production and dissemination of visual data (i.e., moving or still images) has led to an exponential increase in data on situational dynamics over the last decade. Never before in the history of humanity have so many recordings been available that document real-life situations and interactions. In addition, the way people use the Internet for sharing experiences makes much of this data easily accessible. For instance, on YouTube alone, more than 300 hours of new video footage are uploaded every minute (as of 2018), many documenting social situations, such as protest events.

Making use of these novel data types, I analyzed protest marches in Germany and the United States from 1960 until 2010, employing over 1,000 visual recordings. I compared visual data to thousands of documents from protesters, police, courts, journalists, and outside observers. Moreover, I compared data from various sources so that no perspective (of the police or of the protesters) dominated and so that I had several pieces of data on each minute of a protest event confirming what happened. I complemented my analysis through participant observation and interviews.

Interested in in how far findings on situational dynamics can be applied to other instances of surprising outcomes, I then broadened the scope beyond protest marches and beyond violence. First, I studied whether identified patterns are similar or different from other types of collective violence, examining violence in uprisings after police shootings in the United States. Further, recordings from CCTV cameras allowed me to study a type of routinized individual social interaction beyond violence—armed store robberies. In contrast to marches, these robberies follow a brief interaction routine (usually 2 minutes instead of hours), with few actors (usually two to four instead of several thousand). A routine that is forced upon one person by another threatening force and possibly murder should be largely successful. Here, the surprising outcome is when a robbery fails despite one person being armed and dangerous.

In short, I examined whether one can find a convincing explanation for surprising outcomes across several social phenomena and different decades by including a systematic analysis of what happens during the unfolding event itself and comparing situational dynamics to background factors. I started from a sociological perspective, but soon I combined insights and analyses from sociology and other disciplines such as social psychology, criminology, peace studies, international relations, anthropology, and neuroscience. Research from these fields helped me to connect empirical insights into interactions and emotions and culture and expectations in these events.

As a result, this work provides an account of how and why routine interactions break down, leading to protest violence and other types of surprising outcomes. It takes a close-up look at the dynamic processes of how situations unfold and develop. It points to factors that can draw us into violent situations and discusses how and why we make uncommon individual and collective decisions. The discussion of different cases of routine interactions gone wrong will show how unfolding situations can override our motivations and strategies and how emotions and culture, as well as rational thinking, still play a part in these events. It will show that despite situations overriding motivations, agency still exists; people are very much able to control these situations and avoid being caught up in violence, if they know what to look for.

ACKNOWLEDGMENTS

So many extraordinary people have helped me during this study and the ensuing book project. I am very grateful to everyone who has read drafts, commented on ideas, and shared their stories with me.

First, I thank the many journalists, YouTubers, LiveLeakers, documentary filmmakers, protesters, observers, and police officers who shared their time and experiences with me, among them Elke Steven, the activists at Indymedia, and the officers at the "Direktion Einsatz" of the Berlin Police Department. I thank especially everyone who talked to me despite being skeptical of me talking to both sides.

Among my colleagues, I would like to wholeheartedly thank Randall Collins for being a mentor and a friend, for his inspiring work, and for his invaluably constructive comments on my research. I am extremely grateful to Jim Jasper for encouraging me to write this book, and for his many constructive comments on several drafts. I am also thankful to the anonymous reviewers for their fruitful comments. I would like to thank Klaus Eder for being the first supervisor of my dissertation, upon which parts of this book are based, and believing in my research skills when I still had very little idea what I was doing. I thank Debra Minkoff for her always honest, helpful, and to-the-point remarks on this project. I thank Lee Ann Fuji for comments on part of this book, for being a mentor, and a friend. You were such a happy-spirited fighter for diversity in research and supported and inspired so many young women to pursue their dreams in the sciences. You will always be a role model to me and I'll miss you.

I would further like to thank numerous admired colleagues for feedback on specific parts of this book: Elijah Anderson and Martin Lüthe for their invaluable feedback on the uprisings chapter, Claudius Wagemann for his advice on qualitative comparative analysis, and Anette Fasang for her comments on sequence analysis. I am thankful to Jack Katz, Jeff Goodwin, Ion Bogdan Vasi, Harald Wenzel, Gökçe Yurdakul, Harald Wessels, and Silvia von Steinsdorff for their comments on specific aspects of this book. I also want to thank James Cook and Emily Mackenzie at Oxford University Press for their editing and all the support in finishing this work.

Moreover, I would like to thank my parents, Monika and Georg Nassauer, for always believing in and empowering me. Jörg, thank you for your design advice and humor. I am the luckiest person on the planet to have you as my big brother. I thank Barbara and Heiner for rooting for me. Further, I want to thank Uwe for encouraging me when I started this project, and Birte, Marie, Olivia, Sandra, Maria, Melanie, Claire, Val, Philipp, Mascha, Sophie, and many more for encouraging me to have a good time while doing so. Steve, thank you for your uplifting spirit and "just go for it" attitude. It means the world to me.

Last but certainly not least, I want to thank Nicolas Legewie—for everything, from instrumental theoretical, empirical, and methodological feedback, comments on argumentation, logic, research design, qualitative comparative analysis, and style, to moral support and overall happiness. Without you, this book would be nothing like it is. I cannot thank you enough. I am so happy to have you by my side.

Situational Breakdowns

Introduction
SITUATIONAL COLLAPSES AND ERUPTIONS

Rostock, June 2007

The day turned out to be sunny after all. By midmorning, the sun broke through the clouds. Slowly but steadily, protesters gathered at Rostock's main railway station. From there, a sea of colorful banners, puppets, drums, and chants started filling the inner city. Police officers watched the arriving protesters, facing the prospect of shifts of 12 hours or more. Protesters met up with friends in the group they wanted to march with and stood around, chatting. The smoke from tear gas and burning cars and the yelling and screaming were still far into the future—almost unimaginable at the time. It did not seem to cross anyone's mind that in a few hours, clashes would leave more than 1,000 people injured.

Everything seemed to be fine that afternoon in June 2007—just another regular, colorful protest march for a better world. About 40,000 protesters had assembled against the G8 summit in Heiligendamm, Germany. Police were approaching protesters with a tolerant, soft strategy, as they had been directed. Police and protest organizers had negotiations prior to the march, both stating their intentions to remain peaceful.

The march set off at 1 p.m. Protesters headed east along the broad Lange Straße (see map, Figure I.1). The route crossed the inner city on its way to the port, where a large stage for concerts and speeches was set up. When realizing that several protesters, dressed in black and wearing facemasks, had assembled as part of the large march, some officers became slightly unsettled. Due to the soft approach that police strategy dictated, officers were neither allowed to search this group for weapons nor conduct close surveillance. In order to create a peaceful climate, officers did not wear protective helmets. Some units observed protesters collecting stones,

FIGURE I.1. Map of Engagement, Rostock

but they had no authorization to stop them (German Police Union, 2007; Pfohl, 2007). They started wondering: What if the protesters did not play their part? A few hundred meters further along the march, a handful of protesters destroyed the windows of a bank while passing by. Police did not react, but both the majority of peaceful protesters and police officers noticed the broken glass and feelings of disquiet increased.

Many officers guarded the buildings surrounding the protest route. Even without helmets, their riot gear made for an intimidating sight. Helicopters started flying over the protest, creating an uneasy level of noise. When marching down the large street through the inner city (Am Vögenteich, see Figure I.1), protesters realized that numerous stores were barricaded with particle board. For them, the empty wide road ahead began to create a subtle feeling of discomfort. They started to observe the police officers and increasingly looked at each other. Was everything still okay?

The march made a large U-turn and headed west down Warnowufer (see Figure I.1). The port was in sight. On the right side, the large street would open up into a square—water to the right, the stage ahead. The street ran along the left side of the square. Protesters were almost there, nearly at the end of their sanctioned route.

At the bottleneck of the street, right where 40,000 protesters poured out into the square, a police car was parked. Why was it parked *there*, protesters wondered? This was the officially sanctioned protest route. About ten protesters, masked and dressed in black, attacked the car with stones and poles. A few other marchers stopped them. Most protesters assumed that the car was empty, a provocation, parked there to incite an attack by the few who would let themselves get carried away and damage property. Yet an officer was sitting inside, hardly visible. He ducked down instantly and later drove the car away. Consequently, to the police, the attack on the car, the *person* in the car, was a "life-threatening" attack on a colleague (German Police Union, 2007, p. 3). In their view it could have been any one of them who was almost killed. Memories of the 2001 protest in Genoa, Italy, which had resulted in hundreds of severe injuries and one casualty, came to officers' minds (German Police Union, 2007, p. 5). Both officers and protesters in Rostock were now increasingly tense. Something seemed about to happen. From then on, events unfolded quickly.

Several groups of about fifteen officers each repeatedly ran through the crowd at the rally site. These police groups then stood among the crowd silently, without a clear purpose, then retreated to Warnowufer, only to run back through the crowd again. Protesters were confused and afraid, not understanding why officers were entering their agreed-upon territory. The majority of the protesters had not done anything unlawful, yet they were wondering whether the police wanted to arrest them. But if that were the case, they did not understand why no arrests were made. The protesters felt they could not back up, as they were surrounded by water and the stage on the other three sides of the square (see Figure I.1). Several scuffles between police and protesters occurred (Steven and Narr, 2007, pp. 57 ff.). A car parked on the street next to the assembly was set on fire. The wind blew thick smoke over the square. Where did the happy spirit for a better world go? The chanting and the drums? The atmosphere had changed.

The operational command was confronted with a situation getting out of hand. They ordered more units into the inner city. Large numbers of backup police from all over Germany were on standby in the area, stationed around Rostock for the summit. To most of them, this meant average shifts of 16 to 20 hours, with an average of 4 to 6 hours to rest at night in noisy accommodations. To them, the summit also meant an average of two to four hours driving each day to get from their accommodations to their area of operation and back. While working, units had to endure long hours without toilet breaks and in some cases 20 hours without food (German Police Union, 2007).

Now, some of these units hurried to the inner city. Coming from elsewhere in Germany, many did not know their way around Rostock, they had to rely on information from operational command. But with things getting out of hand, operational command was overwhelmed with the unexpected situation. They could not tell units where they were in relation to "the action," nor what they were supposed to do, nor what to expect. They kept changing tactics, ordering units to advance and making them retreat shortly after. Units walked around in the protest area, uncoordinated and tense, and collided with protesters on various occasions.

Clashes between larger numbers of officers and protesters followed. On the street next to the rally site, dozens of protesters threw stones at police officers. Protesters and officers chased each other. Protesters who fell to the ground were kicked and beaten. The police employed water cannon trucks at the assembly square, where, they assumed, the "troublemakers" were hiding. The majority of the 40,000 peaceful protesters were afraid and baffled, caught up in a quickly escalating situation while trying to get away from the tear gas and tumult (Steven and Narr, 2007). To make things worse, officers had mixed CN gas (a stronger version of CS irritant gas) into the water they were spraying (German Police Union, 2007, p.4).[1] Officers perceived that they needed to get the situation back under control. Many feared for their safety and felt abandoned by operational command to fend for themselves. "It was about pure survival," one officer recalled (Pfohl, 2007).[2] Protesters felt attacked by police and trapped in the area at the port, not understanding why police would, in their view, attack the large assembly (Steven and Narr, 2007).

Steadily, the situation escalated further. "It all turned into a full-blown riot," CNN reported live from Rostock (CNN, 2007). At the end of the day, 1,000 people, including both protesters and officers, had to be treated for injuries. "What started this off, since it has been going on peacefully for so long?" a CNN anchor asked his correspondent standing next to the

---

[1] CS gas is a tear gas used by riot police to incapacitate individuals. It causes, among other effects, a burning sensation and tearing of the eyes, coughing, and difficulty breathing. Individual effects can range from mild tearing of the eyes to severe pain, vomiting, or pulmonary damage. CN gas is a stronger version of CS gas and can cause a more generalized reaction, including temporary loss of balance and orientation.

[2] All translations by author.

violence at the Rostock port. "Well that's a very good question!" the reporter responded (CNN, 2007).

Kehl, April 2009

A contrasting protest example illustrates why it is puzzling that protests such as the Rostock march turn violent instead of staying peaceful. On April 4, 2009, protesters assembled at a parking lot in Kehl, Germany, to march against a meeting of NATO in Kehl's neighboring town, Strasbourg, in France. With around 8,000 participants, this was the largest German protest related to the summit.

In Kehl, things did not look good from the start: police had previously declared a strict strategy toward protesters, employing around 15,000 officers. As a consequence, protesters were, among other things, allowed neither to approach police closer than 5 feet (1.5 meters) nor to bring feather dusters or toilet brushes to the march, items often used by protest clowns. Protesters were skeptical: if even clowns were forbidden, this march would not be a piece of cake. Both the police and the media expected violence to break out (see, among others, Schlieben, 2009). Referring to protesters dressed in black who are often assumed to be motivated to use violence, the federal state police chief had told the media previously, "If a black bloc should form, it will be 'processed' here" (Höhl, 2009).

Many protest groups were severely delayed by police checks on arriving buses. Officers checked protesters' ID cards and backpacks before letting them pass. Yet these checks did not change the setup of the protest, as radical protest groups could still attend. Other protesters were waiting for late arrivals, and officers observed them attentively. Stores in the inner city of Kehl were barricaded with particle boards. The protesters appeared serious when meeting with each other.

The march finally set off on its approved protest route to cross Europabrücke, a bridge to France, in order to join the march in Strasbourg. Yet, unexpectedly, police blocked the sanctioned route, stopping protesters 500 feet before the bridge. A hotel had been set on fire right at the other end of the bridge, police officials stated. Smoke appeared from a tall building across the river. Protesters were in disbelief: Why could the march not pass by the building? Why would other protesters set the hotel on fire, as police officials claim? Wouldn't they have realized that their fellow campaigners on the German side might therefore not be able to join their march? Was this a setup?

The protesters were uneasy. They had already waited some time before the march could finally start. Many of them had traveled from other parts of Germany to attend. Now, after only half a mile of marching, the police were standing in their way, on their sanctioned route. They were not only standing there, though; officers had the entire march surrounded, outnumbering the protesters nearly two to one. The protesters felt confined and tense, unsure whether they could actually leave if they wanted to, a member of the Green Party recalled (Achelpöhler, 2009). It was not only marchers who were unsettled, officers were uneasy as well. The protesters had not done anything that would justify restraining them from their right to protest. The route was sanctioned. Now protesters lined up before the police, demanding to pass.

The area got crowded as protesters pushed to move on. In addition, some protesters from behind pushed others in the front row against officers—some seemingly wanting to provoke an escalation of the situation. In one instance, an officer pushed back but immediately raised both hands as a token of peaceful intention or innocence, and the heated situation calmed down again (for visual data, see, among others, Swiola, 2009). Extended negotiations between protest organizers and police officials followed. In the end protesters gave their final speeches nearby and the protest dissolved peacefully.

In Kehl, everything pointed to violence: violence was expected; some police and protesters seemed prepared for it, or even violently motivated; and the circumstances did not work in anyone's favor. Yet violence did *not* erupt. How was this possible?

Situational Breakdowns and Surprising Outcomes

The two marches in Rostock and Kehl illustrate that violence (defined as an action physically injuring or killing another person; see Chapter 1) seems to erupt without forewarning. In one protest police and protesters came together with peaceful intentions and negotiated peaceful strategies, but in the end they beat each other bloody. In the other protest everything pointed to violence, but people parted ways in peace.

Generally, marches in Western democracies follow established practices, leading to between 92 and 98 percent of all protests staying peaceful (see, e.g., Della Porta, 1995, p. 216; McAdam, Tarrow, and Tilly, 2001, p. 9; Tilly and Tarrow, 2006). Western democracies are familiar with people marching through the streets to publicly protest against climate change, racism, and hundreds of other issues. Often they bring colorful posters and chant slogans. After marching, they commonly disperse and go home. Such protests, just as most human behavior, are thus a routinized form of action (Collins, 2005a; Goffman, 2005). However, the Rostock protest illustrates that some protests turn into something else: clashes emerge, stones fly, tasers are used, and tear gas fills the air. Protesters and police engage in physical fighting, and people are injured or even killed. What starts peacefully might end in chaos, beatings, and broken store windows, sometimes leaving hundreds injured. Comparing Kehl and Rostock, the obvious question is: If even the Kehl protest stayed peaceful, why did Rostock turn violent? When and how do demonstrations turn violent, instead of staying peaceful? Why do these surprising outcomes emerge?

While the common assumption would be that societal grievances; the people's strategies, cultures, or motivations; the police:protester ratio; or the presence of violently motivated individuals are key to violence (be it protesters, police officers, or undercover agents), this book will show that these factors cannot systematically explain the eruption of violence. They are too commonly present in instances without surprising outcomes. Motivations and plans generally seem key for how we behave in a situation. Yet such motivations can be overridden by situational dynamics. My systematic analysis of background and situational factors highlights clear situational patterns for how and why surprising outcomes occur, not only during left protests marches but in many other social events as well. Surprising outcomes occur because of situational breakdowns—moments of emotionally charged chaos and poor communication. In these situations, people are confused and overwhelmed because the interactional and organizational routines they usually rely on have collapsed. In this work I maintain that similar dynamics occur across various types of individual and collective violence and other puzzling outcomes such as violence in uprisings or failed crimes (see Chapter 9). However, such instances do not unfold randomly but due to specific patterns and are therefore not beyond our control.

Studying Surprising Outcomes

Even though they affect only a small portion of protests, outbreaks of violence receive extensive media coverage (McCarthy, Clark McPhail, and Smith, 1996; Rosie and Gorringe, 2009). Peaceful protests are hardly newsworthy; violent ones usually are. For some time, social science research has set the same focus, putting the violent outcome they were interested in at the center of analysis. Consequently, most studies on these events sample on the dependent variable, i.e., they limit their analysis to events that end in physical clashes (Reicher, 1984; Noakes, Klocke, and Gillham, 2005; Della Porta, Peterson and Reiter, 2006a). These studies largely point to the prior motivations and strategies as the main reasons for outbreaks of violence. When, for example, several factors precede a violent interaction, studies tend to claim that the most rational factor was key. In the paramount example of violence—murder—a large sum of money seems to be a more convincing explanation than a silly insult (Gould, 2003, pp. 1 ff.). Why would people use violence if not because they planned to do so? Yet this reasoning faces three empirical problems. First, studying only violent protests might overlook that the same factors might be present in peaceful protests. For instance, people who are explicitly motivated to use violence are often present in peaceful marches as well but violence does not occur. Second, even if only peaceful groups attend, a protest can still turn violent. It therefore seems key to move beyond a focus on violent events and compare them to peaceful events. Further, we should look beyond background factors, such as people's motivations and strategies, and investigate whether they matter during a protest, zooming in on the role of situational dynamics.

Analyzing large-scale, left protest marches in Germany and the United States from 1960 until 2010 promises to be especially insightful for such an endeavor. Their analysis allows examining a wide variety of protest events: alter-globalization protests; hippie, student, environmental, and anti-war marches; among many others. These groups have different leaders, organizational structures, and claims and behave differently during protests. Some of these protests are seen as threatening by police from the start, others less so. They occur during specific police and protest cultures—some after the turn of the present century, others in the historic setting of the 1960s. Studying such a variety of groups and marches thereby allows examining the impact that factors such as different police strategies and protest cultures may have on a violent outcome.[3] Analyzing

---

[3] At the same time, these protests are less likely to turn violent than protests in most other democratic (and non-democratic) countries, than most other protest forms, and than protests by more radical protest groups. Factors that lead to violence even in these more unlikely settings are thus likely to be powerful and likely to be at play in other types of protest violence and other types of surprising outcomes as well (for details, see Appendix B). In technical terms, large-scale marches in Western democracies are "deviant cases" (i.e., cases showing a "surprising value," here violence, which are thereby well suited for developing new explanations for an outcome; see Gerring, 2010, p. 647).

these protests, I compared a total of 30 peaceful and violent protests[4]: if the same factors identified in leading to violence occurred in the peaceful protests, they would have limited explanatory power. Comparing violent to peaceful protests is therefore highly valuable to determine whether specific situational or background factors indeed impact violence.

How then to examine everything that happened during a protest and all relevant background factors, such as police strategies, expectations of violence, and many more? To tackle this task, I developed a novel analytic approach relying on recently available video data and all available document data and puzzling them together for each protest to gain as detailed and comprehensive a picture as possible. Due to the mass dispersion of video cameras and their extensive use during almost all types of social events, we are now able to look at protests as they happened, second by second. This pool of video data on various events grows by the minute and can provide insights into how protests unfold. Over 5,700 videos exist, for instance, on YouTube on the June 2007 Rostock protest alone; similar numbers can be found on the Ferguson 2015 uprisings (as of May 2018). They allow one to track who was where, when, doing what (see Appendix A). By employing these novel data to reconstruct the course of protests meticulously, we can observe such events almost as if we were *in* the protest situation, while having the advantage of not being caught up in emotional dynamics, gaining a bird's-eye view of what happened, watching the situation unfold in slow motion, or in as many replays as necessary (Nassauer and Legewie, 2018). Often, videos can complement each other to provide different angles on a situation during a protest event. Various types of document data (e.g., police reports, protesters' accounts, media accounts, police radio traffic transmissions, court data, or observers' accounts) can provide further details what happened.

As an additional tool, Google Maps Street View allows one to take virtual strolls through cities to identify houses and places recorded in videos. Walking along the protest route, I could match the videos (e.g., recorded in front of a yellow building) with the protest route. Identifying where the recording was made, I could then compare the recorded scene with information from protesters, media reports, or police logs on what happened at this intersection. Such technological advances, among other aspects, allowed me to reconstruct minute by minute, or even second by second

---

[4] This number of protests allowed studying each protest in depth and in great situational detail, while at the same time studying enough cases for a systematic comparison of similarities and differences across cases (Ragin, 1994).

what happened in the usually two-hour time frame from the beginning to the end of a protest (or violence eruption). As Figure I.2 shows, to reconstruct protest events in meticulous detail, I thus used all data sources that might help obtain as complete a picture of an event as possible (see also Appendix B). Figure I.2 illustrates how the combination of these novel data sources can be pieced together like a jigsaw puzzle to reconstruct a protest unfolding from beginning to end, or to the eruption of violence (for details on this analytic procedure, developed for this study and then extended into an analytic approach, see Nassauer and Legewie, 2018).

We can then compare the role of these situational dynamics to background factors (also commonly labeled context factors) to violence. What were activists marching against? Did the planning of the protest or its location shape the outcome? Were some of the officers or protesters motivated or prepared for violence? What was the police:protester ratio? Was the police culture at the time prone to harsh police actions, and did police plan to use a harsh strategy at this protest? Were protest repertoires at the time prone to the use of violence, and did protesters plan specific potentially escalating or unlawful tactics for this protest? Did police or protesters expect violence to happen? Document data from all types of sources could provide answers to these questions. In addition, I conducted interviews with participants, photographers, and documentary filmmakers present at the protests and conducted participant observation with police forces responsible for planning and implementing protest policing (see Appendix B).

To explore the range of findings, I then went on to examine whether dynamics to surprising outcomes are similar outside protest marches and violence (see Chapter 9). In doing so, I discuss breakdowns of other forms of collective interactions, studying uprisings after police shootings. Further, I discuss surprising outcomes in non-violent individual interactions by analyzing convenience store robberies. Put in technical terms, I examine the external validity of findings by employing a "most-different" design (this design allows exploring the portability of the situational breakdowns argument; see Gerring, 2010, p. 671).

Motivations, Strategies, and Culture

In analyzing a variety of surprising social outcomes, this book not only sheds light on situational dynamics but also speaks to the role of motivations, strategies, context, and culture in producing social outcomes. A first issue is what role motivations play in leading to such social

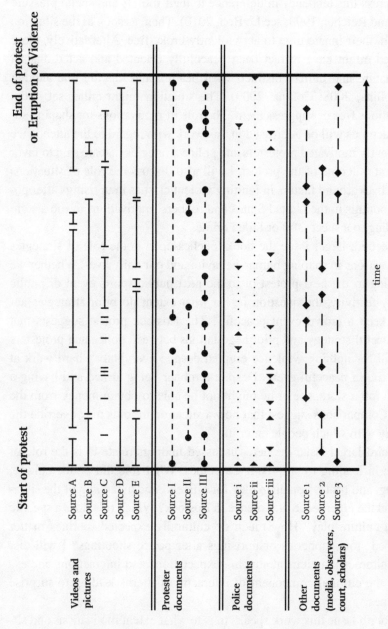

FIGURE I.2. Reconstructing Protest Events

outcomes. Both protesters and police wanted to avoid violence in Rostock, but violence erupted nevertheless. We might assume—as a large part of the media and police do—that people were inherently violent but wanted to suppress this tendency in deference to their morals and social pressure (Stott and Reicher, 1998; see Le Bon, 2010). Then, as soon as the situation allowed, their innate urge to act violently broke free. Alternatively, those involved might have in fact been peacefully oriented and acted against their nature and human instinct when beating and kicking one another (R. Collins, 2008; Collins, 2009). The situation might either set initial motivations free or suppress them. The role of motivations for shaping social outcomes will be addressed in this work with regard to the attendance of violently motivated protesters and police strategies that are said to favor a violent outcome of the protest. I will also discuss the role of situations versus background factors in igniting violent clashes in uprisings after police shootings in the United States and robbers' motivations to rob a store in leading to a successful or failed crime.

A second, larger issue the book touches upon is the role of strategies versus actions in shaping human behavior and our daily lives. Whether we are going to the next protest or to the next public sports event or public holiday festivity, the question is: To what extent do prior strategies actually keep a crowd event peaceful? The Rostock protest suggests that the peaceful strategy and prior negotiations between police and protesters were all for nothing; violence erupted despite everybody's hard work at organizing a peaceful event. Despite a robber being armed and having a plan to rob a store, she or he might not be able to obtain money from the clerk. Comparisons suggest that how a situation unfolds may override the strategy with which people enter it.

A third larger issue the here-discussed findings relate to is the role of culture in leading to surprising outcomes. What role did police culture, training, and professionalism play for officers' understanding of the situation and the emergence of violence in Rostock? Which role does a specific protest culture play? How much do culturally expected routines matter in armed store robberies or uprisings after police shootings? I will discuss culture as an element shaping expectations and interactions and examine the cultural component of interaction patterns leading to surprise outcomes.

A fourth issue this work speaks to is to what extent motivations and situational dynamics play out differently if people are alone (e.g., a robber) or part of a group (e.g., a protester)? Did a certain group effect (McPhail, 1991; i.e., the maddening crowd, see Le Bon, 2010) cause people to act as they did in Rostock in 2007 or Ferguson in 2014, or did they make individual choices during these interactions, hardly impacted by a collective vibe? Do robbers get carried away by their emotions while robbing a convenience store at gunpoint, or are they less likely to respond to surging emotions, since they usually act alone and enforce a situation onto the clerk? I will thus discuss to what extent situational breakdowns are similar when individual or collective actors are concerned and how collective and individual actors' reinterpretation of the situation, their roles, and their counterparts can shape social outcomes.

What's Coming

Chapters 1 to 8 of this book will take a close-up look at protest marches. They will examine the situational unfolding of protests and the role of background factors of violence such as police strategies, protest culture, time period, and people's motivations. These chapters will show the crucial importance of situational dynamics for surprising outcomes. The systematic comparison of protest events suggests that situational dynamics are key in turning protests violent or keeping them peaceful regardless of background factors. Violence erupts in these routinely peaceful interactions independently from police strategies, time periods, protest group composition, or the attendance of people motivated for violence. The chapters will show that violence erupts as people get confused and anxious or feel abandoned or attacked. It is not anger that we usually find in these instances before violence breaks out; people generally tend to show tension and fear before they resort to violence (see also Collins, 2008). The chapters highlight that interactions, reinterpretations, and emotional dynamics during these events are vital in leading to surprising outcomes. They thereby combine key ideas of relational social movement scholars (e.g., Goodwin and Jasper, 2006; McAdam, Tarrow, and Tilly, 2001; Tilly and Tarrow, 2006; Jasper, 2018), situational violence researchers (e.g., Katz, 1988; R. Collins, 2008; Collins, 2009), social identity–interested crowd psychologists (e.g., Reicher, 1996; Drury and Reicher, 2000; Stott and Drury, 2000), and micro-sociological theorists (e.g., Blumer, 1986; Collins, 2005a; Garfinkel, 2005; Goffman, 2005).

Chapter 1 starts by shedding light on protest groups and types of violence. The two subsequent chapters (2 and 3) discuss in detail why neither protesters' motivations nor a harsh police strategy alone can lead to violence in protest marches. Chapter 2 shows how goals and the influence of the "violent few" are often misinterpreted. Some protest groups, like the so-called "black bloc" (in itself a protest tactic, but commonly labeled a protest group), are frequently viewed as motivated toward physical violence against persons per se and solely responsible for it. I discuss that this assumption is misleading when studying physical violence and the "violent few" (in particular black bloc activists), as their key motivations lie elsewhere and their attendance alone is not sufficient for larger clashes to erupt.

The same goes for harsh police strategies; in Chapter 3, I demonstrate that—contrary to common assumptions—rigid police strategies alone cannot cause violence. Instead, low-profile, tolerant strategies may even favor escalation if specific situational patterns occur. Overall, Chapters 2 and 3 will discuss that neither protesters' nor police motivations, strategies, or cultures are key causes of eruptions of violence in marches. Instead, as Figure I.3 summarizes, my study suggests that five interactions

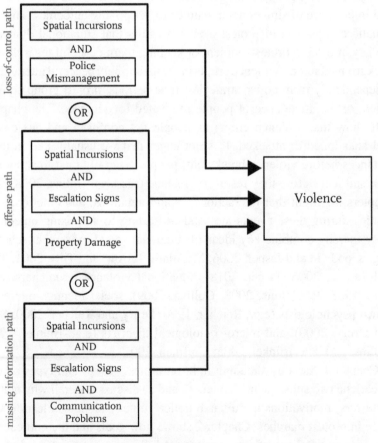

FIGURE I.3. Interactions and Paths to Protest Violence

between protesters and police that happen during protests are crucial for the emergence of violence: spatial incursions, police mismanagement, escalation signs, property damage, and communication problems between protesters and police.[5] They trigger violence if they occur in one of three combinations.

Chapter 4 will discuss the first combination, in which officers perceive losing control over the operation. This is a path through which police actions *during* a protest (rather than prior police strategies) matter for violence: police mismanagement and spatial incursions merge into a loss-of-control path as one path to physical violence. In this path (see upper part of Figure I.3), the organization of police forces is either flawed or breaks down during the protest situation. When the resulting uncertainty and disorientation of officers is combined with territorial invasion by protesters, officers perceive a loss of control over the situation. This loss raises tensions and fear and leads officers to use violence when they perceive a slight advantage over protesters.

The second path, comprised of spatial incursions, escalation signs, and property damage, will be examined in Chapter 5. This combination (see Figure I.3) leads protesters or police to perceive an offense during a protest, which increases tension and fear and leads protesters or police to use violence once they achieve a specific situational advantage (emotional dominance; see R. Collins 2008; see also Chapter 7) in a micro-situation.

Lastly, in the missing-information path, spatial incursions, escalation signs, and communication problems between protesters and police lead to violence. Chapter 6 shows that their interplay is vital; the missing information regarding the other side's goals and intentions in light of escalation signs and spatial incursions during the protest increases tensions and fear, as the lower part of Figure I.3 illustrates. Violence then erupts after specific triggering moments, when one group gains emotional dominance in the situation.[6]

---

[5] Two of these interactions refer to actions initiated by one side (property damage refers to actions by protesters, and police mismanagement refers to police actions). However, I refer to them as two out of five "interactions", emphasizing that both involve crucial in- and out-group interactions. They are perceived and interpreted by both groups and provide a basis for subsequent interaction dynamics.

[6] As this is a first study to examine and identify situational patterns versus background factors, combinations discussed here may not be exhaustive. Other studies may identify additional paths, for example, in studying further protests. Whether alternative paths exist and what these may be can at this point only be speculation. An analysis of a very different type of claim-making (uprisings after police shootings in the United States, such as Ferguson, Missouri, in 2014) did not suggest any additional key interactions beyond the ones identified (see Chapter 9).

Chapter 7 examines in detail the emotional dynamics these three paths create. It discusses how they disrupt routine interactions and thereby raise tension and fear, how violence erupts after specific triggering moments, how emotional dominance is established, and how violent situations end. Chapter 7 also focuses on the degree of violence used; in some protests, people take violence to the next level and beatings seem excessive and unrestrained. In these cases, a specific temporal sequence of interactions can lead to police using excessive force in the form of police riots. Chapter 8 will then discuss practical implications of these findings. The chapter discusses that violent outbreaks can be avoided on the micro-level and presents specific measures to do so, like ensuring a flow of communication between protesters and police and respecting territorial boundaries between the two groups.

Lastly, Chapter 9 will explore the analytic scope of the findings: Do we find similar patterns to be key in other types of surprising outcomes, such as other types of collective activism and beyond collective action and violence? The chapter first discusses my analysis of violence in recent uprisings after police shootings of African American citizens in the United States. These uprisings do not only directly concern police actions and police accountability and therefore possibly lead to different interaction dynamics between the two groups, they also show strong background factors to violence, namely systemic and symbolic racism and racial discrimination and harassment, playing a crucial role in their emergence. Can such background factors then explain why some uprisings turn violent? I argue that such explanations (that these factors automatically lead to physical clashes in uprisings) discredit involved protesters who are—as in other protests—mostly peaceful and overlook the striking presence of situational patterns leading to violence in protest marches discussed in Chapters 3 to 6.

A second part of Chapter 9 discusses successful and failed armed store robberies, suggesting similar patterns of situational breakdowns in these occurrences as well. Here, the surprising outcome is not violence but armed criminals failing to get the money from an unarmed store clerk. Just like protest marches, robberies follow an implicit but universally understood interaction ritual: a clerk hands over money in exchange for not being harmed or killed. The roles in the ritual are clear and not up for negotiation, since one person is armed, threatens violence or death, and thereby enforces the ritual onto the other. However, these situations can still break down, as Chapter 9 will discuss. Like protest marches and uprisings, robberies break down due to interactions, interpretations, and emotional dynamics during the situational encounter (see also Blumer, 1986; Collins, 2005a; Tilly and Tarrow, 2006; R. Collins, 2008). Chapter 9 will show that despite being armed and usually physically stronger, robbers act out of disorientation and fear if the interaction routine breaks down. In each of these nine chapters case vignettes will be discussed in detail, relying on the rich information that video and document data provide. All cases discussed were selected either as especially illustrative of a general pattern or because they deviate from a pattern in some illuminating way.

In short, the book suggests that situational breakdowns make the difference between what manifests statistically as a "robbery" versus an "attempted robbery." They also make the difference between what manifests as a "peaceful protest" or "violent protest," an "uprising," or "violent uprising." That is, similar dynamics of situational breakdowns are at play in protest marches that turn violent, in other types of collective protest activities escalating, and in failed robberies. These findings point to a crucial importance of the micro-level of social phenomena (see also, e.g., Blumer, 1986; Katz, 1988, p. 198; Goffman, 2005; R. Collins, 2008; Collins, 2016c). If routine behavioral rituals of both collective and individual social encounters are disrupted in the situation itself, surprising outcomes occur.

Much like Garfinkel's (2005) breaching experiments,[7] these findings tell us something about the routines that govern social processes. Such routines do not work because of people's motivations alone. Routines and social outcomes are not a given; they are constructed through interactions, their interpretations, and the emotional dynamics of the situation. Further, they need to be maintained on the micro-level, otherwise even the most stable routines can fail and surprising outcomes emerge.

Nevertheless, we are not without control over such unfolding situations, as the Conclusion will discuss. Findings suggest that knowing about the crucial role of situational breakdowns for surprising outcomes can, for instance, help further theoretical discussion in the social sciences and point to implications for future empirical research. They also entail societal implications. Finding interactions that trigger violence in specific combinations can help develop preventive measures. For example, it is quite possible to communicate one's intentions, interpretations, and expectations during a protest so that neither in-group nor out-group members

---

[7] Garfinkel's breaching demonstrations violate commonly accepted social norms and rules, which he claims we are mostly unaware of. By exhibiting how a rule is broken, Garfinkel claims we can understand how it works in the first place.

feel threatened. It is easy to pack a second pair of walkie-talkie batteries if officers are aware of the ramifications of running out of power in the midst of a chaotic protest march. Micro-situational patterns might therefore be an easy entry point to change undesirable social outcomes. The Conclusion will further discuss where these findings stand on the debate of an innate human inhibition to violence and a human peaceful or violent nature, as well as reflect on the findings' broader societal implications.

1 | Protest Groups and Physical Violence

T HE FIRST CHAPTERS OF THIS book examine the eruption of violence in protest marches by left protest groups in Germany and the
United States. These marches are highly routinized events and generally stay peaceful. Although violence is often expected prior to a march,
its outbreak is empirically surprising. This first chapter takes a closer look
at protest groups, their claims, the participants, their relationships to violence, as well as how they are policed. Furthermore, it will discuss what is
meant by *violence*. These reflections provide the basis for analyzing violence in protests in subsequent chapters.

Protest Groups and Police Reactions

Who exactly are the protest groups that this book is concerned with?
I will focus on the analysis of protest marches by left transnational social
movements in the United States and Germany from 1960 to 2010 to examine how protests end in violence instead of staying peaceful (for details
on case selection, see Appendix B).

In the 1960s, the first large transnational left movements after World
War II entered the stage. In many industrialized countries, the 1960s
student movements had claimed a more participative university structure. Worldwide, provocative lifestyles and action turned against the so-
called establishment, against the conformism of previous generations,
and against politics that were perceived as hypocritical. Starting in 1965,
the United States was involved in the war in Vietnam and the civil rights
movement was gaining momentum. In Germany, many Nazis were still
working in the judicial system, among other fields, determining accountability for the Holocaust was slow, and the Frankfurt Auschwitz trials were
still underway.

In both the United States and Germany, the SDS was a key organization in student movements during this time period.[1] In both countries, the SDS concerned itself with working in opposition to the Vietnam war, but it also addressed various global issues: gender and racial inequalities, civil rights, university and environmental issues, and the influence of mass media and consumer society. Societal conventions were called into question, as were sexuality norms. Subversive counterculture and non-conformism became prominent.

In both countries, social movements[2] employed innovative and pro-vocative protest performances (Tilly and Tarrow, 2006, p. 11) such as sit-ins. Protesters quickly realized that minor transgressions of the law could have wide-reaching consequences, and the police reacted harshly to such actions. To many protesters, the distinction between the use of violence against objects as a form of protest and violence against people was im-portant (see, among others, Kraushaar, 1998), and some protest groups occasionally caused property damage. Physically violent clashes between protesters and law enforcement officers erupted on numerous occasions (Busche, 2003), and violent police reactions in turn reinforced the 1960s movements' impression of an authoritarian state.

After a perceived failure of the 1960s movements and because the desired fundamental societal changes were not achieved, activists returned to more manageable claims in the late 1970s and early 1980s (e.g., Brand, 1991; Minkoff, 1995, 1997; see also Vasi and Macy, 2003). The new so-cial movements emerged from the splintering of the 1960s movements and abandoned most of their strong anti-capitalist and revolutionary claims. Still, the emancipation of women, breaking of sexual taboos, peace, envi-ronmental issues, hunger in developing countries, as well as human rights remained essential issues for activists in both Germany and the United States. The protest repertoire (Tilly and Tarrow, 2006, p. 11), however, differed among the various protest groups and their claims: sit-ins, squat-ting, and demonstrations were common. People searched for and found alternative self-determined lifestyles in communes and shared apartments. Unconventional protest forms remained prevalent, but police strategies became more tolerant in both countries. Clashes between protesters and

---

[1] In the United States the abbreviation stood for Students for a Democratic Society; in Germany it stood for Sozialistischer Deutscher Studentenbund (Socialist German Student League).

[2] Social movements are "a sustained campaign of claim making using repeated performances that advertise the claim, based on organizations, networks, traditions and solidarities that sustain these activities" (Tilly and Tarrow, 2006, p. 8).

police decreased during the era of the new social movements (e.g., Della Porta, 1995; Soule and Earl, 2005; Soule and Davenport, 2009).

In the late 1990s the global justice movement (GJM) followed the new social movements in most Western industrialized societies. The GJM seeks to make globalization socially just and stop the deregulation of markets, the curtailing of social rights, and the economic exploitation of humans and nature. Protesters mostly target global forums, such as summits of the International Monetary Fund (IMF), the World Bank, the World Trade Organization (WTO), or the Group of the Eight leading industrialized nations (G8, presently G20), as activists see them as responsible for maintaining an unjust world order (Klein, 2000; Hertz, 2001; Grefe, Greffrath, and Schumann, 2003).

Since participating GJM protest groups and actor coalitions vary widely across the globe, protest performances also vary from country to country and protest to protest: activists employ mostly marches but also include several innovative performances used by the 1960s movements such as sit-ins—frequently employed to block access roads to global political or economic summits. Activists also organize world social forums to discuss alternatives to neo-capitalist globalization. Compared to the new social movement protests, police reactions to these groups became harsher and law enforcement increasingly focuses on surveillance of protest groups (McPhail, Schweingruber, and McCarthy, 1998; Noakes and Gillham, 2006; Gillham, 2011). Violent clashes between protesters and police took place at a number of protests by the GJM—most prominently at protests related to global summits such as the WTO meeting in Seattle in 1999 and the G8 meeting in Genoa in 2001.

Comparing left social movements in Germany and the United States from 1960 until 2010 reveals a number of similarities in protest groups and their claims: in both democratic societies the state generally views social movements as a peaceful form of contentious claim-making (Tilly and Tarrow, 2006). Further, movements in both countries addressed similar global issues (e.g., war, poverty, and globalization) as well as similar domestic issues (e.g., university structure and minority rights). In both countries marches were a common protest tactic throughout the years.

Police organization is also comparable, as both countries' police forces are fairly decentralized. While the United States features a highly decentralized police force in which most crimes fall under the jurisdiction of state police, standard policing practices and stronger federal involvement have increased consistently across US police departments since the turn of the millennium (Rafail, Soule, and McCarthy, 2012). German police are more centralized than US police but still feature one of the most decentralized organizations in Western Europe (e.g., Sweden, France, Italy, and Spain all show much higher levels of police centralization). Thus, in both countries county and municipal law enforcement (in Germany also federal state police units, like the Berlin "operations department") are responsible for the bulk of police work and the training of officers employed in protest operations.

While the high degrees of decentralization led to regional differences in policing, police in both countries nevertheless underwent similar changes over time. First, both countries show a general trend from a philosophy of *Staatspolizei* (police serving the state) to *Bürgerpolizei* (police serving the citizens) (see Winter, 1998; Noakes and Gillham, 2006). Furthermore, in both countries, policing became increasingly professionalized. Lastly, in recent years, police in both countries face increasingly diverse coalitions of protest organizers, creating "mixed motive challenges." This means that groups participating at a march might have very diverse backgrounds and intentions (McPhail and McCarthy, 2005, p. 5). At the same time, recent protests are growing in size and therefore require law enforcement to form coalitions of multiple agencies (state level and national level) in order to police large crowds. Personnel in such coalitions often comes with diverse training, experience, and equipment (McPhail and McCarthy, 2005, p. 8). These recent trends create similar challenges for police officers in both countries.

What Is Meant by Violence?

Just as social movements and police organizations have changed over the past 50 years, so has the perception of violence. In addition, what is labeled *violence* often lies in the eyes of the beholder. For instance, some scholars might define chanting protesters or officers in riot gear as psychological or symbolic violence (e.g., Bourdieu and Passeron, 1973). The fact that protesters usually have to get their protest routes approved can be labeled structural violence (see Galtung, 1969, 1970). The destruction of property might be labeled violence, as can instances when police and protesters engage in direct physical altercations (see Imbusch, 2003). Even within this latter definition of physical altercation, violence can take many forms that are hardly comparable—from a brawl, to torture, to genocide. In short, beyond a general everyday understanding of violence as a physical fight between people, the term violence is very imprecise (Collins,

2008, p. 463) and violence as a single empirical phenomenon does not exist. "Violence" is often used to describe very different phenomena and is rarely explicitly defined (see also Imbusch, 2003, 2004; Reemtsma, 2008). So what kind of violence are we talking about?

I propose a narrow definition as physical interpersonal violence, i.e., actions in which one person causes physical harm or death to another. First, the emergence of physical violence is particularly interesting, as the inhibition threshold for (as well as consequences of) physical violence against a person seems to be generally higher than the inhibition threshold for using other forms of violence. Further, the analytic focus on physical violence allows examining whether other forms of so-called violence, like shouting or property damage, can foster the emergence of physical violence. Third, by defining violence as a physical action that is visible and observable, its beginning and end can be clearly identified and analyzed, which facilitates searching for causes of violent clashes.

For my analysis of protest marches, this means I am interested in physical violence by protesters as well as physical violence by police officers. Randall Collins (2008, 2009) claims that all people need to overcome tension and fear to be able to use violence, and suggests patterns would be similar for protesters and police. I therefore study violence by both sides to analyze whether similar or different dynamics need to be present. My focus is not on isolated incidents but on the situation turning violent, i.e., numerous acts of physical interpersonal violence taking place. During the protests studied, violence is often almost dichotomous: protests either show very isolated instances of individuals shoving each other or large-scale violence with much more than 10 people involved.

Physical violence in left protest marches in the United States and Germany is an empirically rare and therefore surprising outcome. When looking at all types of protest events (including blockades and occupations, which are generally more likely to become violent than marches), between 2 and 21 percent of left and right, moderate and radical protest activities in Germany between 1966 and 2001 feature violent actions by protesters (for a summary, see Bundeszentrale für politische Bildung, 2017; see also Della Porta and Reiter, 1998b; Wissenschaftszentrum Berlin für Sozialforschung, 2011).[3] Even in peak times, only every fifth protest (including all types of protest groups and performances) ended in violence.

---

[3] In Germany, an increase in violence from 2 percent to 21 percent occurred from 1966 to 1968 after the shooting of student Benno Ohnesorg by a police officer at a protest in West Berlin. This incident is said to have increased radicalization and clashes. Numbers then drop to 2 percent in 1969 and stay low until 1980. Another peak of 20 percent is visible in Germany in 1981, when police increasingly

When taking confrontational protest forms (like blockades or squatting) out of the equation and focusing on demonstration marches by left protest groups in Germany (including moderate and radical groups), registered violent offenses by protesters are extremely rare.

Numbers look similar in the United States, with violence rates for protests at 12 percent in the 1960s with a spike of 34 percent in 1967. Numbers have declined since then and have remained under 20 percent since 1973, with around 10 percent between 1983 and 1990 (Soule and Earl, 2005; see also Rafail, Soule, and McCarthy, 2012). McAdam, Tarrow, and Tilly (2001, p. 9) show that in only 2 percent of US protests from 1970 to 2000 did injuries or property damage occur. Violence by officers against protesters occurred in between 10 and 25 percent of US protests from 1960 until 1972 and 2 and 10 percent of the cases from 1972 until 1990 (Soule and Earl, 2005; see also Rafail, Soule, and McCarthy, 2012).

While these statistics have some reliability issues,[4] the numbers show that, overall, physical interpersonal violence at marches is the exception, not the rule. Violence occurs in less than 10 percent of all protests over most years. These numbers include various protest groups—more and less confrontational and more and less radical. If we leave out radical groups and confrontational protest forms and focus on moderate protest marches, studies point to violence rates of below 2 percent.

In short, protest marches in Germany and the United States are highly routinized and overwhelmingly peaceful. It is therefore particularly interesting to explore how such types of routinized peaceful behaviors are disrupted and what might cause protests to end in violence. The subsequent chapters will study the role of violently motivated protesters (Chapter 2), the role of police strategies and police behaviors (Chapter 3), and the role of specific situational interaction dynamics between protesters and police (Chapters 4–6) in leading to such clashes. Further chapters will examine the emotional dynamics these interactions create and the role

---

evicted occupied buildings, which frequently led to clashes with protesters (Bundeszentrale für politische Bildung, 2017).

[4] Overall rates of violence in protests need to be considered with caution, as most studies and databases rely on corporate media descriptions of "violence." Yet media often defines violence only vaguely, and a strong police bias prevails (Greer and McLaughlin, 2010, pp. 1043 ff). Media reports sometimes refer to violence when protesters damage property but physical violence (e.g., injuring a person) did not occur. When reporting on protests in which officers use physical violence against protesters, media sources frequently do not mention the occurrence of "violence" but refer to "police use of force." This makes the reliance on media-based datasets problematic for the study of physical violence by protesters and police. What databases consistently show, however, is that rates of physical violence are low in protests in Western democracies.

of emotional dynamics in violent outbreaks (Chapter 7). They will discuss practical measures to avoid violent clashes (Chapter 8) and expand the analytic scope of the findings by examining situational dynamics versus background factors in violent uprisings and armed store robberies (Chapter 9).

2 | The (Lack of) Power of the Violent Few

"VIOLENCE ARRIVES, DRESSED IN BLACK," reads the *Seattle Times* headline for an article on a recent protest (Bernton and Carter, 2012). NBC Chicago warns, "Police, Peaceful Protesters: Beware the 'Black Bloc' " (Rogers, 2012). Media, politicians, as well as scholars frequently attribute outbreaks of violence to the presence of violently motivated protesters, in recent times dubbed the "black bloc" or vaguely labeled "anarchists": "Agencies warn of possible anarchist activity at conventions," CNN reports (Cratty, 2012). The UK *Daily Mail* ran the headline "Undercover with the Anarchist Mob: How the Mail Infiltrated the Group at the Heart of the Violence" (Martin, 2009). Anarchists or the black bloc are often seen as the root cause of violence in demonstrations in Western democracies—the violent few who stir up the crowd. Describing protest events at the WTO summit in Seattle 1999 where police, among other things, tear-gassed protesters who peacefully blocked intersections, a US TV news anchor spoke of an "anarchist rampage" (Kiro 7—Eyewitness News, 2013, min. 11:38).

The violent few are often considered a main cause of violence eruption at left marches in Western democracies. A common belief is that the attendance of protesters motivated to use physical violence increases the likelihood of physical violence. For instance, in recent protests the mere presence of the black bloc has often been considered to be crucial in leading to violent clashes (Owens and Palmer, 2003; Juris, 2005). Referring to black bloc protesters in Eugene, Oregon, who allegedly committed much of the property damage at the WTO protest in Seattle in 1999, the Eugene police captain stated: "My view of this more militant and violent group is that they are dangerous and violent criminals. They terrorize innocent people. People that have nothing to do with their cause become their victims" (CBS, 2010, min. 6:12).

This chapter will discuss the impact these violent few might have on violence eruption—more specifically whether their presence, or their specific actions, can favor violence. Since it's impossible to ascertain protesters' potential violent thoughts, in this chapter I will use so called "black bloc protesters" as a proxy for violent protesters because they have been frequently seen as the archetype of the violent few in Western protests since the late 1980s. Black bloc activists are easily identifiable by their clothing and attend the majority of larger left protest marches. To study the black bloc's influence on violence, this chapter will discuss protest dynamics and violent outcomes in marches with and without black bloc attendance. I argue that the presence of violently motivated protesters is not vital to causing violence but that the breakdown of routine interactions on the micro-level is. To elaborate on why the common assumption that the violent few can ignite violence does not hold empirically, I will discuss who these violent few are, what they want, and why they may use property damage for claim-making. I will further explore mainstream media's tendency to blaming the black bloc, the effect of the violent few on the eruption of physical interpersonal violence, and more broadly the role of people's motivations for committing violence.

Who Are the "Violent Few"? From the 1960s to the Black Bloc

Protesters potentially motivated to use violence have participated in large left marches alongside other groups for decades. The alleged violent few were also present in protests organized by moderate groups in the 1970s, in which, for instance, members of the *K-Gruppen* or *Autonome* were often assumed to be violently motivated (Della Porta, 1995, p. 41; McPhail and McCarthy, 2005, p. 14). Since the 1980s the alleged violent few are said to be easier to identify due to the emergence of the so-called black bloc. Some of the first identifiable black bloc activists marched in West Germany in the early 1980s (Dupuis-Déri, 2013; Douglas-Bowers, 2014; for pictures, see Dissent, 2014). In the early 1990s the tactic spread from Europe to the United States. In the United States, it received broader public attention at the 1999 Seattle WTO protests. In recent marches in Germany and the United States, black bloc activists frequently participated next to union groups, leftist parties, environmental or feminist organizations, or participants without any specific affiliations (see also Chapter 1).

The so-called black bloc is a loosely organized group of protesters who wear black clothes, sometimes cover their faces, and usually move in tight formations. Black bloc activists commonly wear black hoodies, black sunglasses, and black pants and shoes. While often considered to be a label for a protest group, the term "black bloc" generally refers to a tactic that some protesters use in order to be less identifiable by the police as individuals (Douglas-Bowers, 2014).

But why do activists organize in such a way, and what do they stand for? Can their participation cause an eruption of violence? The discussion of the Rostock and Kehl protests in the Introduction showed black bloc activists destroying property, with some even trying to provoke violence between protesters and police or throwing stones at officers. Hence, in order to understand what role these violent few play in provoking physical clashes, it is crucial to examine what they want and whether their presence, ideology, or use of property damage can be a factor in the eruption of violence.

What Do the "Violent Few" Want?

Anarchism and Vandalism

Recently, a large part of US and German media have used the terms black bloc and anarchists interchangeably—often equating black bloc and anarchists with disruption or destruction, as members of the black bloc frequently engage in disruptive protest techniques such as property damage (Wood, 2007, p. 378). As a Washington correspondent for the BBC claimed: "[. . .] the Black Bloc—several hundred black clad anarchist protesters—did their best to disrupt the U.S. capital" (Anderson, 2002). A further common assumption is that black bloc activists lack any political motivation or conviction and are merely interested in disruption and destruction for sport.

Both motivations—anarchism and vandalism for sport—might at first seem reasonable explanations for pointing to a black bloc connection to violent outbreaks. Yet these assumptions do not adequately portray most black bloc activists' motivations. First, black bloc activists are not necessarily proponents of anarchist theories and may not even be interested or well versed in them. At the same time many anarchists—such as Noam Chomsky, to take a prominent example—are not part of the black bloc. Anarchists in general advocate a society free of dominance of one person over another and oppose hierarchy and authority as a form of oppression of individual and collective freedom (Stowasser, 2007, p. 19; see also Chomsky, 2005).[1] Although anarchist activists oppose structural violence (as black bloc members might, too), this philosophy does not necessarily make them dress in black and destroy shop windows.

While some black bloc members might be anarchists, the black bloc and anarchists are not the same group. At the same time, the assumption that most black bloc activists destroy property for sport or because they enjoy acts of vandalism is not conclusive either, as most black bloc activists who use property damage do so to make certain public claims.

Property Damage as Claim-Making

Black bloc activists commonly claim to send a message via damaging a target (object) that they choose for its symbolic value (Douglas-Bowers, 2014). As diverse as black bloc activists are, many consider damaging property an appropriate tactic and a statement that captures media and public attention. In their view they attack major corporations where it hurts them—in their wallets. Thus, most black bloc members do not regard property damage as violence, since no individuals are injured.

Rather, to many black bloc activists, property damage is a tactic to oppose actual violence. For example, to them, what deserves the label "violence" is the European Union's border politics, leading to thousands of deaths of refugees who drown in the Mediterranean Sea every year. Black bloc activists claim that the EU with its policies is killing desperate people who are fleeing their home countries due to poverty and/or armed conflicts, which are often fueled by neo-colonialist exploitation and arbitrary demarcation. In some activists' view, practices by major Western corporations financing rebel groups in order to exploit a country's national resources further fuel large-scale violence (e.g., Vidal, 2014; Burgis, 2016). Other black bloc activists label environmental destruction as violence, claiming it leads to droughts and flooding, contributing to poverty and conflict.

On a more general level, many black bloc activists also oppose ideologies they describe as "violent," such as racism, sexism, homophobia, and other related practices of discrimination. Others highlight system-immanent

---

[1] Media, police, and independent police review commissions' reports on protests often define anarchism as "using violent means to overthrow the established order" (see, e.g., RNC Review Commission, 2009, p. 2). While the term is frequently associated with violent chaos, Stowasser (2007, p. 19) highlights that anarchist ideology itself does not promote chaos or violent behavior but a society free of dominance, oppression, and violence.

narratives, such as advertising of the ideology that anyone can make it in US society: With the gap between rich and poor growing each year (OECD, 2015), the American dream, they claim, is becoming a nightmare for many. It causes psychological distress by telling people that "everyone can make it," when in fact the system is set up to allow only a few to reach the top. In the activists' view, the American dream narrative suggests that everybody should blame themselves for their suffering, because apparently they are not working hard enough. Hence, many black bloc activists disagree strongly with the system as it is, or at least with many aspects of how it is set up (Dupuis-Déri, 2013).

An extract of an interview with black bloc protesters can illustrate why some activists see property damage as a response to such grievances and as an appropriate protest tactic to publically oppose system-immanent aspects of violence. Six protesters that were part of the black bloc in the Seattle WTO protests in 1999 were interviewed for US television (see CBS, 2010, min. 03:10–04:40). "What does that get you: smashing the windows of a Starbucks, of a Nike store? What's the point?" the reporter asks. An activist replies: "Economic incentive to not hold meetings like that at all— much less in the Northwest. And psychological incentive to reconsider the kind of society that we live in that fills our world with Starbucks and McDonalds." "Let's be frank here, what I am hearing you say here right in this interview is that you advocate violence," the reporter asks the group. Some protesters nod, others shake their heads. One clarifies: "I consider private property to be a form of violence. I consider the state to be a form of violence. I don't think destroying that which maintains violence to be a form of violence." Another adds: "I do not consider breaking a window or spray-painting to be violent at all." "But it's against the law," the reporter replies.

An open letter by a black bloc activist summarizes why using property damage against large corporations is seen by some activists as a non-violent tactic to oppose perceived violent politics:

> Violence is a tricky concept. I'm not totally clear what actions are violent, and what are not. And when is a violent action considered self defense? I believe that using the word violent to describe breaking the window of a Nike store takes meaning away from the word. Nike makes shoes out of toxic chemicals in poor countries using exploitative labor practices. Then they sell the shoes for vastly inflated prices to poor black kids from the first world. (Herron, 2003)

As stated in Chapter 1, definitions of violence can vary greatly. While some define property damage as violent, others define policies that kill refugees as violent, and yet others define ideologies that make people miserable and desperate and exploit them as violent. This book's main focus is on neither of these forms of violence but on direct physical clashes between protesters and police. As this section highlighted, the violent few—recently commonly labeled the black bloc—are frequently accused of being the root cause of such physical violence. While some black bloc protesters might engage in physical violence against officers, it seems that—contrary to common belief—physical clashes with officers are not most black bloc activists' immanent or primary goal. While some black bloc activists frequently use property damage as a means of claim-making, this tactic is neither directly connected to anarchist theorizing nor the expression of an apolitical funfest. The common misconception of the violent few being the root cause of physical clashes can be understood when studying the role of the media in promoting this narrative.

The Violent Few as Media Scapegoats?

Why are the violent few (since the 1980s primarily black bloc activists) often held accountable for physical interpersonal violence if they mostly tend to damage property? A look at media reports of violence in demonstrations makes the fluid definition of violence obvious—often to the disadvantage of the black bloc or protesters in general. When media reports talk about "violence," they do not necessarily refer to physical violence between people. On numerous occasions Western mainstream media report that protesters used violence when they in fact damaged property, hence suggesting black bloc activists use physical violence against persons when they did not. At the same time, media might report that "police respond with force" or "got the situation back under control" when confronted with "violent protesters." What happened, however, in numerous of these cases was that officers used physical violence (described as "responded with force") against protesters who had previously destroyed property (described as "violent protesters") (see, e.g., Harvey 2010). Hence, media do not mention physical violence by police in these protests, but property damage by protesters is referred to as violence. These reports thus often turn common violence definitions around and can suggest that some protesters are disproportionately responsible for a violent outcome.

This reporting to the disadvantage of protesters is partly due to the mass media's hierarchy of credibility, which ranks police accounts much higher than protester accounts. Studies suggest that police officers are aware of a pro-police media bias and know about the opportunities to influence media coverage (Greer and McLaughlin, 2010, pp. 1043 ff.). Therefore it is vital to look behind these reports as to their sources and their sources' definition of violence to verify whether physical violence was actually used and, if so, by whom. It is necessary not to take media reports by their face value but to examine what actually happened by studying videos and different types of document data from various sources on a protest. As Chapters 2 through 8 will show, this can reveal the limited influence violently motivated protesters have on the outbreak of violence and highlight the crucial role that situational dynamics play in the breakdown of routines and the subsequent eruption of violence.

Stirring Up the Crowd? The "Violently Few" and Outbreaks of Violence

To fully answer which role violently motivated protesters might play in leading to protest violence, let us assume that numerous members of the black bloc are using property damage as a means of claim-making and that most are not primarily interested in using physical violence against officers, but that some are. Are these few who are potentially motivated to use physical interpersonal violence (whether part of the black bloc or not) able to cause large-scale violence?

Empirical evidence indicates otherwise: in several protests potentially violently motivated protesters such as black bloc activists did not join the march by moderate protest organizers or were hindered from joining it by the police. Nevertheless, violence erupted, as in the protest against the FTAA in Miami in 2003, where the black bloc was hindered from joining the main march, but violence emerged (see Chapter 5, "Where Were They? When Would They Strike?").

In other protests the violent few were present and seemingly tried to escalate the situation, but still violence did not erupt. Consider the 2009 protest against the NATO meeting in Kehl discussed in the Introduction. Here, visual data show that some black bloc protesters pushed the crowd that was held up by the police from behind so that protesters in the front row were pushed against officers. Presumably, these activists not only wanted to continue their march but some might also have wanted to provoke an escalation of the situation. Officers pushed back but raised their hands to show that they meant no harm. Even though protesters were held back at the street for several hours until the protest was declared over, violence did not emerge.

Comparing violent and peaceful protest marches suggests that the presence of people who appear to be motivated to use physical violence against others cannot by itself lead to violence. Even if people fear, expect, or intend to use violence, interactions between protesters and officers during marches can calm the collective mood. Even if apparent violent protesters are present and aim to provoke violent incidents, protest examples show that they do not succeed if the micro-situation is not favorable. If situational interactions help to keep routines from breaking down, fear and confusion do not surge and violence is avoided (see also Chapter 8).

Moreover, if the presence of violently motivated protesters sufficed to lead to violence, it would be reasonable to assume that they could arrive at a protest and start violence immediately. Why wait? At least they could start violence right away from time to time. However, empirical evidence suggests that violence usually emerges one to three hours after the start of a demonstration. This means even when tensions rise rapidly in some protests and slowly and steadily in others, violence usually breaks out at least one hour after the march has started. Hence, it seems that the mere intentions and motivations of some participants are not enough to lead to violence. Apparently, even for people motivated to use violence, specific situational group interactions, reinterpretations, and emotional dynamics have to occur before violence actually breaks out. When violence does not occur in the critical time frame of one to three hours after the march has started, the emotional mood apparently shifts, and peaceful interactions prevail. As examples will illustrate in further detail (see Chapter 8), people settle into a non-violent routine, they interpret possible new emerging situations more calmly, and the dynamic leads away from the tension and fear that are vital for violence.

Motivations and Physical Violence

The finding that people's motivations are not key to determining their actions—in particular when explaining violent actions—seems very counterintuitive. Before moving to other possible explanations for the emergence of violence, I will therefore briefly discuss why this counterintuitive finding makes sense.

The assumption that people use violence due to the motivations with which they enter a situation is very prominent. Common sense suggests that motivation is a very good predictor of action. Apart from self-defense, why would anyone use violence, if not because she or he wanted to do so? It seems counterintuitive *not* to assume that our motivations are key. If dissatisfied with political circumstances and societal opportunities and faced with injustices, for instance, protest violence becomes more likely, many studies assume (Ransford, 1968; Lodhi and Tilly, 1973; Olzak, 1989; Grant and Wallace, 1991).

Let us first look at examples from everyday life to point out problems with this reasoning and evaluate the counterintuitive argument in the discussion of violence. If we intend to go for a run after work, it is very likely that we will. This presumes, of course, that nothing gets in the way. We might have to work overtime on that particular day or forget our shoes. So we know from banal everyday experience that motivation is not everything. But it still seems to be a very good predictor of behavior. This is especially true if we only look at the instances where people actually do what they were initially motivated to do. If we manage to go for a run after work, we might think that this is not surprising as we were very motivated to do so. If someone carries out an elaborate plan and successfully murders their neighbor, it seems to us that their motivation was key. But what about the times we don't actually achieve what we intended, the times we or other people were just as motivated but things turned out differently? Often someone is committed to murdering another person but this intention is never put to action (see Katz, 1988).

Things get even more complicated if we add more people to the equation. Imagine a group of people—some of whom you know—interacting with a second group of people, none of whom you know. The situation becomes much less predictable, and motivations are even less likely to play out as intended. We find such a scenario if a large group of protesters interacts with large numbers of police officers.

In short, while the roots of human behavior are part of an ongoing, far-reaching discussion, these examples illustrate a counterintuitive pattern: in many instances, motivation is not a good predictor for action because situations unfold differently from participants' initial goals. Even if we can relate to these everyday examples, the notion that motivations have limited impact on our action is still very counterintuitive to our understanding of violence. We usually assume that the most rational motive is the reason for a violent act (Gould, 2003, pp. 1 ff.). Yet many people who are motivated to using violence never actually do so due to the situational unfolding of events (Collins, 2008). Even if violently motivated activists might be present at a protest, violence might not come off, as the Kehl protest illustrated. Research suggesting that structural factors and grievances can motivate people to protest violence faces a further difficulty: many people who use violence might be affected by social injustices or experience grievances. However, an even larger proportion of individuals affected by social injustices do not become violent (Waddington, 1991; Horowitz, 2001; R. Collins, 2008).

Many journalists as well as theoretical scholars emphasize that human beings' violent and cruel nature is always lurking, waiting to break out. According to this perspective, we quickly tap into our (primitive) violent instincts as soon as the possibility presents itself or if social control gives way (Reemtsma, 2008; e.g., Hénaff, 2015; Theweleit, 2015). Humanity's cruel nature is often illustrated with gory detail and conveniently corroborating anecdotes as violence makes for a good story (see Theweleit, 2015). Yet the idea of humans' violent nature seems to be an intellectual predilection rather than a systematic societal pattern. The claim has little empirical basis, as violence, in fact, rarely happens empirically (R. Collins, 2008; see also Pinker, 2012; Ferguson, 2013). In principal, physical violence is an available resource for any person at any time (Eckert and Willems, 2002, p. 1475). There are many occasions where people could engage in violence—yet they usually do not. Research shows that violence is used only by a few people and only in rare situations (R. Collins, 2008, p. 14). In fact, humans regularly try to avoid violent interactions, be it armed robbers (Wright and Decker, 1997; see also Katz, 1991, 1988) or even soldiers (R. Collins 2008; King 2013). If humans do engage in violence, they usually try to keep fights short. In this sense, violence "breaks with ordinary reality" (R. Collins, 2008, p. 130). This finding is crucial for this book, since it suggests that violence is not a common reaction or caused by widespread motivation but that most people—even if motivated—have to overcome certain thresholds in order to be capable of violence.

In summary, while the media, police, and public opinion often attribute the blame for violent clashes to the "violent few" and their motivations (either being anarchist or enjoying destruction for sport), this assumption is not supported empirically. First, anarchists are not the same as the black bloc. Second, many black bloc activists do not seem to engage in property damage for the fun of it, but do so as a protest tactic to express grievances. Chapter 5 will therefore look at people's observable actions that might or might not make a difference to a violent outcome and discuss the role of property damage in inciting violence in more detail.

Further, although black bloc activists might engage in property damage as a tactic for contentious claim-making, this does not mean that physical violence against officers is per se part of their protest repertoire. Some protesters might participate in marches primarily to engage in violence with officers. But even then the violent few alone do not seem to suffice to provoke larger clashes.

These findings suggest that motivations and background factors impacting these motivations form weak predictors of when people will carry out violent actions, since they are too commonly present in instances where violence does not emerge. Further, people do not necessarily carry out the action to which they were motivated: not in the case of implementing personal plans, like an after-work run, and even less so in the much more drastic action of using violence against a fellow human being or collective violence against another group. The limited relevance of (violent) motivations can explain this book's counterintuitive argument that the violent few are not key to the outbreak of violence and that explanations for violence must be searched for elsewhere.

3 | The Police's Fault?

I F PROTESTERS ARE NOT PRIMARILY to blame for eruptions of violence, what about the police? After all, they are responsible for ensuring orderly protests. Or might officers even intentionally escalate things to put protesters in their place?

Police Strategies and Police Actions

One way in which officers could be responsible for outbreaks of violence is the policing strategy their command chooses for a protest. Policing styles in Western democracies were rather strict and repressive in the 1960s, became more tolerant in the 1980s, and then more repressive again around the turn of the millennium, with an increasing focus on surveillance (Noakes and Gillham, 2006; Starr and Fernandez, 2009; Gillham, 2011). For some time, studies assumed that protests are more likely to escalate when officers use these strict and repressive strategies, so-called escalated force policing (Della Porta and Reiter, 1998a; Gillham and Noakes, 2007). Using this logic, numerous studies employ the emergence of violence as an indicator to determine ex post facto which police strategy had been used (McPhail, Schweingruber, and McCarthy, 1998; Della Porta and Reiter, 2006; Noakes and Gillham, 2006; Rafail, Soule, and McCarthy, 2012). If officers used violence, the argument sometimes goes, the police strategy must have been escalated force policing.

This is a tautological argument; escalated force policing is argued to lead to violence and is often defined as a strategy that quickly employs violence. It does not come as a surprise, then, that studies find that strategies, tactics and violence are connected. But the argument also lacks empirical foundation; some studies suggest that arrests and use of force by police officers *increased* during periods when officers use a non-dominant strategy (Soule and Davenport, 2009). It therefore remains contested whether policing strategies really impact the emergence of protest violence, or how significant they are in causing an escalation. Given the extensive literature on the topic claiming that police strategy is vital in leading to violence in protests, the issue deserves a closer look.

Police Strategies and Their (Non-)Implementation

Looking at what happens during a protest, moment by moment, shows that protesters' motivations alone do not lead to the eruption of violence (see Chapter 2). A close-up look at police strategies leads to a similar observation: it shows that planned police strategies are rarely implemented during an operation and in some of the analyzed protests officers' actions even clearly contradict the predetermined strategy.

At several protests prior to which a lenient, hands-off strategy was announced (negotiated management policing), officers did not communicate with protesters and used strict and formal tactics—in many aspects they behaved contrary to the announced and planned strategy (see also Wahlström, 2011). Similarly, at several protests where police had announced an escalated force strategy, officers were cooperative and communicative. Yet findings suggest the key is not that police deliberately make false announcements about their planned strategy but that internal police procedures seem responsible for this divide.

For instance, at the Kehl march in 2009, police declared a low-tolerance approach, including a number of restrictions: protesters were not allowed to approach within five feet of officers or to bring toilet brushes. However, officers did not enforce these rules during the operation, but were in fact rather forthcoming and tolerant in their interactions with protesters. Their actions during the operation directly contradicted the planned strategy. This march and other protest examples suggest that prior decisions of high-ranking police officials do not determine the behavior of officers on the ground when they are confronted with specific interaction dynamics. Kehl officers simply did not see a reason to implement harsh tactics when confronted with colorfully dressed, relaxed, and happy protesters. When in the situation, the announced minimum-distance rule between protesters and officers or a ban of large banners seemed inappropriate for the operation.

Why might strategies have such a limited impact? At the end of Chapter 2, I discussed why (protesters') motivations alone are not vital to causing violence in protests. It seems only logical to assume that it helps if we translate our motivations into strategies. Strategies can guide the way we handle a situation and therefore how a situation will unfold. Going back to the everyday example discussed above, I can keep a tight schedule at work and pack my sports gear the night before as a strategy to follow my motivation to go for a run after work. This will increase the chances of my intention becoming action.

Yet the protests in Rostock and Kehl suggest that strategies can be fragile. Police officers in Rostock employed a tolerant strategy—up to the point where they felt that protesters were not playing by the rules and the situation was getting out of hand. Protesters used peaceful strategies—up to the point when they felt that the police were provoking them and possibly playing and attacking them. In Kehl we saw that police had the strategy of not being "velvet glove" with protesters, e.g., if you bring a toilet brush, you will get arrested. Yet, the situation unfolded as a collaborative effort and constructive exchange of how to proceed—toilet brush or no toilet brush.

My participant observation with German police officers involved in planning and implementation of crowd policing suggests that such differences in strategies and action can be explained by two organizational aspects on the side of the police. First, interaction dynamics, not strategies, guide police operations, and operational command has some leeway in how to react to operational dynamics. During my participant observation, many officers stressed that the proportionality principle is key—at least in recent police protest operations in the German capitol. For instance, a Berlin police officer in charge of planning and organizing large-scale protest operations explained that proportionality in accordance with the situation is vital for an operational commander to decide what her or his platoon should do. Other officers up and down the chain of command expressed this assertion in separate talks.

Furthermore, unit leaders are generally given some leeway in achieving their specific objectives in order to be able to adequately react to changing situations during an operation. While thresholds for intervention are set in the mission report, it is up to commanders to determine how to carry out the specific task they are given (e.g., securing or clearing an area or accompanying the march up front). Thus, officers interviewed with experience in policing large crowds repeatedly described operations as dynamic interactions and police actions as responses to protesters' behavior. Due to the principle of proportionality and the operational commander's leeway in achieving an objective, a direct line from the broader strategy to specific actions during an unfolding operation does not exist in most operations.

Second, I found that broader operational strategies[1] are often not communicated in detail down the chain of command. Officers in the front lines are usually briefed first and foremost on their specific objective during an operation, rather than the overall strategy. In operational briefings, officers in the front lines are instructed what they are specifically ought to do in the field. To pursue tasks like "accompany march up front" or "secure area X," these officers do not need detailed knowledge on talks taking place on the highest police planning level or the talks between the highest planning level and the leader of their unit. While officers receive a written report during operation briefings, police officers (interviewed by sociologist Peter Ullrich) stated that these reports are often not read in detail (see also Arzt and Ullrich, 2016; Ullrich, 2017). Therefore, a further reason for a non-implementation of strategies might be that officers do not always concern themselves with what the planned strategy entails. A former officer explains:

> Well, I think, I am not sure if the [. . .] units and in general the operational commanders are even sure about the tactic, or if they are even aware of, this view, this other view, they get an operational order, which indicates certain guidelines, whether they read it, or not, we don't know. [. . .] Whether or not they are even interested. So there is, I think, there is a divide between those standing in the front lines, and those experiencing it from the planning and strategic level. (Peter Ullrich,[2] personal correspondence with author)

In short, the principle of proportionality, commanders' leeway, and the communication down the chain of command might explain the gap between police strategies and actions. While operational commanders might have had less leeway in the 1960s and the principle of proportionality might have been less important then, officers in the front lines at these protests might have had even less knowledge of the overall strategy during the more hierarchical police structures of the time than they have today. These aspects might have led to similar gaps in planning and implementation across decades.

---

[1] The current common police strategy in Berlin is by default de-escalation. Specific tactics, however, vary.

[2] The interviews took place as part of Ullrich's research project, "Video Surveillance of Assemblies and Protests" (German: "Videoüberwachung von Versammlungen und Demonstrationen").

Escalated Force Policing Equals Violence?

Findings suggest that during an operation officers often do not act according to the policing strategy chosen by the command due to the principle of proportionality and unfolding situational dynamics. But what if they actually *do* employ a rigid strategy? My analysis suggests a counterintuitive finding: a tolerant strategy (i.e., a strategy to keep the peace) rather than a rigid strategy might actually favor the outbreak of violence under specific circumstances.

Consider the Rostock G8 protest in 2007. Police had announced a hands-off strategy, which was then implemented. The strategy was described as a "de-escalation strategy" (see, e.g., Ramelsberger, 2007): tolerant, reactive, and informal. Tension among officers and protesters then increased due to several factors in the unfolding of the event. The situation escalated, and violence broke out. Many studies on protest policing would assume violence would not erupt in times of a negotiated management strategy. Why did violence nevertheless break out in Rostock?

In Rostock, and several other protests, a negotiated management strategy contributed to an escalation by increasing tensions. In line with the planned tolerant strategy, officers did not stop protesters who collected stones, and they did not wear helmets, although some thought they should (German Police Union, 2007). When officers observed protesters covering their faces or smashing the windows of a bank, officers in the front lines felt unable to adequately respond. They perceived that their command had let them down as a result of management problems and a lack of precautions and overview. After the protest, the German police union accused the police command of having used officers in the front lines as "cannon-fodder" (Beikler, Hasselmann, and Tretbar, 2007). The interaction dynamic during the march led to the officers' impression that their command's low-profile strategy had been a mistake. This perception of feeling let down by operational command increased tension and fear drastically. Hence, in Rostock, the lack of precautions due to a negotiated management strategy added to tensions that arose due to unfolding interactions with protesters (German Police Union, 2007). After a build-up of tension and fear, officers used violence, in particular, where and when they established emotional dominance (i.e., when police–protester lines broke, in situations when officers outnumbered protesters, and when protesters turned their backs or fell down; for more information, see Chapter 7).

The Rostock protest illustrates that a tolerant strategy might amplify tension among officers, if other tension-increasing interactions accumulate during the protest. Nevertheless, case comparisons suggest a tolerant strategy itself does not lead to violence. In many protests a tolerant strategy was used successfully and the protests stayed peaceful. A tolerant strategy is also generally preferable, since it creates a more pleasant atmosphere for protesters and officers. If an escalated force strategy is announced, protesters—many of whom invest their free time to protest for what they see as a better world—might be criminalized from the start. When fearing harsh police reactions in response to minor transgressions or perceiving a high probability of violence, some citizens might not even attend a march although they agree with its purpose. Both scenarios cannot be in the interest of democratic countries, which depend on political participation by the civil society. For officers in the front lines, policing a protest might also be more pleasant if they do not need to react harshly to any form of transgression but can instead expect more easygoing interactions with protesters and if they can support them in their right to protest. While a negotiated management strategy can thus amplify tensions under specific circumstances, it is generally the preferable strategy.

Police Strategies and Agents Provocateurs

When analyzing the potential impact of the violent few on the emergence of violence in Chapter 2, I studied all potential effects that the presence, ideology, and performances of the violent few could have on a violent outcome. In a last step, I examined what impact it would have if some of the violent few actually wanted to provoke and use violence against officers. Similarly, when looking at police influence it is vital to shed light on the issue from every angle and examine all possible scenarios in which police motivations and strategies might impact a violent outcome. Another way in which police strategies could impact interactions between protesters and police is in the use of agent provocateurs.

While police might not officially adopt a harsh strategy to escalate a protest, they might do so by employing undercover agents who commit illegal acts in order to incite protesters to do the same. While I found evidence in only one protest that operational command officially ordered physical violence, the possibility of undercover agents being present and trying to provoke violent acts cannot be ruled out in most protests. Yet nothing points to such individuals playing a crucial part in the emergence of violence in social protest marches in Germany and the United States.

Comparisons suggest agent provocateurs might, just like the violent few, inflict property damage, which can—as one out of five key interactions (see Figure 3 in the Introduction)—favor the emergence of physical violence between people. But these individuals cannot alone provoke violence. For instance, some might try to escalate the situation by pushing protesters against the police line, as happened in Kehl. Still, violence does not automatically follow. Some might damage property but physical violent clashes do not ensue. Thus, whether some violently motivated protesters are actually agents provocateurs matters on a normative level, but it does not seem relevant for finding answers as to why large-scale violence occurred during these protests. As empirical evidence suggests, the violent few (be they black bloc protesters or agents provocateurs) seem unable to incite large-scale violence on their own.

Illustrating this argument, a German police psychologist was asked in a radio interview whether agents provocateurs might have caused violence to erupt in the Rostock G8 protest in 2007. He responded: "There is a possibility that *agents provocateurs* were present. [. . .] But in this situation no specific provocateurs were needed [to cause an escalation]" (Roelcke, 2007). The situation unfolded a certain way—with or without provocateurs—and, as I will argue in detail (see Chapters 4–6) the situational breakdown of usually-relied-upon routines was key for violence to break out.

On the whole, strategies seem to have similarly limited consequences as motivations when it comes to causing violence in protest marches. It therefore seems much more useful to focus on how strategies unfold, how they change due to interactions, or how they are overrun by situational dynamics.

Protest comparisons across decades show there is something distinctive happening among police during these unfolding situations that severely increases the chance for violence across protests. While the prior police strategy or use of agents provocateurs do not seem vital for a violent outbreak, it does matter how the police operation itself unfolds. In particular, mismanagement within the police during the operation seems to be a crucial factor for violence emergence.

Police Mismanagement

Police mismanagement is one of five situational interactions during marches I identified to be crucial for the emergence of violence in protests (see also Figure 3, Introduction). Police mismanagement refers to operational command lacking overview and/or a clear course of action during an operation or communication problems occurring among police units.

Police mismanagement occurs independently from the prior police strategy, meaning it can occur if prior plans aimed for a tolerant or a rigid police strategy. Either way, police mismanagement increases tensions on the side of the officers, and the perception of mismanagement can contribute to a change in officers' perceptions of themselves and their role in the protest. Officers might initially see themselves as doing their job, but police mismanagement can have the effect that they increasingly see themselves having to defend their physical integrity, thereby increasing tensions and us–them boundaries between them and protesters. A closer look at several protests in which police mismanagement took place helps illuminate this concept, its various forms, and its consequences for violence.

Rostock, 2007: "That Was Operational Idiocy"

The Rostock G8 main march in 2007 started out in a friendly mood. In pictures protesters and police seem relaxed; they mostly observe their own group, their shoulders down and loose, they are talking to each other or laughing (see also Introduction). Yet this collective mood among protesters and officers changed in the course of the protest. Police mismanagement during the operation was one factor contributing to this development.

A common-sense assumption would be that police units are in frequent contact with command during an operation, know where they are, and carry out specific orders given to them. However, in Rostock, and a number of other protests, things looked quite different. The operational command could not tell officers where they were, where to go, or where other units were. Officers recall these stressful instances: "Suddenly we were surrounded by masked people and were apparently right in the middle of the assembly at the port. We did not see any other units. Later we were bailed out by [another unit] that hadn't noticed us earlier and were themselves surprised to meet us there" (German Police Union, 2007, p. 4). Many officers report they were left to their own devices in highly chaotic operations. In addition, units felt let down by operational command. When requesting backup, one unit was told by command to "make it to the waterfront." Yet the waterfront was located at the other side of the square, which was filled with tens of thousands of protesters. "You will find a maritime salvage cruiser there," the reply continued (German Police Union, 2007, p. 4). The unit felt mocked and desperate.

Units that received backup by water cannon trucks were not better off. The unit, which was lost in the middle of the assembly, continued: "Later water cannon trucks arrived and mixed CS gas into the water. Units on the street were not notified of this action" (German Police Union, 2007, p. 4). Thus, officers sprayed their colleagues with CS gas and several officers needed medical assistance due to their own group's miscommunication.

Further, when the situation at the port became increasingly chaotic, officers on the ground felt special units, trained to react to crisis situations such as the one unfolding in Rostock, were badly needed. Yet these units were employed to guard specific buildings and therefore were not available in order to help out at the port.

Amid increasing disorder, various unit commanders at the scene had to use their private cell phones to find out what their assignments were. In an interview with a large German magazine, an officer later recalls fits of sweating and heart racing during these chaotic situations (Pfohl, 2007). A police psychologist later criticized command for reacting highly inflexibly, although the operation was planned and prepared for two years in advance. Bottom line, he states: "That was operational idiocy" (Pfohl, 2007).

New York, 1988: "Not Well Planned, Staffed, or Executed"

Police mismanagement like that in Rostock is no exception. A different protest, in a different country and during a different time period, provides an illustrative comparison: the protest against the Tompkins Square Park curfew in New York City in 1988. This march ended in what the *New York Times* (1988) later called a "police riot." While the protest, its context, and its course of events will be discussed in more detail (see Chapter 4), some incidents taking place during this protest can further exemplify what can go wrong on the side of the police during an operation.[3]

In 1988 a curfew was to be implemented in New York's Tompkins Square Park. By organizing a march, activists aimed to protest the curfew

---

[3] In Germany, data on potential mismanagement is usually available from the German police union, among other sources. In the United States, police mismanagement is usually indicated in after-action reports or civilian investigative panels. Hence, while the sources differ, information on potential police mismanagement can generally be obtained for both countries.

and the perceived gentrification of the neighborhood. Because the police department was severely understaffed, most officers at the march were young and inexperienced. Protesters marched to the park, but once they arrived they did not disperse but entered the park in which the curfew was to take place. As the situation got out of hand, a police headquarters was quickly set up in the middle of the park and more units were ordered to the scene. As a consequence, newly arriving backup units had to pass through a throng of protesters just to reach the temporary headquarters and receive orders. Only then could they find out whether the crowd through which they had just walked was actually dangerous or not. Similar to the Rostock event, such management failures at the Tompkins Square Park protest caused distress on all sides.

Moreover, once backup units arrived at the headquarters, many of them did not find high-ranking officers to receive information or orders from. Officers in charge were either "absent from the scene or unable to cope with the situation" (Pitt, 1988). The *New York Times* (Blumenthal, 1988) reported that in the middle of unfolding clashes, the deputy chief went to use the bathroom of a police station a mile away and remained absent for some time. The commanding police officer was able to reach neither the commissioner nor the mayor during the night of the clashes (Solomon and Levin, 2008; Daily Beast, 2010). A later report by the New York Police Department showed that "hundreds of police flooded into the area, though they 'had not been briefed about the event . . . were not equipped for such an encounter . . . were not under the direct supervision of a superior officer' " (*New York Times*, 1988). Breakdowns in command and communication occurred. Police commissioner Benjamin Ward later confirmed that the police actions were "not well planned, staffed, supervised, or executed" (Purdum, 1988).

St. Paul, 2008: "No One Was Seeing the Big Picture"

Police forces today are certainly better organized than they were in the 1980s. Nevertheless, police mismanagement still occurred in recent protests. Consider a third example of police mismanagement: on Monday, September 1, 2008, about 10,000 protesters marched in St. Paul, Minnesota, to protest the Republican National Convention (RNC) being held in the city. A mobile squad unit in riot gear watched the peaceful main march. Yet, about 200 to 500 activists diverted from the march into nearby areas, smashed store and car windows, and threw newspaper boxes onto the street. Officers responsible for the surrounding area hence witnessed severe property damage by protesters. They were not wearing any protective gear and were unprepared for this sort of trouble. They felt they badly needed the mobile squad units to support them. However, these units could not be reached, as the police had established two separate dispatch centers, one for the convention and one for the rest of the city. The idea was not to be overwhelmed by the amount of incoming information—a legitimate concern, as the Rostock protest illustrated. Yet, the dispatch centers could not communicate with each other (Fox 9 News, 2008). Officers therefore witnessed property damage, but were unable to call the mobile squad for backup. While the squad unit watched the peaceful march, the disorder took place just around the corner. "No one was seeing the big picture," Fox 9 News reported (2008, min. 0:30). While two centers were located only 20 feet apart, the communication breakdown between them continued for two hours. More and more people joined in the property damage around the march route. When police finally reacted, they responded with force, using pepper spray, tear gas, and, in some cases, rubber bullets in arresting nearly 300 protesters.

This example illustrates the role of internal police communication as a crucial aspect of police management. In St. Paul, the two command centers' inability to communicate was a key element in police mismanagement. Cross-case comparisons show that internal police communication is usually disrupted or breaks down for two main reasons: overflow and technical problems. First, communication might break down if too much information needs to be handled and processed at a single command center. As soon as disturbances take place, the large amount of information reaching the command can lead to paralysis. Command then loses oversight over the operation in real time and cannot support units on the street anymore. This was the case in Rostock, for instance.

A further problem at longer operations in the context of global summits can be technical problems. Large-scale protests, such as in St. Paul, show that communication can be difficult if units from different parts of the country take part. Since these units usually operate on different radio frequencies, it can be impossible for them to communicate or reach each other if necessary (see, e.g., City of Miami Civilian Investigative Panel, 2006, p. 19; Miami Police Department, 2004, pp. 25 ff). Other technical problems include communication breakdown during the operation, for instance, if walkie-talkie batteries go dead or police radio communication is interrupted. Such seemingly "small" difficulties can create major problems: units are suddenly cut off from communication with other units. When police orders and tactics change due to new developments, different units might have different information and contradicting orders on how to (inter)act with protesters and other citizens—e.g., if one unit has old information that protesters should disperse to the south and one has more recent information that they should disperse to the north. While one unit sends protesters one way, they are then stopped and told by a different unit to double back. This scene occurred during the Miami Free Trade Area of the Americas (FTAA) protest in 2003 (City of Miami Civilian Investigative Panel, 2006, p. 20). It was impossible for protesters to comply with both units' orders, putting both protesters and officers under stress. Some police units are more used to these types of dynamics and unexpected situations, in which one might temporarily be cut off from communications, than others (e.g., police units in the capitols, who face high numbers of protests annually, are usually more experienced in policing such large-scale events). But depending on how tense and out of control the situation gets, even experienced officers are certainly not immune to being affected by these difficulties.

As these examples show, police units do not always need to communicate extensively, but communication becomes particularly important if the operation does not go as planned. If the last message that a unit received over the police radio was that the situation was getting out of hand and then they are suddenly cut off from radio traffic, left on their own with their batteries dead, tension on their part inevitably increases. When units suddenly find out that protesters have destroyed other parts of the city while they watched the march and thought everything was in order, tensions will certainly rise.

While numerous case examples indicate that some forms of police management problems seem rather prevalent, a number of police commands seem somewhat unaware of lessons from prior operations. This leads to almost identical complaints in several after-action reports coming from several decades (National Research Council, 2004; see also Braga and Schnell, 2013). Hence, although mismanagement is a situational factor, it has a cultural component. Resource management and flow of information are relevant aspects of police culture and organizational structure. If mismanagement occurs, these structures of police organization do not work in the protest situation due to bad planning and unforeseen situational dynamics.

While police mismanagement cannot alone cause violence to break out, it is a vital part of a combination of situational factors that systematically leads to protest violence. If it occurs together with incursions into the other group's space, mismanagement can severely increase tension and fear. It can thereby cause police to perceive that situational routines have broken down and can lead to violence by police officers. This loss-of-control path (see Chapter 4) is one of three paths to violence (see also Chapters 5 and 6).

4 | Losing Control

C HAPTERS 4 THROUGH 6 OF THIS book will show how combinations
of specific interactions during protest marches can create moments
of emotionally charged chaos, where communication is poor and
misunderstandings arise. In these situations, people feel abandoned and
attacked, confused and in distress—tensions and fear rise. Such a breakdown of situational routines can cause protest violence to erupt. One of
three situational paths that leads to a perceived breakdown of routines and
the emergence of violence in protest marches emerges when police mismanagement occurs together with spatial incursions. This combination
forms a loss-of-control path to violence. The same underlying dynamics
of situational breakdowns exist in the other two paths to violence (see
Chapters 5 and 6), in other types of violence, such as uprisings turning
violent, and in non-violent surprising outcomes, such as failed robberies
(see Chapter 9). The following sections will discuss how spatial incursions
and their combination with police mismanagement form a loss-of-control
path to violence in protests.

Invasions

The 33rd G8 summit took place on June 6–8, 2007, in the Grand Hotel
Kampinski at a Baltic Sea spa in Heiligendamm, Germany. On the agenda
were, among other topics, the financial markets, the African continent, and
environmental issues.

From January 2007 on, a fence—eight miles long and eight feet
high—was built around the summit site, including barbed wire, motion
detectors, and CCTV cameras. The expenses for the fence amounted to
some 12.5 million euros. The total tab for the three-day summit came to
92 million euros. The taxpayer-financed fences and security measures left

citizens to protest far from the summit—in the city of Rostock, 12 miles (20 kilometers) away. Nevertheless, demonstrators managed to organize a week full of protest marches in and around Rostock, direct action at the fence, and an alternative summit with speeches and over 100 workshops.

As described in the Introduction, on the day of the large opening march, Saturday, June 2, protesters marched to the port and a police car was parked on the protesters' assigned route. The mood among the crowd got tense, as the car was parked on what protesters perceived as *their* protest space. This tension increased further, when units started running into the assembly square—the *protesters'* assembly square—for no apparent reason. Such interactions, where one side invades the other's associated or negotiated territory, can be called "spatial incursions." *Spatial incursions* seem to be vital for leading to violence in protest marches. The following three sections will clarify what spatial incursions are, why they are crucial for the outbreak of violence, and why, despite this crucial role, they cannot lead to violence on their own.

Spatial Incursions

Public, often urban space usually forms the stage for protest marches. It is where protest happens. But at their core, demonstrations are also *contests* over space. Protesters use space to publically make their claims: by marching on streets and public places they aim to reach a broader audience for the societal grievances or political claims they want to address. The citizens' right to claim public space to express their concerns or demands is ensured by their constitutional right to protest. Disturbing public routines to draw attention to a cause is the essence of a public protest march. Space is thus a primary objective for protesters. The common protest chant: "Whose streets? Our streets!" expresses this focus.

Space is also important for police. Everyday police work focuses on space. When officers are called to a potential crime scene, their first action is to draw attention to themselves and mark their territory (Jacobsen, 2001). One of their first tasks is to conquer the space in which they conduct their operation. At a crime scene, for instance, tape is used to mark that the space now "belongs to" law enforcement for a certain amount of time. Space further plays a role for officers' assessment of operations. For instance, when planning an operation, German police usually assess seven criteria (in the following order): the mission, the occasion, the legal situation, space, as well as time, weather, and their own and adjacent forces (Jacobsen, 2001). During protests, the control over space is also a primary objective of police (Zajko and Béland, 2008, p. 723). Illustrating this notion, the police chief at a protest in Washington, DC, replied to public criticism over a large pre-emptive arrest during the protest, by stating, "We didn't lose the city, so as far as I am concerned, it was worth it" (Montgomery, 2000).

Because both sides of a protest march care about space, its use is usually negotiated prior to the event, especially since the advent of negotiated management policing during the 1980s. Moderate, generally peaceful protest groups usually register their protest marches with the police, who allocate specific parts of public space to protesters for a limited amount of time. Both sides thereby agree upon the use of public space in the form of a protest route. Protesters are able to use specific public streets and places to make their claims heard. They are allowed to interrupt certain societal routines—like street traffic—for a specific amount of time. But police are still responsible for regulating the use of public space, as public space "belongs to" the city. Protesters are not allowed to use public spaces beyond the ones agreed upon, as this is usually perceived as causing too severe disruptions of public life. Which spaces will be allowed also depends on officers' assessment of protest groups (e.g., if groups are considered more or less radical).

Spatial incursions consist of either police or protesters moving into the other group's space during a sanctioned march. For instance:

- In Rostock spatial incursions occurred when police parked a car on the protest route and ran into the protesters' assembly space.
- At the 1988 protest against the curfew in New York's Tompkins Square Park, the march was precipitated by a dispute *over* the public park, which was then entered by protesters.
- At the Brokdorf protest in Germany in 1981 (see Chapter 6), protesters entered the construction site of a nuclear power plant during a protests against the plant. The construction site had been declared off limits by the police and was surrounded by a fence.
- At the 2003 Miami FTAA protest, police pushed protesters away from the fence of the FTAA summit site and toward the "green protest zone." The moment one protest group tried to take down a fence that surrounded the FTAA summit site, officers employed rubber bullets and tear gas canisters.
- At a 1995 Rutgers protest in New Jersey, violence erupted after protesters occupied the intersection of Route 18 South and River Road. Police later claimed officers wanted to clear the road for a pregnant woman who needed to get to a hospital.

- In Frankfurt, Germany, at a demonstration against education fees in 2008, protesters left the sanctioned protest route and ran toward a nearby highway. Violent clashes ensued.
- In other protests, demonstrators ran toward or attempted to enter official or public buildings such as the Pentagon in the Vietnam War protest in Washington, DC, in 1967, the America House in the Berlin protest against the US invasion of Cambodia in 1970, or the state parliament in a student protest in Hanover, Germany, in 2008.

It is important to emphasize that such incursions do not imply that opposing sides make physical contact or that people get close to each other in order to fight. They simply refer to a violation of spatial zones assigned to the other group. The Kehl protest is a perfect example that such incursions do not necessarily entail physical contact and violent clashes. Here, police cut off the sanctioned protest route and interfered with the other group's space: protesters were even pushed against officers, but violence did not occur. In other protests, the other group's space is invaded without the two groups getting close to each other. This underlines that spatial incursions do not imply physical proximity and that physical contact does not equal violence. Individuals can just as well fight from a distance by throwing stones or tear gas while remaining in their "space."

When committing spatial incursions, people usually realize what they are doing but are unaware of the possible consequences. Spaces are usually clearly defined prior to the march, and spatial borders are often marked during the march itself: police lines might indicate where the protesters' space ends, or loose lines of officers may be placed on the sidewalk. Marchers usually follow a loudspeaker van that indicates where the march is heading. When protesters or officers then leave their space, they presumably know that they do so. Hence, when protesters, for instance, leave the protest route and run toward the highway, or when they block the street during a march so delegates cannot attend a summit, they probably know that this is not the space they previously agreed upon with police. But protesters may be unaware of the drastic consequences of such actions. To the same degree, officers know that the assembly space of the rally is the space attributed to protesters and that blocking protesters on their assigned route means blocking their space. Yet officers, too, seem to be mostly unaware of the strong escalating effect of such spatial incursions.

Spatial Incursions and Violence

Out of the five interactions identified as leading to violence in demonstrations, spatial incursions have the most drastic impact on the eruption of violence. They are a necessary condition for violent outbreaks in peaceful protest marches in my study. This means they cannot alone cause violence, but they are present in every path to violence (see also Appendix B).

The strong impact of incursions into the previously negotiated space of the other group makes sense when considering the role of space as a personal safety zone. Having someone seemingly invade and disrespect another's space generally produces strong feelings and concerns. People's space is their comfort zone, their safe haven. When a home is robbed, for example, the owners often do not only suffer material loss; they also suffer from the violation of their *space*. Studies also found that stick-up robbers tend to conduct robberies in areas close to their homes, even if this increases the chance of being recognized and arrested. Yet they know the area; it is their turf, so they feel more comfortable there (Wright and Decker, 1997). It does not come as a surprise, then, that protest space is important to people and that turf violations have a drastic impact on how they react to a situation.

But what about spatial incursions elicits in people as drastic an action as violence? Due to the frequent prior negotiations between protesters and police in Germany and the United States and talks about the protest route, both groups are usually conscious about what their designated space is. Thus, when spatial incursions take place during a protest, they can easily be interpreted as the other side not respecting an agreement, acting unfairly or irrationally, and not being trustworthy. People are disturbed in *their* turf—the space the other side had agreed to respect. Consequently, if police interfere with protesters' territory or if protesters interfere with police territory, tensions rise. In some protests it is the police who worry: Why are protesters leaving the assigned route? Do they want to commit property damage in another part of the city? Officers are responsible for preventing unlawful behavior and keeping traffic flowing in the rest of the city. Could protesters even be preparing an attack on officers? If they do not follow the route that was sanctioned and rules that they agreed to, who is to say what they will do next?

In other marches, protesters worry due to spatial incursions by the police. For instance, in Rostock, police units started walking through the protest to later stand in the middle of the crowd without any clear purpose.

Protesters felt their space was invaded. A video (Fels, 2007) shows that they observed officers carefully and some raised their hands as a sign of de-escalation to show that they did not mean to harm the approaching officers. Protest observers from a human rights organization concluded that officers' running through and standing among protesters was "apparently the main reason for the situation to escalate at the port" (Steven and Narr, 2007, p. 56). Yet, these instances were not the only spatial incursion that raised tensions in Rostock. As a police psychologist stated when describing the Rostock escalation,

> Until [protesters saw the police car parked on their space] the protest was mostly peaceful. An atmosphere between carnival and the Love Parade.[1] [...] Then there was this car at the square. Apparently some of the protesters saw this as a challenge. The car was attacked, a group of officers tried to intervene, then events came thick and fast. (Deutschland Radio, 2007)

Protesters asked themselves: Why did officers park the police car on *our* protest route? Are they looking to start a confrontation? Why do units keep walking through *our* assembly? Do they want to make arrests? What have we done to justify officers entering *our* territory? (see also Steven and Narr, 2007).

Visual data show how severely tension and fear increased due to both sides' spatial incursions, in addition to other relevant interactions: at the beginning of the protest, both police and protesters look happy, relaxed, and mostly focused on their own group's actions (for coding emotions, based on facial expressions and body postures, see Appendix B, Table B2). Pictures show protesters smiling, their shoulders down and relaxed, others talking to each other in a relaxed mood, and police officers interacting with different protest clowns in a friendly manner (Davinca, 2007; Jubilee Australia, 2007; Transnational Institute, 2007). Yet when police officers ran through the protesters' assembly space, protesters showed characteristics of tension and fear. Videos and pictures (Jamsven, 2007; Léglise-Bataille, 2007) show their eyes are tense and wide open, their upper eyelids raised, their lower eyelids raised and tense, and their brows raised. They show open mouths and drawn-back, tensed or stretched lips, postures and movements that are tense, their

---

[1] The Love Parade was a large German electronic music parade. It was notorious for a cheerfully excessive atmosphere, participants' colorful and revealing clothing, sex in public, and excessive use of drugs.

shoulders drawn up. All these are indicators of fear (see Appendix B, Table B2; see also Ekman, Friesen, and Ellsworth, 1972). Officers show the same emotion expressions. Small units move even closer together. Pictures and videos (Jamsven, 2007; Léglise-Bataille, 2007) show that they start standing back to back to avoid possible attacks from behind. Some officers show wide-open eyes, mouths stretched back. Officers move their heads a lot in these instances to see every potential danger in their vicinity. Shortly after these tense situations and displays of fear, violent altercations erupted in Rostock.

In short, spatial incursions drastically disrupt peaceful protest routines and contribute to changing emotional dynamics. They cause confusion and suspicion and raise tension and fear. These specific emotional dynamics later feed into tipping points to violence (see Chapter 7). In contrast to background factors, such as motivations, cultures, or strategies of protesters or police that showed by themselves to be insufficient to lead to violence (see Chapters 2 and 3), such interactions during the protest event are closely related to the eruption of violence. While spatial incursions cannot lead to violence on their own, they trigger violence if they occur in specific combinations with other situational interactions, as the next sections will emphasize.

Territories and Protest Dynamics

Spatial incursions are crucial for the emergence of violence. But despite their importance, they cannot cause violence on their own. Take the example of the migrants' rights march on June 4, 2007, in Rostock. During this march, protesters faced spatial incursions by the police. Nevertheless, the protest stayed peaceful. Just like the main march to the Rostock port, the migrants' rights march was part of the protests against the G8 summit. This protest is particularly interesting, since it took place only two days after the main march, in the same context and place, with similar police forces and protesters, and even with the violent outbreak of the main march in mind. Despite all this, the march remained peaceful.

Protesters assembled at 2 p.m. near Rostock City at a deportation facility to demand a global right to free movement. Protesters wanted to gather at the facility in order to march from there to the inner city. Walking to the starting point of the march, protesters saw police lined up at both sides of the road. Most media were waiting in the inner city. Before the march set off, the police closed in around protesters and accused black bloc protesters of having collected stones. Police declared that they would not let the march start, since some protesters might be armed. Water cannon trucks started to line up on the street leading to the inner city—the sanctioned route on which protesters wanted to march. Tensions rose. Police kettled protesters, a tactic where large cordons of officers contain a crowd within a limited area. The de-escalation team of the police withdrew without notifying protesters of their reasons. Protesters were confused and started to be fearful. They observed the lines of officers closing in around them with distress. They perceived they could not leave if they wanted to. Hardly any onlookers or media would see an escalation here on the outskirts of the city, as most were waiting in the inner city for the march to arrive.

To reply to the accusation of being armed, numerous black bloc protesters stripped down to their underwear to show they did not have any stones or other weapons.[2] Others already came barely dressed, claiming that police used protesters' covering their faces as an excuse for employing harsh tactics. Pictures show protesters standing around in their underwear, with slogans like "naked aggression" or "shoot here!" written on their naked bellies or backs (Süddeutsche Zeitung, 2007; HiveMind, 2008).

After about one hour, the march was finally allowed to start (Mitteldeutsche Zeitung, 2007; Steven and Narr, 2007). Protesters marched several hundred meters, only to be stopped once more by the police near the beginning of the inner city. Police officials stated that the protest turnout was much larger than expected; therefore, the march would not be allowed to enter the inner city. Protesters were baffled. It was a very hot day; they were standing in the sun for hours on end; some had even stripped down to show their peaceful intentions. Many were now left feeling frustrated and betrayed. The route was negotiated, it was sanctioned, and the bigger-than-expected turnout to support migrants' rights should have been a triumph for them, not an obstacle. Protesters felt trapped and worried. Yet after a total of four hours of negotiations, the groups dispersed peacefully at 6 p.m. (Steven and Narr, 2007, p. 70).

---

[2] One reason for this de-escalating behavior could also be that protesters wanted to protect undocumented refugees in the march from being arrested should the situation escalate. Nevertheless, it is unlikely that such a motivation—if it existed—was key for keeping the march peaceful: first, the march shows a common pattern that suggests the specific situational unfolding was crucial for avoiding violence. Second, undocumented refugees might also have been attending the large main march against the G8 meeting in Rostock two days earlier. At the time, this did not hinder some activists from covering their faces, or committing property damage.

While the right to protest was severely curtailed, there is also a positive message to the story: violence did not erupt at this march. Communication between protesters and police played a crucial part in de-escalating the situation (see Chapter 8 for details). Most importantly, however, the example shows that, while spatial incursions drastically influence marches by increasing tension and fear, they alone cannot cause violence to erupt. This is true even though just two days earlier police and protesters had clashed at Rostock's port.

The comparison illustrates that people can become tense if spatial incursions occur. Yet if they are informed about reasons for spatial incursions, or if they feel equipped to handle turf incursions by the other group, they will not perceive that routines have broken down, and interpretations of being threatened and high levels of fear will not follow. Cases suggest that additional interactions need to occur together with spatial incursions for people to interpret the situation in a specific way. The main march in Rostock on June 2 is an example in point.

The Loss-of-Control Path to Violence

One path to violence in protests is a combination of spatial incursions and police mismanagement, which can be called a "loss-of-control" path. This path captures a dynamic specific to police forces, which leads officers to use violence against protesters. The other two paths (see Chapters 5 and 6) can lead to violence by either protesters or police.

While Chapters 2 and 3 discussed that people's motivations and strategies alone are not key for violence, the subsequent discussion of police mismanagement and spatial incursions indicated that these two interactions can contribute to leading to violence. While neither of the two interactions can lead to violence on its own, their *combination* is sufficient to lead to violence (see Appendix B): if organization of police forces is flawed or breaks down and the resulting uncertainty and disorientation coincides with a perceived territorial invasion by protesters, officers feel they are losing control over the area they are policing. They fear the operation could fail and protesters could harm them. This interpretation, caused by the combination of spatial incursions and police mismanagement, leads to violence as it changes emotional dynamics. After a perceived loss of control and following reinterpretations and increased levels of tension, violence erupts in specific micro-situations (see Chapter 7).

Tompkins Square Park Protest: Losing Control over the Park

Tompkins Square Park is located in Manhattan's East Village neighborhood. It is a 10.5-acre square with grass, trees, and benches. While the East Village was home to squatters, artists, landlords, blue-collar families, merchants, and young professionals and a center of counterculture in the 1950s and 1960s, it symbolized New York's decline in the 1980s. Tompkins Square Park, which was part of a high-crime area, became a stand-in for the entire neighborhood. Homeless encampments were built, and the area was a hub for drug trafficking. In August 1988, a curfew was to take effect in the park after 1 a.m. so that homeless people and other citizens could not stay in the park overnight and thereby could not live there permanently. This planned curfew touched issues of homelessness, gentrification, and the future of the neighborhood.

Hence, a protest against the first night of the curfew was set for August 6, 1988. Activists started marching around 10.30 p.m. and arrived at the park holding banners to protest the gentrification of the neighborhood. Activists then entered the park—a territory assigned to the city and police—which was a highly symbolic space for both sides because the claims of the event concerned the park and its curfew.

In addition to this spatial incursion, examples of police mismanagement abound at this protest: the police were understaffed and many of the officers present were inexperienced. Most were unable to get advice from more experienced officers, because the temporary headquarters were difficult to reach. Further, many commanding officers were absent. Command and communication among police broke down (see also Chapter 3, "Police Mismanagement").

Officers faced a territorial invasion they could not respond to. They perceived a loss of control over the operation, and the resulting perceived powerlessness made them apprehensive and tense. Eventually, in what the *New York Times* called a "police riot" (1988), officers attacked protesters, bystanders, and residents alike. Many left the scene bloody and baffled (for videos, see, e.g., Solomon and Levin, 2008).

Vietnam War Protest: Trying to Guard the Pentagon

Together with the protest examples from the 1980s, 1990s, and the first decade of the millennium discussed so far, a protest in the 1960s can highlight the relevance of situational dynamics and illustrate the loss-of-control path across decades.

From 1955 until 1975 the Vietnam War was under way, leaving about 3.8 million people dead. The United States was involved in a ground war from 1965 that led to estimated total casualties of around 2,450,000 people (Rummel, 1997). While most American citizens supported US involvement in the war in the early 1960s, public opinion shifted over the course of the decade. In the summer of 1967 polls revealed for the first time that less than 50 percent of Americans supported the war. Nevertheless, the US involvement increased.

Against this backdrop, on October 21, 1967, about 100,000 protesters gathered in Washington, DC, for a permitted rally and subsequent march to the Pentagon in protest of the war. The march was organized by a loose coalition of over 100 different groups, from students and anti-war veterans to Vietcong sympathizers and pacifist hippies. Of the 100,000 protesters in attendance, about 40,000 eventually marched to the Pentagon.

The US secretary of defense, Robert McNamara, had ordered a low-profile strategy for the operation: initially only about 3,000 law enforcement officers were on open duty for the march of 40,000 protesters. As a contingency plan, 5,000 to 6,000 officers were on standby, hidden inside the Pentagon. Another 12,000 soldiers, marshals, and police officers were on standby in the region (a common strategy in both negotiated and escalated force policing styles). The officers guarding the Pentagon waited for the march in a tranquil picnic-like atmosphere, lying on the grass and chit-chatting with each other (U.S. Marshals Service, 2011). Tensions rose later and rather suddenly.

At noon the rally took place in front of the Lincoln Memorial on the National Mall in Washington. The march then set out in the afternoon. When protesters arrived at the Pentagon after 2.5 miles, they faced security forces that guarded the building behind a rope line. The forces announced that anyone crossing the line would be arrested. While one group tried to exorcise the Pentagon and make it levitate, other protesters approached the police line and some put flowers on the bayonets. When a few protesters tried to cross the thin police line to enter the Pentagon, they were arrested and beaten. Isolated scuffles took place, but no large-scale violence had yet occurred. Other protesters started sit-ins in front of the building. According to some sources, some protesters threw vegetables.[3]

At this point the operational commander wanted to deploy the hidden forces inside the Pentagon to support their colleagues outside. This,

---

[3] According to the U.S. Marshals (2011) some also threw rocks and bottles at officers. Yet this information is unconfirmed by most other sources.

however, was not possible right away: the request had to be approved by the Department of Justice, which took 20 minutes. During these 20 minutes, the event outside became increasingly tense. When the reinforcements finally arrived outside, the situation was already chaotic. Security forces responded very violently and used tear gas against protesters. Major clashes erupted and lasted until the evening. Several soldiers and marshals were hurt, and over 100 protesters had to be treated for injuries.

Consider the event in the light of spatial incursions and police mismanagement: spatial incursions occurred in the form of protesters trying to enter the Pentagon—a highly symbolic non-public space—which unsettled officers greatly. In addition, there was police mismanagement when backup units could not be employed as needed (Vogel, 2007; U.S. Marshals Service, 2011). The combination of both interactions led to officers outside as well as inside the Pentagon being tense and fearful: the officers inside the Pentagon knew that their operation and safety were at risk, but they could not see what was happening outside and thus could not react to the potential danger. The thin line of officers outside could not have held back thousands of protesters had they actually tried to enter the Pentagon. Officers knew this in advance and when relaxing on the lawn throughout the day, but now, in the light of spatial incursions and police mismanagement, this fact suddenly made the situation appear seriously threatening (Leen, 1999). Pictures of the encounter indicate how even armed soldiers show tension and mild fear when protesters try to stick flowers into a soldier's bayonet rifle. Some of the soldiers' eyes are widened, baring the white of the eyes, their upper eyelids raised, their lower eyelids tense, their bodies tense and stiff (see, e.g., ThingLink, 1967; Radnor, 2014).

Further, officers felt that their operational command had let them down, since they could not get support from their colleagues on standby. The *Washington Post* later reported:

> Ironically, Pentagon officials were so preoccupied with presenting a tolerant image that they kept thousands of soldiers hidden inside the building. During the critical early stages of the confrontation, a thin line of MPs outside the building was overrun, and the commander couldn't get reinforcements in place quickly. (Vogel, 2007)

In short, tensions rose when officers could not react to spatial incursions due to police mismanagement—a recurring pattern across protests that turn violent. The officers' situational perception of losing control led them to perceive a breakdown of the routines they usually rely on. Units inside were waiting to be deployed, knowing that the situation was escalating but not seeing what was happening. Units outside were feeling threatened, desperately waiting for reinforcements to arrive. This increased tension and fear on the part of both groups was key to the emergence of large-scale violence. After this increase of tension and fear, thousands of additional soldiers finally arrived outside the Pentagon in a moment of surprise to find chaos. When arriving outside, they were highly emotional, now in a dominant position, and reacted very violently (see Universal Newsreel, 2010, for visual footage).

These situational dynamics and their interpretation can also explain why a rigid police strategy alone is not vital for the emergence of violence (see Chapter 3): such a strategy can generally *support* the officers' feeling of being in control through pre-emptive, clear, and rigid actions toward protesters. A tolerant policing strategy, on the other hand, can contribute to officers' perceptions of losing control when spatial incursion and mismanagement occur, as in the 1967 Pentagon protest in Washington, DC, or the G8 protest in Rostock in 2008. Yet systematic case comparisons suggest that what is key to surprising outcomes such as protest violence is not prior strategies or motivations but breakdowns in situational routines, which lead to moments in which chaos, confusion, and fear prevail. Members of one group then overcome their inhibition threshold for violence if they establish emotional dominance over the other group—for example, when lines break up or individuals of the other group turn their back or fall down (see Chapter 7).

Feeling Powerless

When the combination of police mismanagement and spatial incursions is present, officers use violence—not only at the Tompkins Square Park or Pentagon marches, but in every protest in my study. The feeling of powerlessness seems a vital component leading to violence by police. Police, as part of their professional routines, are deeply concerned with feeling and presenting themselves as being in control of a situation (e.g., Rubinstein, 1973). When officers' space is violated during a demonstration, they tend to perceive that protesters do not respect agreements, or even plan to attack them. Both would undermine the officers' objective to stay in charge (see also Zajko and Béland, 2008). Protest comparisons show that police mismanagement then limits officers' means of handling spatial incursions. This inability to respond leads officers to perceive a loss of control.

The perception of a loss of control takes place due to processes common to most social interactions: officers interpret actions by protesters and assign meaning to them, as well as to the overall situation (Blumer, 1986). They may then reinterpret their own role according to their interpretation of the situation. For example, officers may initially define themselves as people who do their jobs to be able to pay the rent or as people who help citizens in need. Yet if officers perceive losing control during a protest, they might feel attacked by protesters and reinterpret their own role as needing to defend their physical integrity.

At the same time, people's perception of their own group's heterogeneity generally changes during such reinterpretations. Although police as well as protesters are usually a mélange of fragmented groups, conflict increases perceived unity among groups (Reicher, 1997, 2001; Stott and Drury, 2000). When faced with perceived conflict, groups come to perceive their in-group increasingly as a coherent entity that is being attacked by a homogeneous out-group (see Drury and Reicher 2000; Stott and Drury 2000; see also Blumer 1986).[4] For instance, when confronted with perceived conflict, protesters are more likely to assume that their in-group is not a mélange of different activists (e.g., the Green Party, feminist groups, global justice groups, and many others), but a homogeneous group ("the protesters").

The same dynamic takes place on the side of the police. Police units from different parts of a country often have different levels of experience and may come from different police cultures with different training. They are often initially skeptic about colleagues whose collaboration they require at larger protests. Yet, in the face of threatening actions by protesters, their perception of group homogeneity increases. Officers are more likely to overlook that colleagues belong to units from different parts of the country or other branches of law enforcement and may express their happiness about units from a different federal state helping them out (e.g., German Police Union, 2007, p. 4). Studies in social psychology show that conflict not only leads to self-perceptions of being more homogeneous, it also generally increases the solidarity of the in-group (e.g., Reicher, 1997, 2001; Stott and Drury, 2000). In protests, such solidarity can further help

---

[4] Studies show that participants rarely define their identity in terms of specific traits but usually in positional terms and through moral and practical aspects of their position. When the assessment of the other group changes, their own position changes accordingly. This leads actors to treat the out-group more homogeneously, a process that can further increase perceived unity among the out-group (Reicher et al., 2004).

groups overcome their threshold of confrontational tension and fear and use violence when confronted with a perceived hostile out-group.

Lastly, a perception of powerlessness and a reinterpretation of the situation and one's own role affect emotional dynamics. The reinterpretation of the other, the self, and the situation changes so-called universal (Ekman et al., 1972) or reflex (Jasper, 2006) emotions. Universal emotions refer to seven emotions identifiable and differentiable in a person's facial expression across different cultures: anger, fear, sadness, surprise, happiness, contempt, and disgust.[5] A change from happiness to fear could be seen in the Rostock visual footage discussed in Chapter 4 ("Invasions"). These universal or reflex emotions are commonly distinguished from background emotions, such as moral emotions (e.g., compassion, outrage, shame) and moods (emotional filters for perception, decision, and action), which also play a role in protests by causing affective loyalties to one's own group and distinctions to the out-group (Jasper, 2006, p. 17, 2018). In contrast to moods or affections, universal human emotions, such as fear, are usually object-related and triggered by the interpretation of a certain event or situation during the protest (Batson, Shaw, and Oleson, 1992; Jasper, 2006).

If officers reinterpret the situation as one of a loss of control, cases show they become frustrated, confused, and fearful. For instance, after spatial incursions and police mismanagement occurred in the Rostock G8 protest, an officer recalled in an interview with the German magazine, *Der Spiegel:* "An operational fiasco I have never experienced before in all my time of service! It was about pure survival." Another officer stated, "We were so scared, it is a miracle that the fear didn't make us go nuts" (Pfohl, 2007). In Rostock, the combination of spatial incursions and police mismanagement led officers to assume that routine interactions have broken down and thereby generated fear.

The perceived loss of control and the resulting fear then make the slightest opportunity to regain control of the immediate situation appear worth taking. Such opportunities arise in particular if a triggering moment occurs in which one side perceives emotional dominance (i.e., has a

---

[5] Psychologist Paul Ekman and colleagues (1972) showed that respondents across cultures and countries identified the same facial expressions as belonging to certain emotions in a set of photographs. This was also true for preliterate tribesmen not exposed to specific media depictions of emotions (Ekman, Friesen, and Ellsworth, 1972). These seven emotion expressions might be universal, as we need to interpret other people's emotions (such as anger) reliably in interactions to react accordingly. Researchers found that blind persons as well as newborn infants display these seven emotions in the same way. While a researcher always needs to interpret these universals in context (Ekman, 2003, pp. 4, 217; von Scheve, 2012), they can provide vital tools to analyze emotion expressions in comparable cultural settings.

situational advantage over the other), for example, when people turn their backs or fall to the ground. Videos of the Tompkins Square Park protest show protesters being hit when screaming "I am going down" (Telengard, 2007). Others are kicked after they fell to the ground or are hit on the back of their heads when running away (see also Chapter 7).

A Police Culture of Control

Before moving to the second path to violence (Chapter 5), the question remains: Why do officers rely so heavily on being in control, and how do their training and professionalism impact this situational path to violence?

Loss of Control: A Rarity

Let us remain in the 1970s to first illustrate that it takes a lot for officers to perceive they are losing control. Despite US public support for the Vietnam War having declined during the late 1960s, the war still continued in 1971. The United States had been fighting in Vietnam for more than 10 years and was close to invading Cambodia, which further escalated the conflict. Nonetheless, the anti-war movement was in decline from the late 1960s on. Many were tired of demonstrations, as they felt they had little impact on the US involvement in the war.

In this context protesters assembled for a march on April 24, 1971, in Washington, DC. The press expected a generic anti-war march—there had been so many marches over the past years. Yet the April 1971 protest turned out to be much larger than expected: about 500,000 people came to march for peace. On videos, protesters can be seen everywhere—in trees, on statues, in fountains (CBS, 2009; Ling, 2012). Protesters seem enthusiastic. Mostly dressed in hippie clothing, some sing "give peace a chance" and some draw peace signs on each others' naked chests. Others take a bath in public fountains. During the event, protesters even enter the Pentagon and lower its flag (Gilcher-Holtey, 2001). Remember what happened when the Pentagon was *almost* entered by protesters in the 1967 protest—the attempted territorial invasion had drastic consequences.

However, no escalation occurred in 1971. Police refrained from any actions against this territorial invasion; as police mismanagement did not take place, they felt in control. Officers saw no reason to feel particularly anxious or fearful. They were very well prepared for a mass arrest of another group, the so-called May Day Tribe, which had planned direct action right after the march (*New York Times*, 2012). The May Day Tribe had planned to block intersections in order to shut down government meetings. However, due to the Tribe's thorough organizing of when and where to start their direct action, police, who had been surveilling them, also had the knowledge they needed to foil their plans.[6] During the hours after the march, police conducted the largest mass arrest in US history and pre-emptively arrested every person who could possibly have become involved in the direct action: 1,200 protesters were taken into custody (*New York Times*, 2012). Hence, officers felt completely in charge and well prepared during the march. Protesters in fountains and some inside the Pentagon— who cares? The police operation was still going according to plan. Their key focus was the May Day Tribe.

Hence, although interactions in this protest differed from the peaceful routine in that protesters invaded space, tensions did not rise because officers perceived no loss of control. My comparison with violent protests indicates that officers do not perceive losing control easily or often. In the Vietnam protest in 1971 they would presumably have perceived a loss of control had police mismanagement also occurred—as in the march to the Pentagon four years earlier or the Tompkins Square Park march in 1988 discussed in Chapter 3. Since mismanagement did not take place at the Pentagon march in 1971, officers felt in charge, and they had every reason to perceive that they could rely on situational routines.

For protesters who participated in the march, all was well, too. During the march most footage shows no visible police. Protesters seem happy and excited (CBS, 2009; Ling, 2012). Protesters expected the march to be smaller and were then enthusiastic and happy when so many attended. Officers, on the other hand, expected the march to stay peaceful and ex-pected to arrest the May Day Tribe later on. Although the pre-emptive arrests can be regarded as problematic from a legal and normative stand-point, the protest illustrates the importance of the interactional routine maintaining a feeling of safety for participants and the stability of emo-tional dynamics. It shows that if the specific interactions identified as

---

[6] May Day Tribe protesters were one of the first groups using what was later often labeled "Seattle tactics": Peaceful direct action, blocking intersections, organization through affinity groups, etc.—in addition, they let their cars run out of gas at key intersections to block roads. The so-called "Seattle tactics," named after the direct action tactics employed by activists at the WTO 1999 protests in Seattle, were also used in other protests during the 1960s, 1980s, and 1990s (Gillham and Noakes, 2007, p. 343). The common claim that the tactics of the Direct Action Network used at the WTO summit in Seattle 1999 were something completely new to the police and therefore mainly respon-sible for the severe clashes on November 30, 1999, is therefore doubtful.

leading to violence do not occur in combination during a march, officers do not easily feel they are losing control. But why do officers care so much about not being in complete control, even if only for a short time?

Police Culture and Police Objectives

Police, as part of their professional routines, are generally deeply concerned with being in charge of a situation. Establishing control is a key part of police culture, not only during protests, but in any kind of police operation (see also Rubinstein, 1973; Terrill, 2003; Gillham and Noakes, 2007, p. 341). Studies highlight that "there is an institutional imperative for control in police encounters that characterizes policing in general" and that the importance of control is "pervasive and manifest" (Earl and Soule, 2006, p. 148).

In protest contexts officers expect to be in charge and in control and they expect protesters to comply. If protesters do not comply, police become uneasy. Hence, officers in Western democracies perceive and interpret a loss of control within the context of their training as well as within the context of their expectations when policing protest groups. Officers— like protesters—experience protest marches through a cultural scheme and interpret situations and actions in a certain way because of this scheme (Jasper, 2014, p. 7 ff). While "culture in general does nothing" (Collins, 2005b, p. 1), it impacts police training and protest repertoires as well as police and protesters' expectations of protest situations. Officers' cultural backgrounds and professional expectations thus inevitably color their interpretation of events (see Blumer, 1986).

This focus on control has two implications. First, officers' job performance is often measured by how well they control the situations and the persons they encounter (Earl and Soule, 2006). Second, officers—US police in particular—directly connect the objective for control with officers' safety and tend to interpret a loss of control as dangerous. In this social construction of danger, objective risks are quickly exaggerated, since officers tend to equal losing control with being in danger (see also Earl and Soule, 2006, p. 149).

Since protest marches are routinized, generally peaceful social events, things rarely get out of control. If officers do lose control, they therefore tend to become confused, anxious, and afraid. In their view the fear response to a loss of control is rational. For instance, my analysis of visual and document data shows (and interviews with officers confirmed this finding) that officers during the Rostock G8 protest 2007 perceived they had reliable information that suggested they were losing control and were thus in severe danger. In hindsight the danger people were in may not have been as drastic and their actions may thus look irrational from a researcher's point of view. But if we trace the situational dynamics step by step, we see that these actions were rational from their point of view, as officers did not have a full overview of what was going on. Officers were highly alarmed as situational circumstances indicated that they might lose control or have already begun to do so (Earl and Soule, 2006).

The perception of danger plays a role in this path leading to violence, since it is precisely such a "reasonable belief" of being in danger that is frequently used in police guidelines on when to use force against protesters. Force should be used if an officer perceives that "a reasonable police officer in the same circumstances and experiencing the same informational input would feel the same level of danger and the same need to use force" (Civilian Investigative Panel, 2002, p. 77). US police training moreover indicates a necessity of using force against protesters if civilians have a diminished ability to "control themselves" and must therefore be "forcefully controlled" (McPhail and McCarthy, 2005, p. 8). Officers' objective of regaining control when confronted with spatial incursions and police mismanagement therefore makes the slightest opportunity to do so seem worth taking—including using physical violence.

In addition, officers face a further amplifying effect with regard to in-group dynamics: because they possess superiority in armaments and combat training, they are better equipped for the use of force than protesters and are also trained to work in small units, making them well equipped to "retake control" by force. These aspects can further increase their feeling of solidarity in tense situations, creating a further "us" versus "them" dynamic toward protesters.

Police Training and Professionalism

What relevance has police professionalism for the outbreak of violence, if police training and culture impact the loss-of-control path by forming a lens for situational interpretations? Officers' training can be seen as a way police culture impacts situational interpretations, interaction dynamics, and social outcomes. Training heavily influences what officers expect and how well they are able to react to situational dynamics during a protest. The professionalization in German and US police in recent decades might therefore decrease the likelihood of officers' perceptions of being overwhelmed by the situation. We might assume that better training for worst-case scenarios and for situational losses of control will diminish officers' strong emotional reactions and therefore reduce chances of violence eruption. This might be especially true for some police units. For instance, the Berlin police face high numbers of large protest marches each year. Their level of experience and professionalism not only differs from police districts in less experienced federal states (which police fewer such events) but is also visible in how they de-escalate even marches considered to be notoriously violent, like May 1 protests (see also Chapters 8 and 9)—in particular since focusing more strongly on situational control tactics and situational communication since 2012. US police departments, such as in Washington, DC or New York, also show higher levels of experience, as they police large crowds on a regular basis and face more potential worst-case scenarios. These units might be less prone to perceiving a loss of control.

At the same time, even in times of higher professionalism, officers tend to face logistical difficulties (e.g., walkie-talkie batteries going dead, command losing overview and being unable to provide officers with essential information) or unexpected scenarios (e.g., protesters leaving the protest route). While training might thus decrease chances for police mismanagement, mismanagement can and does still occur during operations of experienced units. In addition, protest comparisons indicate that police training generally intensifies a focus on control. Given that the occurrence of a loss-of-control path (police mismanagement *and* spatial incursions) is rare and that increasing professionalism and police training can increase expectations of control, feelings of confusion, helplessness, and fear might even be intensified through professionalism and training, once control seems to be lost.

When conducting participant observation with the German police, I talked to an officer with experience in company-sized police reserve units as well as in operational planning. He illustrates this point by stating that experience helps, while strong routines can hinder good operations: if an officer is too routinized (not only in protests, but also in other police operations), an unexpected situation might hit the officer all the more unexpectedly. Hence, strongly expecting routines may lead to even more severe confusion when routines break down. When an officer involved in planning large-scale operations on a high level started talking about an operation turning out to be different than expected, I asked: "What happens when things go unexpectedly?" He responded: "That an operation goes unexpectedly is very rare, but if it that happens, that's very bad and that's something you later see on TV." Due to this dual impact of training and professionalism, which diminishes mismanagement but increases expectations of control, protest comparisons across decades suggest that violence is relatively unaffected by levels of police training and professionalism.

This detailed look at different protests in the first path to violence has highlighted situational dynamics that underlie not only the loss-of-control path but all three paths to violence: violence during protests erupts due to a breakdown of routines people normally rely on. More specifically, unplanned situational interactions lead to interpretations, interpretations produce emotions, and specific emotions trigger violence when emotional dominance is established. While the discussion showed that interpretations are shaped by cultural expectations, and that spatial incursions as well as police mismanagement have a cultural component, the analysis indicated that motivations and strategies constitute background factors that can be overridden by situational dynamics. Findings hence illustrate the crucial importance of the micro-level of protest marches in leading to violence.

Since the focus on control is crucial for officers' daily routines, a loss-of-control path can only lead to violence precipitated by officers, while either side can precipitate the other two paths that lead to violence (Nassauer, 2018c). The following two chapters will discuss these two paths. Each path consists of previously unplanned combinations of interactions between protesters and officers that occur in the hours between the start of a protest and the outbreak of violence. Chapter 7 will consider in more detail which emotional dynamics these three paths produce in the seconds and minutes before a violent outbreak occurs and how the temporal dynamics of such interactions can affect the intensity of violence.

5 | Expecting the Worst

IN THE SECOND PATH TO violence a somewhat different dynamic is at play than in the loss-of-control path—one that leads either side to perceive that the other is up to no good and thereby causes confusion, tension, chaos, and violence. This chapter will discuss that, contrary to common assumption, prior expectation of violence cannot lead to a self-fulfilling prophecy. No matter what the expectation or media predictions of dire outcomes prior to a march is, the outcome in terms of violence seems barely affected. What happens *during* the event seems to matter more for the actual unfolding of the march and the eruption of violence. An examination of the actual expectations of escalation during the operation suggests that escalation signs during a protest are the third factor out of the five introduced earlier (see also Figure 3 in the Introduction) that can favor violence in protests. If escalation signs combine with spatial incursions and property damage, people perceive an offense. This perception increases tension and fear and leads to violence when individuals or small groups establish emotional dominance.

"Where Were They? When Would They Strike?"

In various marches, protesters had been portrayed as a violent mob before the start of the demonstration. Although these protests were often organized by moderate protest groups, police soon expected anyone attending the protests to be potentially violent (see also Starr and Fernandez, 2009, p. 43). In some cases, as in the protest against the FTAA meeting in Miami in 2003, every person in the city was under constant observation by police days before the protest even started (Crespo, 2006, p. 20). Potential protesters were followed closely through the streets and searched repeatedly by officers. The expectation of violent actions remained on the day the protest started. A participant recalls: "The walk into downtown was like sticking your hand in a bush that you know has an animal in it that is going to bite you. Everyone knew it was going to be bad, [. . .] Where were they? [. . .] When would they strike?" (Harvey, 2010). Everyone was expecting the worst.

Interestingly, in both the peaceful and violent protests in my study, mainstream media behaved similarly prior to many demonstrations; most corporate media (TV, radio, print, and online newspapers) expected violent outbursts—although protest marches rarely end this way. This expectation can be explained by a "good" news story requiring notorious, consequential, or extraordinary events (McCarthy, Clark McPhail, and Smith, 1996, p. 480; Ryan, 1999). Protest violence matches these criteria. Thus, large parts of the media usually predict clashes and discuss possible dimensions and consequences of such violence. If violence then occurs, media usually report on the protest (though mainly on the violent clashes). If no violence occurs, media coverage of the protest is often sparse. Even if the protest is very large but peaceful, corporate media might not report on the event at all (see, e.g., Wenner, 2002).

In addition, police officials commonly inform media prior to protests that violence is to be expected. Police then also tend to display objects captured in raids—sometimes as mundane as bicycle chains—as indicators for mayhem to come (see Hayden, 2003; City of Miami Civilian Investigative Panel, 2006, p. 10). The corporate media's often uncritical echoing of these warnings can favor a background atmosphere of panic and fear.

For example, before the peaceful Pittsburgh G20 protest in 2009, media repeated concerns by police that protesters might use elaborate, violent techniques. According to a security consultant, some of the protest groups involved would be using "long poles from behind to stab at police officers . . . a la the Romans" (Lojowsky, 2009). Before the Brokdorf protest in 1981, German national evening news media discussed statements by politicians that suggested that protesters might take hostages and set farmers' houses on fire (Das Erste, 1981, min. 14:00). None of these actions occurred in these protests, nor were long poles used for stabbing officers in any of the protests I studied.[1] Regardless of a similar expectation of violence, the Brokdorf protest turned violent, while the Pittsburgh demonstration stayed peaceful.

---

[1] I did not study the use of arson in detail, but setting buildings on fire seems to occur rarely in protests by these groups. In my sample, the Brokdorf protest in 1981, where protesters set a sewage disposal plant on fire, seems to be an exception in this regard.

Through such media expectations of violence, protesters—many of whom invest their spare time to promote what they consider a better society—might be criminalized from the start. Moreover, such expectations can have a negative influence on officers in the front lines, as they might buy into the media expectations of violence and be nervous from the beginning. They are also more likely to face tense protesters, which can further amplify officers' tensions.

However, comparisons suggest that expecting violence *prior* to a protest cannot by itself cause violence to erupt. Even if the worst is expected and anticipated, most protests stay peaceful (depending on the year, the protest group, and type of protest between 80 percent and 92 percent of protests in Germany and the United States from 1960 to 2010 stayed peaceful; see, e.g., Della Porta, 1995; Waddington, 1998; McAdam, Tarrow, and Tilly, 2001; Tilly and Tarrow, 2006).

Take the protest against the Group of Twenty (G20) finance ministers and central bank governors meeting in Pittsburgh, Pennsylvania, on September 25, 2009. Prior to the march, newspapers headlined: "G-20 Protest Plans Raise Alarm in City" (*Pittsburgh Tribune Review*, July 11, 2009), "Hospital Coordinator Anticipates Unknown During G-20 Summit" (*Pittsburgh Post-Gazette*, September 10, 2009), and "Pittsburgh Steels Itself for G-20 Protests" (*Wall Street Journal*, September 11, 2009) (Lojowsky, 2009). In fear of protest violence, museums and theaters, colleges and universities closed. The school board even decided to close all 66 Pittsburgh public schools during the summit days and considered buying terrorism insurance for several buildings (Nereim, 2009). "I'm scared for the children's safety," a member of the board stated (Smydo, 2009). Parents were afraid to let their children play outside.

However, none of these fears materialized, and the event remained peaceful. Most people were relaxed or even happy during the protest, focusing mainly on their own group's actions. Passing through downtown, the march resembled a convivial parade (for visual data see, e.g., G20 Peoples March, 2009; People's March Reaches Downtown Pittsburgh, 2009). Many observers were watching the march along the road, while protesters marched in the middle of the street, holding banners and chanting. Officers communicated with protesters if needed. Although media—and therefore many onlookers and participants—expected violence to occur, the interactions during the protest suggested no imminent escalation. This prevented a surge in situational tension and fear. A prophecy set up to be self-fulfilling did not take place.

Compare the different expectations of violent clashes in two major US protests and their insignificance for protest violence to illustrate why a self-fulfilling prophecy is not evident: the Seattle protest against the WTO in 1999 and the Miami protest against the FTAA in 2003. In Seattle the global justice movement stepped into place visibly for the first time. They had brought unexpected tactics with them (although, as depicted in Chapter 4, "A Police Culture of Control," similar tactics had been used by the May Day Tribe in 1971 and other protest groups in the 1970s and 1980s). Through direct action they surprised officers, blocked intersections, and managed to enforce a shutdown of the WTO summit. The Seattle Police Department had failed to plan for a worst-case scenario. When they—in their view—experienced just that, panic among officers broke out. Here was a city center out of their control, the operation a failure. Violence was not particularly expected, yet due to the way the protest unfolded, clashes occurred.

The Miami FTAA summit took place four years after Seattle, in 2003, so that the Miami Police Department had the Seattle events vividly in mind. They knew how much could go wrong—maybe a little too well so. The Miami Police Department was overly prepared. They had studied and planned possible worst-case scenarios and kept protesters under close surveillance, creating a tense atmosphere around the summit from the start. "Seattle wishes it could have done more to prevent what took place and Miami realizes it should have done a bit less," a report later summarized (Chamberlain, 2005, p. 10).

Regardless of the very different expectations and respective preparations, the result—in terms of violence—was the same: violent clashes erupted in Miami just as they had in Seattle. While violence was expected in one protest and not in the other, a clear pattern can be found across cases ending in violence: officers faced extraordinary situations that went against the routines they commonly rely on. They faced situations that were confusing and that caused them to believe they were in danger. This belief and the resulting increase in tension and fear was a key contributing factor to violence in both protests.

The comparison of these two cases illustrates that, no matter what the expectation or media predictions of dire outcomes prior to a march, the outcome might look the same. What happens *during* the event seems to matter more for the actual unfolding of the march and the eruption of violence. Expecting the worst prior to the march can turn out to be the actuality, as in the 2003 FTAA protest in Miami, or false, as in the protest against the G20 meeting 2009 in Pittsburgh. Having no expectation of escalation can turn out to be true in the event, as in the Washington Peace March in 1971, or a false assumption, as in the Seattle WTO protest in 1999. It seems that expecting violence, contrary to common belief, does not necessarily cause a self-fulfilling prophecy.

Escalation Signs

An examination of the actual expectations of escalation during the operation provides a different story. Studying protest marches in cross-case comparison suggests that *escalation signs* during a protest are the third factor that can favor violence in protests. What is meant by "escalations signs"? Escalation signs refer to actions perceived as foreboding harmful actions. For instance, if protesters collect stones as bluster, officers tend to interpret this action as a sign of escalation—as in the G8 protest in Rostock. In other protests, putting on facemasks is interpreted as another sign of escalation: "Many of them put on black face masks, sunglasses and helmets, making them unrecognizable, like gangsters," a police officer at a 1970 Berlin protest against the US invasion in Cambodia stated (ZEIT online, 1970).[2] Such actions are often displayed by some members of one group and perceived by the other as signs of immanent escalation. This interpretation occurs although no escalation has happened yet and although such actions (e.g., police driving around with sirens and putting on gas masks, or protesters covering their faces and collecting stones) do not necessarily lead to the group later exercising violence.

For example, pictures show some groups of protesters in Rostock dressed in black, with hoodies pulled down and their faces covered (Amies, 2007; IGuerilla, 2007a). German police commonly distinguish between protesters "ready to use violence," "prone to use violence," and "peaceful" and assign the colors red, yellow, and green to these groups. The expected numbers of protesters in the red (and yellow) group are usually communicated to units in briefings prior to an operation, and actual numbers are then communicated during the operation. Protesters dressed all in black with hoodies and facemasks are generally considered to be part of the red group. If these protesters then also collect stones, officers interpret this action as a sign of escalation.

---

[2] While these actions also are in violation of the ban on wearing face covers and hence by law require a police reaction, police frequently decide not to enforce this law—still, they perceive face covering as a sign of escalation.

Other actions that can be interpreted as an imminent sign of escalation are if protesters throw firecrackers in the direction of officers (as happened at a protest against the opera ball in Frankfurt on February 26, 2007) or if police receive bomb threats. For instance, officers in the Rutgers student protest in 1995 faced 45 fire alarms and one bomb threat on the day of the protest. Police also might observe protesters carrying gas cans or sticks (Brokdorf protest, 1981), reports might mention protesters collecting stones (Rostock G8 Main March, 2007), or radio transcripts might show that officers observed a truck with concrete blocks they interpreted to be potential weapons (Seattle WTO main march, 1999). Hence, such signs of escalation seem to be consciously recognized by participants and are often either discussed in subsequent documents (e.g., German Police Union, 2007) or mentioned in police radio communications (e.g., City of Seattle, 2008).

Protesters can also perceive specific actions by police as escalation signs—for example, if officers drive around with sirens for no apparent reason. At the Tompkins Square Park protest, a fire truck would arrive and depart every few minutes and more and more police cars and officers gathered quickly, which unsettled protesters as they assumed something was going wrong or about to go wrong. In addition, protesters recognized a helicopter aiming its spotlight at the tops of buildings, asking themselves whether it was looking for snipers. Pictures show that the appearance of officers in riot gear can look just as intimidating or menacing as some activists' clothing: in some protests officers wear full body armor with protective vests, sticks in their hands, helmets on, and dressed in black (e.g., in Seattle; see CNN, 1999; Sayoc, 1999; Tresyk, 1999). If police in addition suddenly start driving around with sirens, or put on gas masks for no apparent reason, protesters interpret these actions as signs of an imminent escalation.

Some police units, such as Berlin police, seem aware of potential escalation signs caused on their part and focus on their avoidance to de-escalate protests—in general since the 1980s but in particular since 2010. For instance, without knowing of the aspects I am studying or my interest in situational dynamics, different officers during my participant observation mentioned (some complaining, others praising) that Berlin police no longer drive water cannon trucks—still heavily used in protest policing in other federal states—into protest areas due to their threatening effect. Several Berlin officers also mentioned that they are frequently asked not to put their helmets on if not really necessary due to the helmet's potential threatening effect. Thus, participant observation suggests escalation signs seem to be recognized by some police forces and—if units are interested in de-escalation—can be consciously avoided.

If escalation signs occur on either side, they have strong escalating effects across protests. If either side interprets actions as foreboding harmful behavior this increases tension and fear. The police radio traffic from the Seattle WTO operation on November 30, 1999, illustrates the effect escalation signs have on emotional dynamics. In Seattle, officers were informed continuously about more and more actions by protesters that they interpreted as escalation signs. Consider only the most drastic notifications between 7:00 a.m. and 8:00 a.m., when protest events had just begun:

> 7.01 am: 10+ people seen with gas masks [. . .] 07.29 am: 1000+ people, 10 seen handing out objects [. . .] 7.30 am: Bomb threat to hotel reported [. . .] 7.42 am: Report of person with accelerants [. . .] 7.44 am: 100 people moving east, pushing dumpster [. . .] 7.49 am: Report of person with Molotov Cocktail [. . .] 7.50 am: Truck with concrete blocks. (City of Seattle, 2008)

It is easy to imagine the impact such notifications, in particular in such rapid succession, can have on someone. Further, such notifications came in increasingly quickly, the more the operation got out of hand. Notifications became increasingly imprecise and more menacing. For instance, at 9:20 a.m. radio traffic notified officers about "two people on roof"; at 10:20 a.m. a notification only stated "suspicious package" (City of Seattle, 2008). More and more vague yet menacing notifications reflect the increasing fear and suspicion on the part of the officers in Seattle. A committee report summarizes the effect of escalation signs during the Seattle operation as follows:

> There were repeated threats of bombings, and armed attacks, bomb scares, reports of shots being fired, demonstrators with Molotov cocktails and purchases of flammable liquids. In retrospect, we know that most of these serious problems did not materialize. But officers on the streets at the time had serious reason to be concerned for their safety. (Citizens' Panel on WTO Operations, 2000, p. 4)

As a response, tension and fear is visible in people's faces and bodily postures. Pictures show people's brows raised, raised upper eyelids, tense lower eyelids, officers looking around frequently, officers clinging to the batons in their hands (Shunpiker, 1999; CBS, 2010; see also Appendix B, Table B2). Escalation signs were one factor that increased tension and fear and thereby favored the outbreak of violence in Seattle and other protests. While escalation signs cannot lead to violence on their own, they form a path to violence when occurring together with spatial incursions and property damage.

Broken Glass

Breaking store windows or destroying trash cans can be a tactic used by protesters to make political points or to underscore their political purposes, or it can be a spur-of-the-moment action without a political message. In some cases of property damage during marches, windows of banks or major corporations are destroyed; in others trashcans are set on fire; rarely, a car is set on fire or a store is looted. In general, property damage refers to protesters damaging or destroying objects by hitting or kicking them with their fists or feet, with the help of objects, or by setting them on fire. Regardless of its underlying message in the eyes of protesters (see Chapter 2), *property damage* is a fourth vital factor in the emergence of physical violence in protests, since it systematically raises tensions and fears.

For one, property damage raises tensions among police officers. Officers know that they have to react to this disturbance of the law. This puts them in a tight spot. In addition, most officers perceive protesters who inflict property damage to be "violent" (see, for example, law enforcement labeling property damage as "violence" in RNC Review Commission, 2009, p. 2).[3] Many officers worry when seeing property damage: Who says that the protesters will stop at inanimate objects? Police worry whether property damage is an expression of the fact that protesters do not respect the rules and might turn against them. A statement by the German police president on TV illustrates this common perception by officers. Asked by a journalist why officers "clubbed peaceful protesters" in a demonstration

---

[3] While police officials frequently make such equivalencies of "property damage" and "violence" publically, court documents indicate that they do differentiate if specifically asked. At a protest against the IMF and World Bank in Washington, DC, in 2002, the police narrative was that officers responded to "violence" by protesters (in the form of property damage). However, during his deposition on the Pershing Park arrests, an assistant chief was asked: "Were [protesters] peaceful?" He responded, "Not particularly aggressive." Asked "Did you notice any violence?," he responded, "No," (Council of the District of Columbia, 2004, p. 116), indicating that he was aware that "property damage" and "violence" are different actions.

against education fees in Frankfurt in 2008, the police president replies: "If property damage is committed at a demonstration, if protesters light up objects, then I don't know if you can call that a peaceful protest!" (RTL Hessen, 2008).

Reporters often share officers' views and assume property damage might lead to an attack on people as well. "It was a frightening moment and I think I was in shock," a reporter said about her shaky panicky voice live on TV when observing protesters smash the windows of a Starbucks in Seattle. She was afraid that the looting protesters might intend to harm others, including herself (Kiro 7—Eyewitness News, 2013, min. 11:59).

In addition to assuming that property damage goes hand in hand with attacking their physical integrity and being supported in that conception by most mainstream media, police also tend to perceive that property damage by a few might bring out the worst in all the other protesters (see Stott and Reicher, 1998). If many protest groups march together and some individuals destroy property, officers fear that these violent few will "highjack" the crowd. They assume that they will lead initially peaceful marchers to become violent as well, and that the whole crowd may snap. "Something disengages in their brain," "the most mild mannered person . . . behaves like some sort of imbecile," according to UK officers (Stott and Reicher, 1998, p.517). This means that many officers tend to attribute property damage (as well as physical violence) by a few individuals to their rational calculations, while they tend to understand crowd violence as the result of a mindless irrational mass following these violent few. "The peaceful protesters lost control of their march because of these rioters, and that continues to be the pattern," a St. Paul police department's public information officer told the media after the 2008 protests against the Republican National Convention turned violent (Stirland, 2008). The above-mentioned distinction by Berlin police between red, yellow, and green protesters suggests that Berlin police makes similar assumptions in part: while not assuming that all protesters can be hijacked, the implicit assumption seems to be that the "yellow" protesters (prone to violence) can potentially turn "red" (motivated to use violence), whereas research would suggest "red" protesters most likely stay "green," while "yellow" as well as "green" protesters can also turn "red" in specific situational circumstances (e.g., Collins 2008; Stott and Reicher, 1998).

As discussed in Chapter 2, it can be disputed whether the violent few are primarily interested in physically clashing with police or stirring up the crowd. If they are, we can attest that they are not very good at making physical clashes happen: black bloc activists are frequently present at large-scale protests, but they rarely clash with officers. Nevertheless, many police tend to view the black bloc as violent anarchists who can stir up the crowd if they intend to (see also Chapter 2). This view of the irrational mob that follows its violent urges when provoked is heavily inspired by sociologist Le Bon's (2010; originally 1895) crowd theory. His long-prominent approach explains violence through the irrationality of collective actors: being in a crowd strips actors of their ability to think rationally, and actors then use violence since they respond to mindless instincts. These assumptions were supported by early studies in biology and psychology, assuming that violence is an immanent human urge (for an overview, see Bauer, 2011, among others). However, recent research in social psychology and sociology rejects this assumption, arguing that violent people act (boundedly) rationally (R. Collins, 1993, 2008) and do not lose their identities in a crowd (Reicher, 2001). Yet, while Le Bon's view is outdated in social science research, it is still held as a strong conviction by many people, including some police and mainstream media. And even an empirically incorrect and outdated conviction can have consequences. According to the Thomas and Thomas theorem (1938),[4] "If we define situations as real, they become real in their consequences." Applied to protests this means that officers who assume that protesters are all *potentially* violent will likely act accordingly. Police will subsequently treat all protesters differently and more antagonistically than if they assumed them to be peaceful. They will also perceive and treat protesters as a more homogeneous group than they are. Many protesters will then feel that they are treated unfairly by police, which again enforces stronger us–them boundaries on both sides (Reicher, 1996, 2001; Drury and Reicher, 2000; Reicher et al., 2004). The use of property damage thereby has wide-reaching consequences for officers' interpretations of the role of protesters, their emotional states, and subsequent actions.

To make matters worse, property damage also visibly raises tensions among the majority of protesters who refrain from damaging property, as well as among bystanders. After property damage occurs, protesters are aware that police have to react to this transgression, but they do not know what kind of reaction will follow. Will the police disperse protesters? Will they arrest them or even employ force against the entire crowd? Will the

---

[4] Commonly labeled the Thomas theorem and ascribed to W. I. Thomas, this theorem was first mentioned by W. I. Thomas and his wife and research partner, Dorothy Swaine Thomas, in their 1928 work *The Child in America*. I refer to it as the Thomas and Thomas theorem to acknowledge both authors (see also Smith, 1995).

situation escalate? Do officers know that it was only a small group of individuals who committed property damage and that most participants at the march do not condone these actions?

Furthermore, protesters fear a bad image for the protest: if property damage occurs at a march, most media tend to focus on property damage instead of the message marchers were passionate about and wanted to communicate (Giuffo, 2001; see, among many others, Boykoff, 2006; Cicco, 2010; Boyle, McLeod, and Armstrong, 2012). Thus, visual data show how protesters get upset by property damage as well: in Seattle about 100 out of approximately 50,000 protesters caused property damage worth $3 million (Cheh, 2005, p. 5). Several protesters tried passionately to stop them—some verbally, others physically (for videos, see Bijitaq, 2007; Independent Media Center, 2011). They were not wrong to fear an escalation: although property damage alone cannot trigger violence, it can cause violence to erupt in combination with spatial incursions and escalation signs by breaking situational routines and causing confusion and fear. Just as in the loss-of-control path, this combination leads people to a specific interpretation of the situation, which causes distinct emotional dynamics, as the following section will show: protesters or officers perceive that an offense by the other group is taking place.

Pre-emptive Strikes

In 1999 in the United States, the historic "N30," or "battle of Seattle," took place, an event we are already familiar with by now from previous chapters and a key event in the global justice movement.[5] A wide coalition of protesters gathered on November 30, 1999, to march against the meeting of the World Trade Organization in Seattle. As in Rostock, police officials and protesters had met in advance to organize and ensure a peaceful event. The primary march started at 12:45 p.m. and arrived downtown at Union and 4th Street by 3 p.m. At this point violence erupted. Officers clubbed protesters, although the latter had participated in an obviously peaceful march. Officers cleared intersections using batons, pepper spray, and tear gas. Protesters built barricades, and some threw objects at police. How did it come to this? In Seattle a number of escalating interactions combined: spatial incursions, escalation signs, police mismanagement,

---

[5] As other protest examples discussed in this book, this march will be described in detail as it is ideally suited to illustrate key dynamics of the path. Moreover, the event and the causes of its escalation into violent conflict have been the subject of extensive media coverage and public debate.

property damage, and communication problems between protesters and police.

The direct action network (DAN) was up early; at 5:30 a.m. the first groups were seen. Their goal was to shut down the WTO meetings, as they were seen as causing an unjust world order that exploits humans, animals, and nature. Equipped with "sleeping dragons" (devices for chaining arms together), among other things, protesters walked to the inner city, chained their arms, lay down in a circle, and blocked key intersections. Some used bicycle locks around their necks to chain themselves together (*Seattle Times*, 1999b), while others linked their arms and sat on the floor.

The protesters' aim was to prevent delegates from attending the conference, and to that end they had entered a public space not assigned to them. Police units were surprised by these actions. They had negotiated with protest groups in the weeks leading up to the event, but the DAN had not participated in the negotiations—and for good reason, since their tactic worked much better via this surprise effect.[6] Yet when initially only 400 to 600 Seattle police officers faced about 50,000—partly civilly disobedient—protesters, officers felt unprepared and betrayed. Tension and fear surged.

Thus, in Seattle the fact that protesters so significantly outnumbered police officers further increased officers' perception of being in danger. However, while the size of the protest or a ratio in favor of either group can contribute to escalation signs, a ratio in favor of protesters cannot solely explain violence by officers or vice versa. While the ratio is often impossible to assess exactly or reliably (police and protest organizers often report very different numbers), protest comparisons suggest that the ratio alone cannot lead to protest violence. In my study, violent protests occurred in a variety of ratios; in some many more protesters than officers were present. For instance, in Brokdorf, Wilstermarsch, 1981, around 100,000 protesters outnumbered 10,566 officers. At the WTO protests in Seattle, 1999, around 50,000 protesters initially outnumbered 400 officers. In other protests ending in violence the ratio was almost balanced, showing around 500 protesters to 450 officers (Tompkins Square Park, New York, 1988), or around 3,000 police to 2,000 protesters (IMF "people's strike," Washington, DC, 2003). At the same time, there are peaceful protests with approximately 40,000 protesters outnumbering around 10,000 officers

---

[6] Their plans might have been foiled, were they to become known to police. This happened, for instance, on April 24, 1971 (see Chapter 4), when officers knew about the May Day Tribe's plans for direct action and arrested thousands of protesters in advance.

(Peace March, Washington, DC, 1971), or even 50,000 protesters and 2,500 officers (emergency laws, Bonn, 1968), just as there were peaceful protests with only 9,000 protesters to 14,600 officers (NATO, Kehl, 2009). In short, there seems to be no pattern directly linking the police:protester ratio to violence. In line with these findings, in a report on the people's strike protest in 2002 (Council of the District of Columbia, 2004, p. 108), a legal counsel points out in his testimony that in protests in the year 1971, police were not overcharged to deal with 100,000 protesters, but in the years 2000 and 2002, they claimed to be overcharged with 15,000 or even 3,000 protesters. His assessment illustrates that the ratio alone is not key. However, in some cases, as in Seattle in 1999, the ratio can contribute to tensions perceived due to escalation signs.

Escalation signs also occurred throughout the day on November 30 in Seattle, when officers heard news about possible bombings, about aggressive protesters with Molotov cocktails, and about units having to withdraw from areas. Officers received such bits of information from colleagues over police radio in quick succession (City of Seattle, 2008). Such escalation signs had a drastic influence on the emotional dynamics in Seattle, as they visibly amplified tensions. Officers had no precise knowledge of the situation, but one of the few things they believed they knew for certain was that they were in danger (City Council's WTO Accountability Review Committee—Panel 3, 2000, p. 4; WTO Accountability Review Committee, 2000, p. 12).

In Seattle, police mismanagement further aggravated the tense situation. Logistical problems led to shortages in officers' food and water supply as well as to insufficient rest for officers. Police leadership did not take action when the situation got out of hand, and the operational control lost real-time knowledge of what was happening in the streets. The WTO Accountability Committee later found that officers were "victims of poor planning and leadership in the field" (WTO Accountability Review Committee, 2000, p. 4).

In addition, a very small percentage of protesters committed property damage in Seattle. These actions again increased tension among the officers, as well as among protesters. Shop windows of chain stores like Starbucks, Niketown, and the Gap were smashed (Nelson, 1999; Offby1, 1999; *Seattle Times*, 1999a; Pilz, 2007; BattleInSeattle, 2008), and some stores owned by major corporations were looted. On numerous such occasions police are not visible but other protesters tried to prevent the damage. For a long time, protesters found easy targets, unprotected by the police, which contributed to officers' increasing anxiety (for a general discussion of how police underenforcement of the law can impact escalation, see Gillham and Marx, 2000). Other pictures show police officers in gas masks, sticks in hand, standing in front of downtown office buildings. Protesters had spray-painted on the wall behind them: "We are winning" (Nadir, 1999).

Lastly, communication problems between protesters and police manifested in these increasingly chaotic situations, making each side less aware and increasingly skeptical of the other group's intentions—in particular in light of other escalating interactions, like property damage. This skepticism led to a surge in rumors about the other side, such as protesters allegedly preparing Molotov cocktails or flammables they would use against officers. The Seattle Accountability Review Committee (2000, p. 12) later assessed that "investigators found the rumors of 'Molotov cocktails' and sale of flammables from a supermarket had no basis in fact. But, rumors were important in contributing to the police sense of being besieged and in considerable danger" (for details on communication problems and rumors, see Chapter 6).

Case comparisons, the analysis of background factors, and the reconstruction of the moment-by-moment unfolding of Seattle events suggest that what led to the strong increase of tension and fear in Seattle was the perception of an offense. This perception was created through a combination of spatial incursions, escalation signs, and property damage. Police mismanagement occurred as well, which did not help the situation. Consequently, an offense path and a loss-of-control path operated simultaneously in this protest and overlapped. Either path alone could have triggered clashes. Some cases, like Seattle or Rostock, are overdetermined in this way as two paths occur, either of which could have triggered violence (for more detail on the loss-of-control path in Seattle, see Chapter 4).

In the offense path the dynamic interplay of the three factors (spatial incursions, escalation signs, property damage) leads collective actors to interpret that an offense is taking place. This perception changes emotional dynamics during the protest. If property damage occurs alone, officers can react to these actions (although case comparisons and my participant observation suggest that police react differently to law-breaking, depending on the situation; see also Earl and Soule, 2006, p. 150). At the same time, protesters might become tense when only property damage occurs, but the routine interactions they expected are not fundamentally disrupted. Hence violence does not automatically ensue.

Yet if property damage occurs in the offense path, it provides actors with evidence that dangers perceived through escalation signs and spatial incursions are real. Reports speak of "highly emotional circumstances" due to such combinations (WTO Accountability Review Committee, 2000, pp. 2, 8) and of officers perceiving themselves to be in "serious danger" (City Council's WTO Accountability Review Committee—Panel 3, 2000, p. 4). In Seattle, document data confirm what visual data (Shunpiker, 1999; see also Kaiser, 1999b, 1999c) and police radio transcripts (see City of Seattle, 2008) suggest: officers felt attacked and were fearful due to their interpretation of the combination of these three interactions. In their view, the expected situational routine had broken down and could not be relied on anymore. People became tense, anxious, and fearful.

More than seven hours had passed in Seattle from the start of protest activities until violence erupted in the main march. During these seven hours tensions increased drastically. Seattle police then used violence against protesters of the main march around 3 p.m. Pictures show officers leaning over cowering groups of protesters, firing rubber bullets. Tear gas fills the air, some officers fire bullets into the crowd while standing on SWAT cars, others casually walk up and down and pepper-spray protesters from close distance. At 3:30 p.m.—30 minutes after the officers first used violence against the march—Seattle Mayor Paul Schell declared a state of emergency. In the view of the city and police officers, the situation had escalated that far that the National Guard was brought in. After-action reports by the Seattle City Council later use the word "panic" to describe Seattle police officers' state of mind before clashing with the main march (WTO Accountability Review Committee, 2000, p. 12). This high level of fear also becomes evident from radio communication, a committee later stated, as well as from the police's "inflated crowd estimates, which exceed the numbers shown in videotapes" (WTO Accountability Review Committee, 2000, p.12). Videos show officers clinging to their batons, indicators of fear in their faces, shoulders drawn up, looking over their shoulders frequently (Shunpiker, 1999; see, e.g., CBS, 2010, min. 1:05).

Reports later concluded that officers' perception of an offense was unjustified. In hindsight, there was no reason to be that fearful. Nonetheless, this immense fear was rational in the view of the officer, due to how the event unfolded, given the information they had at the time, and given the interactions with which they were confronted. The limited impact of motivations and strategies for such surprising outcomes, in contrast to the strong impact of situational patterns, suggests that these are not simply hate-driven acts (although it cannot be ruled out that individuals feel hate or a desire for violence) but mainly a result of routine breakdowns.

In summary, a situational breakdown occurs in the offense path, just as in the loss-of-control path. Yet in the offense path (unlike the loss-of-control path), officers still feel in charge of the operation. The emergence of property damage does not change this perception, as officers are trained to react to such transgressions (and if mismanagement does not occur, they also feel they can react to them). In the offense path, the crucial dynamic is that one of the two groups feels attacked by the other, which increases tension and fear on the part of its members. This path can lead to violence by officers as well as protesters. Thus, a different pattern of combined interactions causes situational routines to break down and consequently a different interpretation leads to an increase in tension and fear. This illustrates that different processes can lead to the same violent outcome. What unites both paths discussed so far is that by occurring together, specific combinations of interactions during the protest produce the same emotional response of tension, discomfort, and fear due to the perception that routines have broken down. This increase in tension and fear is a vital step in the eruption of violence.

6 | Uncertainty

The Others' Intentions

The third and last of the three paths leading to protest violence is what I call the missing information path. Previous chapters have shown that distress occurs if individuals perceive that the other group might attack them or if officers perceive they might lose control over the operation. But uncertainty can be just as stressful and can be a further dynamic leading to the perception of situational breakdowns, in which people are confused, fearful, and overwhelmed. When police and protesters cannot communicate with each other at crucial moments, they start to wonder what the other side is up to. If "the other" has previously behaved strangely, imaginations can run wild. Actions by the other group are now meticulously observed. If one group is already suspicious, minor actions can be taken as an indicator of the other planning something malicious. Time seems to move more slowly as fear increases (Grossman and Christensen, 2008). Did they just talk to each other and then look over here? Protesters worry; officers worry. What is the other group's intention?

Communication problems between protesters and police, meaning an interruption of the routine flow of information between police and protesters, can foster these dynamics. Communication problems can occur due to technical problems, for example, when communication is interrupted due to equipment malfunction or is not acoustically clearly understandable. Communication can also be impaired because of content problems, for example, when the information given in announcements remains unclear.

Communication problems between protesters and police play a role across protests ending in violence. In the Rostock G8 protest in 2007, demonstration organizers at the rally's main stage announced at one point that they were not able to communicate with the police. In the Brokdorf protest in 1981, a case discussed further in the following sections, officers ceased communication at a certain point in time, and protesters did not know why officers stopped talking to them. In other examples, such as a protest against a fundraiser for President Bush in Portland, Oregon, in 2002 or at the Miami FTAA protest in 2003, police orders to disperse were not announced loud enough for protesters to hear. Hence, protesters did not understand what was said and consequently could not comply. Failures in communication might not be problematic if the protest goes as planned. Yet not knowing about the other side's intentions and plans can have a strong impact on emotional dynamics if things do not go according to plan, and each side needs reassurance about the other's intentions.

In instances of low communication, rumors can spread rapidly and can further escalate situational dynamics. Consider two examples of rumors and escalation: the first is an incident from police officers' operations on parole, in which officers respond to a call about a person, apparently suicidal, who has behaved strangely on a road for nearly an hour (Boyer, 1999; R. Collins, 2008, p. 113). In this event, on March 27, 1998, around 2 a.m., the person parked his car next to the road, got out on the ramp that connected the road to a freeway, and waved around an air pistol. He was drunk and disoriented due to a medication he was taking that had side effects when combined with alcohol. He called his wife, telling her he did not quite know where he was and she tried to explain to him how to get home. Police were informed that the man on the ramp was apparently armed and potentially posing a threat. Over the course of one hour, this information became more and more extreme and threatening. Police radios crackled with information about the man shooting at a police helicopter as well as shooting at officers. His behavior was reported to be increasingly dangerous. Apparently at no point did police communicate with the man, which could have resolved their fears, given that he was confused and only in possession of a BB gun. Testimony shows how fearful officers were after a quick succession of constant and increasingly drastic communications of rumors. The longer the situation went on, the more rumors increased and the more officers were fearful. Around 3:15 a.m. officers perceived that the man was pointing a weapon directly at them. Others reportedly heard his weapon hitting the concrete and metal next to them.

In response to this perception, they shot him 106 times. Fifty-five of the wounds were fatal. Other shots hit nearby apartment buildings in which residents were sleeping.[1]

This example illustrates that the longer rumors circulate, the more drastic they usually become (see also, e.g., Rydgren, 2007) and the more fear increases. Eventually, all information that does not fit the extreme narrative gets dropped and all new information is interpreted as evidence of this narrative. Rumors can thereby add to a spiral of escalation. Just before fatally shooting the man, officers were in fear for their lives, although the man was alone, only had a BB gun, and was disoriented and suicidal.

Rumors can also be at play during demonstrations. Here, too, they usually have an escalating effect. The protest against the FTAA meeting in Miami in 2003 provides a second example. A participant recorded the following scene on video (Indymedia, 2004): officers accompany dispersing protesters and tell them to walk on the sidewalk. While walking, one of the protesters leaves his banner on the sidewalk. He quickly but carefully leans it on an adjacent fence. The action is barely noticeable in the video. Nonetheless, officers directly perceive this act as a behavior with harmful intent and immediately start communicating rumors. Walking next to the protesters, one officer shouts to others, "They're trying to hurt us, guys! Be careful, they're putting things in the way!" The action, which is in itself rather insignificant, is interpreted as a potential threat, since one side does not have information on the other's intentions and generally mistrusts them. The rumor that protesters want to hurt officers is directly communicated to the policeman's own side, and clear us–them boundaries are established. "*They* are trying to hurt *us*" (emphasis added): people understand and support their *own* group. But *the others* might be a very different kind of animal—they even leave banners on the sidewalk to inflict pain.

After specific interactions during the protest and no communication between the two groups, the other is anxiously observed. In one protest example, a journalist recalls:

> [The officer] was a big, big guy and was wearing a bulletproof vest and a police-issued riot helmet, but I really think he was scared of the skinny, dreadlocked bandana clad protesters. He had this look of panic on his face, like he had been in a scuffle with the Viet Cong. (Scahill, 2003)

---

[1] Such wild gunfire can be another indicator of how panicky officers were (see Collins, 2008).

Continuous communication, on the other hand, allows tensions to cool down. If each side knows the other's intentions they usually do not have to observe their every move. The protest against the NATO summit in Kehl in 2009 (discussed in the Introduction) exemplifies how communication can be vital to calm tensions and fears. In Kehl, police and protesters were in constant negotiations about how to proceed and how to solve the situation together. They constantly informed their own groups via loudspeaker about their intentions, the other group's intentions, and the joint negotiations. Rumors could not emerge and therefore did not escalate the situation as in Miami, since the intentions of the other and the state of negotiations seemed clear the entire time. Even in an increasingly tense and crowded situation in Kehl, extensive communication avoided perceptions of threat, kept tensions at bay, and strongly favored the peaceful outcome (for details on keeping a protest peaceful, see also Chapter 8).

Missing Information

If spatial incursions, escalation signs, and communication problems between protesters and police occur together, they form a missing information path to violence. My study suggests the missing information is the third combination of interactions during a protest that breaks the established situational routine, strongly increases tensions and fear, and thereby favors violence. As in other paths, the interplay of the interactions is vital: the missing information regarding the other side's goals and intentions in the light of escalation signs and spatial incursions seems crucial. In the other two paths discussed in previous chapters, the interpretation of a perceived development (a loss of control) or action (an offense) raises tension and fear. In the missing information path the lack of knowledge about developments and planned actions in the light of spatial incursions and escalation signs seems to unsettle police and protesters and thereby leads to tension and fear and a violent outcome.

Brokdorf Power Plant Protest, 1981

One example of how the missing information path leads to violence is the demonstration on February 28, 1981, in Wilstermarsch, Germany. This protest was not only very influential in German history, it is also well suited to illustrate the inner dynamics of a missing information path. The protest was part of a movement against nuclear energy that formed in the 1970s. When nuclear power became more and more popular after the first oil crisis in 1973, groups opposing nuclear energy organized across Germany and managed to delay the construction of power plants. By 1979, approximately 100,000 protesters marched in German cities such as Bonn and Hanover.

In Brokdorf, which is in northern Germany, the construction of a new nuclear power plant was planned. The building permit was issued in 1976, but construction soon stopped because of protests. In 1981 the construction was due to start again, and further protests were announced.

The demonstrations against the plant on Sunday, February 28, 1981, were first legally banned in the area of Wilstermarsch. Yet one day prior to the march, the administrative court in Schleswig overruled this ban, thereby sanctioning the march. Some hours after this decision, however, during the night from Friday to Saturday, the administrative appeals tribunal in Lüneburg again legally prohibited protests throughout the whole region. Consequently, when arriving for the rally on Saturday morning, most marchers did not know whether the rally would actually be legal or not. This created a confusing scenario from the start. Interestingly enough, years later, in 1985, the Federal Constitutional Court declared the protest ban unconstitutional. The so-called "Brokdorf verdict," a landmark decision by the court, still shapes the rules of the freedom of assembly in Germany today. On the day of the protest, however, the march was illegal, but most participants were unaware of the ban, as police sanctioned the protest impromptu.

Marches started at 10 a.m.: protesters had to march 7.5 miles (around 12 kilometers) from the town of Wilstermarsch to the construction site of the nuclear power plant. Taking place in the cold north German winter, it was less than 14 F (−10°C). The fields in the rural area around the power plant were speckled with snow and ice. Strong cold winds swept over the frozen cropland. The fields were empty. Many protesters took their bikes to ease their passage over the long route. Chants and singing seemed useless, as onlookers would not hear them from far out on the fields. Protesters marched together, wrapped in thick winter clothing, their clouds of breath in the cold air in front of them.

Pronounced escalation signs occurred throughout the march: police observed protesters collecting stones, shovels, ropes, and anchors. They saw a car unloading gas containers. Protesters saw officers rehearsing landing operations with helicopters and were confused by a checkpoint on their route, out in the fields. Around 11:30 a.m. one of the two marches was stopped by a police barricade of containers filled with sand 4 miles (around 6 kilometers) from the actual construction site. Protesters were allowed to pass if they agreed to be searched by police and to leave all poster poles and other objects, which might be used as weapons. Later, however, at 2 p.m., the entire police checkpoint barrier was removed by police order and protesters could pass unsearched. Protesters helped to get the sand out of the containers so that the protesters' speaker vehicle could pass the checkpoint. While doing so, the protesters' loudspeaker van asked marchers to stay calm and cool. Nevertheless, some protesters were confused about why the police had elaborately constructed a checkpoint only to then remove it with the help of protesters—even more so since the protest was not legally permitted, but then sanctioned inpromptu. Could this be some sort of trap? The German news magazine *Der Spiegel* (1981) later asked whether people can in fact be liable for prosecution if they participate in an illegal march but the police grant them access to the prohibited area. The situation was confusing to several participants, making them increasingly suspicious about the other group's intentions.

At the checkpoint, communication was still working. Police and protesters engaged in "relaxed interactions" as pictures and documents confirm (Kleinert, 1984; Schröder, 2012, p. 20). Protesters perceived officers to be very friendly and very committed to "diminishing tensions" through communicating with them (Kleinert, 1984, p. 75). Despite these earlier interactions, communication between the two sides stopped when protesters arrived at the construction site—obviously a highly symbolic space. "A wall of silence" lay over the scene, and "helplessness, perplexity, and resignation spread" (Kleinert, 1984, p. 81). Protesters were confused. Why did communication stop? At the same time, officers were informed to expect violence from the protesters at this point (Schröder, 2012, p. 23).

No one knew what would happen next, as if no one anticipated actually arriving at the site after the legal scuffles and a draining march in unfriendly temperatures. Now, out in the middle of nowhere, protesters having arrived at the construction site, communication ceased. Protesters recall: "Everyone seemed to be waiting for something to happen," and "[s]lowly an unsettling feeling emerged: this cannot go well." Observers summarize: "Protesters were suspicious: Is this a trap?" (Kleinert, 1984, pp. 82, 79, 71). Another protester states that groups of protesters discussed uneasily what officers might do next (Kleinert, 1984, p. 81). The missing information about the other side's goals in the given circumstances strongly increased tension and fear.

Suddenly some protesters tried to enter the construction site by climbing its fence. Some tried to pull down the fence with tracer ammunition. In fact, protesters would not have been able to destroy much on the site, since construction had not yet started. They would most likely not have squatted on the site because of the exceedingly cold temperatures, even by day. Nevertheless, this spatial incursion seemingly tipped the interactional and emotional dynamic. Police reactions suggest that protesters crossed an invisible line, resulting in the immediate deployment of force as more protesters climbed the fence. Violence erupted at 3:15 p.m. at the eastern side of the construction site. Police gave three orders to disperse and started to use water cannons and tear gas against protesters at 3:35 p.m.

In what followed, protesters set a sewage disposal plant located next to the power plant construction site as well as a construction trailer on fire. The situation escalated further, and police ordered quick-reaction forces to arrest the presumed leaders of the protest. When a police officer in a quick-reaction force chased a protester, both broke through the ice of a frozen canal that surrounded the construction site, and several protesters attacked the officer with poles. Pictures of the scene made the news throughout the next days and weeks: the officer in a thick jacket, gloves, and a helmet with an open visor is stuck in the approximately 9-foot-wide canal (around 2.5 meters). The icy water rises up to his knees. He tries to climb out of the water up the steep 3-foot-high bank (around 1 meter) with both hands. Behind him hundreds of protesters stand closely at the other side of the canal, watching. Above the officer, at the edge of the ditch right where the officer tries to climb out, a protester stands, a wooden slat in both hands, targeting the officer's head from above. Another protester stands behind the officer in the ice-cold water in the middle of the canal. He grabs the officer's jacket with both hands. To the left and behind the officer, another protester—also standing in the water, wearing a white jacket and a helmet—swings a shovel to hit the policeman.[2]

Eventually, other protesters helped the officer out of the canal and brought him to the protesters' medical tent. At first, police assumed that the officer had been kidnapped and that protesters were trying to lure police into a trap when protesters requested an ambulance for the officer. They did not know what the protesters were up to and were extremely suspicious. It took police command 90 minutes to overcome their doubts and send a helicopter to the protesters' medical facility in order to get the severely wounded and hypothermic officer to a hospital. This example

---

[2] The picture can be found online, e.g., at http://static.apps.abendblatt.de/flips/magazin/2011/magazin2011_08/files/mag08.pdf (p. VII, above left).

illustrates how missing information in the light of spatial incursion and escalation signs led to profound and persistent mistrust.

Subsequently, police started using helicopters to disperse protesters, flying very low over their heads. Protesters were running over the empty fields in every direction, helicopters chasing them. Others engaged in physical fights with officers. Helicopters arrived and unloaded backup units. At 5 p.m. the last marchers started to leave the area. Retreating protesters were chased by police by land and by air. At 6 p.m. a helicopter landed right in front of a retreating group around a loudspeaker van and arrested them. Several participants speak of scenes like those in a "civil war" (Fritz51202, 2010, min. 03:35; see also Kleinert, 1984). Confrontations continued until the evening. About 200 people were reportedly injured and 240 arrested. Even though the nuclear power plant was placed into operation in 1986, the year of the Chernobyl disaster, the protests against Brokdorf were a success for the movement: Brokdorf was the last nuclear power plant commissioned in Germany.

Where Communication Stops and Mistrust Begins

The protest description illustrates that what seemingly led to this eruption was foremost the missing information on the opposing sides' goals in the light of escalation signs and spatial incursions. This missing information severely increased tensions—a pattern visible across protests turning violent. Communication problems between protesters and police, just like property damage, seem to be a way in which escalation signs build tensions on both sides. Not knowing the intentions of the other group due to communication problems makes escalation signs and spatial incursions more menacing and thereby severely disrupts routine interactions. Such situational breakdowns lead to moments of chaos, confusion, and fear, in which people are overwhelmed, because the organizational routines they usually rely on have collapsed. For example, in Brokdorf tensions emerged due to escalation signs perceived throughout the day. Police mismanagement and communication problems added to tensions. In pictures, video, and document data, participants are very tense and greatly unsettled, describing helplessness, suspicion, and confusion (see among others *Der Spiegel,* 1981; Kleinert, 1984, pp. 81, 82; Norddeutscher Rundfunk, 2011; Schröder, 2012; ZDF Heute, 1981). Attempts to enter the construction site then tipped the interactional dynamic in the light of missing information.[3]

---

[3] Interestingly, while spatial incursions seem to be a spur-of-the-moment idea in many other protests, they seem to have been intended by at least some protesters prior to the march in Brokdorf. Some,

Communication can cease for different reasons. In Brokdorf, actors seemingly had decided to stop communicating. In other protests, communication ceases due to technical issues. The results are similar: a breakdown of communication between protesters and police can lead to severe distress in light of escalation signs and spatial incursions. A remark by a photojournalist at the FTAA protest in Miami suggests how important it is to possess the will as well as the technical means to communicate, once the situation gets confusing or tense:

> If you've got 3, 4, 5 or more helicopters above you, you're in small narrow streets with buildings with sharp hard surfaces that bounce back the sound, and the noise at street level from the marchers and the police makes it almost impossible to hear anything. If there were any commands or instructions issued by the police, no one heard them. Yet, had the police had any sort of portable sound system, they could have announced something like this, "Attention everyone. We are not going to arrest you. We are not going to pen you up in the street. If you will turn around and look, you will see that the access to Biscayne Boulevard has been cleared." (Crespo, 2006, p. 48)

Communication can help transmit that the micro-order is still in place and allows actors to reply to certain patterns of routine behavior. Communication can also transmit that the situation might be confusing, but that actors are working to get the system running again. Thus, if communication exists and uncertainty is not perceived, protests are more likely to stay peaceful, even if other escalating factors take place. In Kehl, for instance, spatial incursions occurred, yet both police and protesters communicated so much that protesters became bored by the various announcements. Extensive communication kept tensions at bay, as each side was reassured of what the other side was planning.

A further example that illustrates the crucial role of communication in maintaining situational order and avoiding a missing information path is the protest for migrant's rights on June 4, 2007, in Rostock (see also Chapter 4, "Invasions"). Here spatial incursion took place and escalation

---

for instance, brought grappling hooks to the march—an action very likely taken in order to enter the construction site if one were to get to it. Yet case comparisons suggest that whether spatial incursions were intended prior to the march (and then executed or not) or not (and then occurred spontaneously), spatial incursions alone cannot cause violence (see Chapter 4). Instead, the combination of spatial incursions with other situational factors was key in Brokdorf to cause a perceived breakdowns in situational routines that led to confusion, distress, and fear.

signs occurred when police assembled water canon trucks right in front of protesters on the sanctioned route while protesters were kettled outside the inner city. Despite these actions, police and the protest organizers' lawyer were in constant negotiations with each other. Although fewer announcements were made in the Rostock migrants' march than in Kehl, communication was flowing. Further, both sides had representatives that could speak for their group and pass information on to their group, as well as a joint position to the other. Thus, no particular interpretation arose from the other group's actions that could have sparked confusion, rumors, and violence. Tensions were kept at bay, and after hours of negotiations, police and protesters parted in peace.

In short, in the missing information path, spatial incursions, escalation signs, and communication problems between protesters and the police lead to violence. They do so because the missing information regarding the other side's goals and intentions in light of escalation signs and spatial incursions during the protest increases tension and fear. Interpretations of the situation and the intentions of the other change, rumors spread, and the other group is more and more anxiously observed. In cases in which a missing information path occurred, participants perceived a situational breakdown of usually-relied-upon routines, and violence was then used, in particular against people who fell down or ran away (Kleinert, 1984). In Brokdorf both police and protesters used violence when in a dominant situation. Three protesters attacked the isolated officer that fell into the canal. Police attacked in similar instances of situational advantage. An officer recalls the actions of one of his colleagues: "On the street there was a woman lying on the ground, and she was hit by an officer. He was hitting her without any reason, although she was lying there, crying. [. . .] She had run away earlier. [. . .] And then she fell, and he started hitting her" (Kleinert, 1984, p. 96). Instances like physically attacking a crying person who has fallen down seem to occur without any clear rationale and thus appear hard to explain other than by rage and hate. Yet these instances show specific situational emotional patterns. These patterns will be the center of the following chapter.

7 | In the Tunnel of Violence

Don't Turn Your Back

All three paths discussed in Chapters 4 through 6 cause routine interactions to break down by leading to emotional dynamics that trigger violence. The following sections will further introduce how the described paths impact emotional dynamics in the hours leading up to violence and how emotional dynamics then cause violence to break out. This chapter will discuss the precipitating micro-situations step by step, following the temporal order in which they appear during a protest from the start of a march until violence erupts and ends.

Tension and Fear

Visual recordings show that people are usually relaxed and focused on their own group's actions at the beginning of generally peaceful demonstrations. They often show facial expressions that indicate happiness: cheeks are raised, diagonal folds extend from tip of nose to the corners of the mouth. Their postures are relaxed, and several smile (Ekman, Friesen, and Ellsworth, 1972; see also Klusemann, 2009; R. Collins, 2008).

In the peaceful protests in my sample, this emotional state usually remains stable throughout the demonstration. For protests that turn violent, people's emotional state changes during the protest, as seen in the Rostock main march (see Chapter 4, "Police Mismanagement"; see also Introduction). At some point calm behavior is replaced by hectic movements, such as people clustering with their own group, looking around frequently, contracting all muscles. People feel in danger and show characteristics of stress, tension, fear, and panic before violence emerges: e.g., raised brows, open mouths, upper eyelids raised, lower eyelids tense, lips stretched back, and drawn-up shoulders (see Indymedia, 2004, showing officers displaying pronounced fear in the protest against the FTAA in Miami in 2003; and Jamsven, 2007, showing protesters displaying pronounced fear at the march against the G8 in Rostock, 2007—in both scenes violence emerges shortly thereafter).

As Randall Collins (2008, p. 2) shows, tension and fear are the primary emotions found in pictures of combat situations. This leads him to claim that the common cliché that anger is directly linked to violent behavior is inaccurate. Even in the bodily postures and facial expressions of soldiers at the moment of violence, fear and tension are much more common than anger (R. Collins, 2008, p. 69). Collins suggests that tension and fear increase due to a human inhibition threshold toward violence. People display confrontational tension and fear before the outbreak of violence, not only because they fear getting hurt but also because they fear hurting others. Confrontational tension and fear therefore inhibit the outbreak of violence in most situations.

When looking at protest violence, tension and fear seem more closely linked to the use of violence in demonstrations than do anger or hate. Yet my analysis suggests that fear seems to occur not only due to an inhibition toward violence right before the outbreak of violence, as Collins (2008) suggests, but also due to the breakdown of routine interactions, which causes people to reinterpret situations and to experience disorientation, helplessness, and fear in the hours and minutes before violence. Police and independent committee reports on demonstrations frequently use the word *panic* to describe the psychological state officers are in prior to using violence (e.g., WTO Accountability Review Committee, 2000, p. 9). Protesters seem to experience similar states of confusion and fear prior to using violence in most instances.

As we have seen, tension and fear occur due to specific interactions between protesters and police. These interactions are interpreted to imply that established and expected social routines have broken down and cannot be relied on any longer. When people perceive a loss of control, an imminent attack from the other group, or a lack of information on the others' intentions in the face of unsettling events, tension and fear rise. This rise is systematically visible in videos and document data of events (see, e.g., Citizens' Panel on WTO Operations, 2000; Indymedia, 2004; CNN, 2007; German Police Union, 2007; Jamsven, 2007; Solomon and Levin, 2008; Independent Media Center, 2011).

A protester at the International Monetary Fund (IMF) protest in Washington, DC, in 2000 describes both groups' fears when interacting:

We are afraid of the police: they have guns, clubs, tear gas and pepper spray, and all the power of the state at their disposal. They can beat, gas, or jail us with relative impunity. What's hard to grasp is how much they are afraid of us. Some of our group are wearing black and covering their faces and they look like the folks in Seattle that broke windows and made the police look bad. Mostly, I think, the police are afraid of the unknown. Someone in the crowd could have a bomb. Those bubbling vats in the convergence kitchen could be homemade pepper spray instead of lunch. Those bottles of turpentine could have some nefarious purpose other than removal of the paint used in banner making. (Starhawk, 2002, p. 27)

Triggering Moments

If specific group interactions increase tensions and fear in the first phase, tension needs to be released through emotional dominance over a weak victim in the second phase for violence to erupt (see R. Collins, 2008). What is meant by emotional dominance? Emotional dominance is visible in people showing a confident body posture, a high rate of activity, and a strong physical presence in contrast to an unconfident, less active victim (R. Collins, 2008; Collins, 2009). Emotional dominance does not mean that a person has physical dominance—a physically inferior person can also gain emotional dominance—but that the person perceives her- or himself and is perceived by others to be dominant in the situation and possesses situational advantage.

Hence, emotional dominance can be established in micro-situations regardless of whether the person has an actual physical advantage or not. It refers to the *situationally* weak and the *situationally* dominant people and could therefore also be called "situational dominance" or "perceived dominance" (although I stick to Collins's [2008] term in the following). Collins notes in an interview with Walby and Spencer (2010, p. 98) that the expression used in sports of one side "having the momentum" is quite accurate for describing these instances. In most cases this gaining of emotional dominance seems to be an opportunity presenting itself, rather than a conscious technique of individuals.

To start violence, Collins (2008) claims, a micro-interactional turning point needs to occur, in which one side overcomes confrontational tension and gains emotional dominance. Collins (2008, 2009, p. 599, 2012, p. 4) found that attacking the weak through the establishment of dominance is one way in which confrontational tension and fear is overcome and violence breaks out. During protest events, several triggering moments can systematically foster emotional dominance and protest violence: the breakup of police–protester lines; one side being outnumbered; and people falling down. These three aspects are not exhaustive, and other triggering moments for violence might exist.

Lines Breaking Up

First, the breakup of police–protesters lines can trigger violence. Officers usually try to form a clear, straight line when moving forward. However, before a violent confrontation breaks out, these straight lines tend to become loosened. Visual footage of various cases shows that the police lines are straight when approaching protesters (see, e.g., Indymedia 2004). As long as these solid lines exist, isolated individuals who attempt to provoke the other group (e.g., by making insulting gestures) usually do not succeed. When solid lines exist, people are more likely to confront each other face to face, which increases the inhibition threshold for violence as the face acts as a weapon against violence (see R. Collins, 2008).

The NATO protest in Kehl (see also Introduction) is an example of a protest in which lines stayed intact, a triggering moment did not occur, and violence did not emerge. Remember that at this march violence was expected; police had announced a rigid strategy, and protesters were stopped on their assigned route that crossed a bridge to Strasbourg. At the bridge police–protester lines stayed intact and protesters and police faced each other in tight situations. Yet most of the time, officers and protesters stood face to face, with about 3 feet (1 meter) of space between them (see Savkoeln, 2009, min. 0:52). Protest organizers can be seen making announcements in a calm manner, their body postures relaxed. No triggering moment occurred. Neither protesters nor police officers established dominance during these situations: people looked at each others' faces when being shoved, and no one turned their back, stumbled, or fell— triggers that could otherwise lead to the perception of a weak victim (for visual footage see, e.g., Swiola2, 2009). My analysis suggests that violence did not emerge in part due to this lack of emotional dominance— in part also since no combination of interactions was completed to form one of three paths to violence, and thus a particular interpretation among participants that the situational routine had broken down did not take place. This means that violence did not break out even though both sides were in immediate physical contact with each other in a stressful situation and over an extended period of the time, and even though some protesters tried to provoke an altercation by pushing participants into the police line. Yet even the physical contact and the attempted provocation by some protesters did not lead to violence, as a triggering moment was missing.

If lines break up, however, individuals can establish emotional dominance and attack the situationally weaker opponent. Situations are more likely in which a single member of one group is alone with several members of the other group. Individuals are isolated and appear to be weaker targets than when the two groups face each other in coherent lines. Moreover, if lines break up, people are more likely to turn their backs than in a stand-off and run away. Thus their faces—otherwise increasing an inhibition threshold for violence (Collins, 2008)—are not visible. In numerous marches, such as the Miami FTAA protest, Rostock G8 protest, and the Tompkins Square Park protest, many people received blows to the back of their heads, indicating that they were not facing their attackers after lines had broken up. For instance, in the Tompkins Square Park protest, pictures show a tall protester wearing a black, sleeveless shirt, facing police officers. The back of his head shows a gaping wound from a blow to the head. Blood is running down his neck and shirt. The officers who face him hold their sticks in hand (DeRienzo, 2008). Similarly, videos from Rostock show protesters being hit on the back of their heads while running away: a man in a dark jacket tries to run from an officer. The officer holds on to the protester's jacket with one hand, swinging his stick with the other to hit the protester on the back of his head (IGuerilla, 2007b). In such instances, violence is more likely due to the lack of face-to-face confrontation.

Falling Down

Second, falling down can trigger violence. In several instances, when a protester falls down or struggles to regain footing, one officer—usually the one closest to the protester—hits the person who has fallen. Right after the first attack, other officers start hitting that person as well, usually much harder. This is visible in footage and shots of the Tompkins Square Park and Seattle WTO protests (Solomon and Levin, 2008; e.g., CBS, 2010; Daily Beast, 2010; Independent Media Center, 2011). Often officers who might not have seen what has happened join in and pile on (see also R. Collins, 2008, p. 89).

The Miami FTAA protest of 2003 is one of many examples: a protester has linked his arms to another protester's arms while slowly retreating from the advancing police line. He has turned his back to the officers, bends his knees, and is about to sit down. The reason for this action is unclear. Immediately after he moves toward the ground, four or five officers start hitting and kicking him. Again, the closest officer starts; the officers nearby join in (for visual footage, see, e.g., Indymedia, 2008, min. 01:54).

Another video example from the FTAA Miami demonstration shows a protester stumbling in a highly chaotic situation in which officers and protesters stand close to each other. He almost falls down, turns his back to the officers and ducks in an evasive motion, at which point the officers start hitting him (see, e.g., Indymedia, 2008, min. 03:52). After a time of standoff, by falling down or stumbling the protester seems to become a weak victim. Tension is then released through violence toward this easy target.

Both incidents in Brokdorf 1981 described in Chapter 6 are a further example of the emotional pathway of attacking the weak: an officer describes how his colleague hit and kicked a woman who fell to the floor and was crying—a clear instance of emotional dominance over a weak victim. In the described instance of the officer in the ditch, three protesters are in superior tactical positions: one standing above the officer blocking the nearest escape route, one next to him outside the officer's line of vision, one standing right behind him. They surround and outnumber the isolated officer and seem better armed. They swing their shovel and wooden slat against the situationally weak victim.

Being Outnumbered

Lastly, as the Brokdorf example suggests, being outnumbered in a situation seems to be a further trigger to favor emotional dominance and the outbreak of violence. Individuals are often outnumbered after tension has built up and lines have broken down. My observations support Randall Collins's (2008, p. 10) finding that only a small proportion of the people present in a situation actually fight with each other. In no case in my sample did all individuals on the scene join in a fight. A cluster of between three and seven attackers against one target is common when lines have broken up, as it clearly allows dominating one individual (R. Collins, 2008). Usually after one officer starts, other officers tend to pile on. As one of many examples, take the scene that a protester in the Tompkins Square Park protest described. An officer had hit him between the legs: "Naturally, I went down, and after that there were at least six other cops kicking me and beating the hell out of me with their sticks" (DeRienzo, 2008).

Such examples suggest that tension and fear as well as clear emotional dominance precede physical violence. Reporting on a protest against the emergency laws in Berlin in 1968, a magazine article illustrates tension and fear as well as emotional dominance before the outbreak of violence: As soon as protesters "ran away, or—as scattered individuals—were outnumbered," they experienced "officers' readiness to beat them up," the journalist notes (*Der Spiegel*, 1968). "Our fear animated the officers to swipe,'" an interviewed activist states, and the commanding officer at the same protest recalls high levels of fear on the side of his officers, too: "Our guys had naked fear written on their faces," he recalls (*Der Spiegel*, 1968). Both sides in this demonstration were scared, and both used violence against the other in dominant micro-situations.

Becoming a Weak Victim

The three triggering moments can also occur together: the breakup of police-protester lines, someone falling down, and being outnumbered. For instance, a press picture (Junge Welt, 2007) from the Rostock G8 protest in 2007 shows that police–protester lines have broken up. While running away, a protester has fallen and is now lying on the ground on the parking lot. The picture shows more than a dozen officers in riot gear who come running through a narrow passage onto the parking lot. They heavily outnumber him. When the first officer reaches him, he aims to kick the fallen protester hard. He has a baton in his left hand and takes a full body swing to kick the protester. The protester seemingly tries to protect his stomach by crouching on the ground, potentially trying to kick the officer's leg with his right foot. It is unclear what the protester has done earlier. Regardless, the officer would now have had the opportunity to arrest him. As the protester poses no immediate threat to him, the use of force is not the prescribed police response. However, the clear establishment of dominance after an increase of tension during the protest might explain his reaction.

This indicates that specific triggering moments are dangerous after a buildup of tension, as they allow one group to establish emotional dominance. While in some examples (as the woman falling down in Brokdorf; see Chapter 6, "Missing Information") the victim is also physically weaker, emotional dominance and physical dominance do not always coincide: a physically weaker person can gain emotional dominance over the other and carry out violence, and a physically stronger person can be unable to gain emotional dominance and can therefore be unable to control the situation or use violence (Wright and Decker, 1997; see R. Collins, 2008). Gaining emotional dominance means to "beat the enemy psychologically before beating them physically" (Collins, 2016a, para. 14). Individuals become weak victims by getting on the ground, falling, stumbling, and being outnumbered. If this happens, tension is likely to be released through violence toward these weak victims, who were previously seen as dangerous. When one person is in distress and attacks another individual who is crying and lying on the floor, routines have broken down and emotional dominance has been established.

This does not imply that people follow their mindless instincts, however. Quite the opposite, people's interpretations in the immediate situation are highly important to lead to these situations, since they determine whether individuals perceive danger in the first place. Without perceived danger and the perception that routine interactions cannot be relied on anymore, tension and fear would not increase. As discussed in Chapter 4, people's perceptions of themselves, the context, and others seem to change in these very specific situations that are outside any ordinary routines. Their perceptions change due to their interpretation of in-group and out-group actions and emotion displays (see Blumer, 1986). In addition, people form a homogeneous view of the out-group and tend to stereotype the "other" as dangerous (see Drury and Reicher, 2000; Hylander and Granström, 2010a), thus becoming tense and fearful.

Consequently, the context of the protest, the police, and the social movement culture in Western democracies affect these interpretations and thereby influence these situations. Culture plays a part in such instances, but not in the broader sense with which the term is commonly used, meaning a certain police or protester culture necessarily leads to violence. Rather, culture can be seen as a toolkit of symbols, stories, rituals, and worldviews that people use to solve different kinds of problems and that broadly shapes action by defining what people want (Swidler, 1986; Jasper, 2009). It is thus important to examine how cultural expectations and routines actually play out in specific situational dynamics. Further, how a person perceives and interprets the situation (due to their cultural expectations) also impacts their emotions. Because humans are socialized into expressing "adequate" emotions in certain situations, emotions are a further part of culture playing a role in emerging situations (Shott, 1979).

In short, instead of necessarily following a specific desired intention, people seem to decide on a course of action based on their interpretations and arising emotions *during* the event. These interpretations are shaped by specific interaction dynamics. Interaction dynamics, interpretations, and the resulting emotional dynamics are crucial not only for violence to break out but also for sustaining it.

The Intensity of Violence

Emotional dominance can also help explain why violent clashes vary in form and intensity. Comparing the protest against the WTO meeting in Seattle in 1999 and the protest against the G8 meeting in Rostock in 2007 can illustrate this finding.

Recall that in Seattle some alter-globalization protesters used disruptive techniques—and a few also committed property damage—to hinder delegates from attending the conference (Citizens' Panel on WTO Operations, 2000). Officers then used pepper spray and batons to disperse protesters. After using violence for some time, Seattle officers appear to have perceived total dominance over protesters. Several officers walked around calmly and pepper-sprayed and hit everyone on the scene. In one video recording (PicAxe Productions, 2000, min. 04:52–05:15), a unit marches through a group of protesters. One protester gets on the ground, his arms over his head. The officers seem to be just passing through the street. While they could walk around him, or step over him, one officer walks right over the protester by stepping on his lower back. The officer behind him also steps on the protester. They calmly continue walking, straight, without considering the crowd of protesters around them. One of the officers runs into a protester on the sidewalk, and their shoulders collide. While the protester turns around confused, the officer calmly continues walking. No major injuries seem to occur, but the incident appears cruel.

In another incident, a TV channel recorded an officer dragging and pushing a Seattle protester to the ground. The protester, who wears a bright checkered shirt and light-brown baggy pants, seems unarmed and goes down, lying on the pavement, non-resistant. Lying on his side, he brings his knees up to protect his stomach, his hands over his head. The officer and his colleague, both wearing helmets and in full riot gear, seem uninterested in arresting him but start clubbing him with their batons: one directly targets the protester's head, the other targets his stomach and ribs with blows. A third officer joins in and starts hitting vigorously (PicAxe Productions, 2000, min. 04:30). Again, the incident looks brutal and hate-driven.

These incidents, among several others, suggest the dominance that Seattle police felt after using violence against unresisting protesters for some time. While unarmed peaceful protesters crawled on the ground, officers shot rubber bullets at them from close range or emptied their pepper spray bottles over them in a body posture that shows self-assurance and calm, shoulders down and relaxed (e.g., Kaiser, 1999a). My analysis suggests that what looks like actions spurred by feelings such as hate and anger in fact can also be explained by strong dominance over a weak victim (R. Collins, 2008). While police officers might have hateful intentions at numerous protests, violence breaks out if specific situational patterns take place.

Compare, for instance, the violent incidents in Seattle and those in the main march in Rostock in 2007. In Rostock, both sides engaged in physical violence. Dozens of protesters threw stones at officers and clashed in direct physical confrontations. As a CNN reporter comments in a live recording, protesters "throw everything they find at police" (CNN, 2007). In the video police groups chase protesters, and, if they catch them, they beat and/or arrest them. In several incidents, police and protesters stand about 65 feet (20 meters) apart and repeatedly attack and retreat. Protesters throw objects at officers, and officers run toward protesters and chase, arrest, and hit them with batons. Dozens of individuals are involved in violence with the police, chasing and being chased, breaking up the sidewalk and throwing stones at officers. While officers in Seattle show dominance over victims after some time of violent interaction, most officers in Rostock look tense, stressed, and afraid right before and while clashing with violent protesters. Here, violence is two-sided and chaotic.

My analysis suggests that the balance of emotional power within the situations might explain these different violent behaviors. Police officers in Seattle seem to feel complete emotional dominance over non-resisting protesters after using violence for some time, and this dominance is reflected in their actions. While black bloc activists engaged in property damage in Seattle, it seems they did not engage in violent clashes with officers on a larger scale. In Rostock the emotional strengths were more balanced. Both sides used physical interpersonal violence in a constant back and forth—whenever the micro-situation offered a perceived advantage. Since neither police nor protesters were able to establish clear emotional dominance over the other side, these instances look different from those in Seattle. They suggest that emotional dominance can impact not only the outbreak but also the manifestation of violent action.

Studying protests from Germany and the United States, I observed slight differences in the intensity of violence. As Chapter 1 pointed out, protest groups and policing in Germany and the United States are similar in many ways. Nevertheless, in the rare cases where violence occurs in generally peaceful protests, some German protesters seem to be better prepared for violence and more motivated when engaging in it, while some police seem to be better prepared for using force in the United States. This might also be because the black bloc and the tactics of property damage and direct action have a longer tradition in Germany and other European countries than in the United States (see Chapter 2) and the stronger focus on control in US policing. Some protesters in German marches seem to be more motivated than protesters in the United States to use physical violence when the situation presents itself. Remember, for example, the Brokdorf protest in which protesters brought tracer ammunition and anchors to get over the fence around the nuclear power plant construction site. In one instance three protesters hit the officer in the ditch with shovels. At the Tompkins Square Park protest, which occurred during a similar time period in the United States, protester violence looks less planned and less harsh. Although some protesters allegedly threw bottles and stones at the Tompkins Square Park confrontation, they seemed less prepared for violence, fewer protesters participated, and the intensity of protester violence seems to have been much lower, while police involvement in violent clashes was much higher.[1]

Nevertheless, as Chapters 4, 5, and 6 have illustrated, the same situational paths are visible in both countries. These paths seem to override such country-specific aspects or police or protesters' motivations or strategies. Emotional situational triggers, such as the break-up of police lines or people falling or being outnumbered seem similar in both countries over decades. Lastly, we also find similar cross-national patterns in the way violent situations end, as the following section will show.

How Violent Situations End

Isolated violent interactions between people during large-scale violent clashes are usually short-lived, often lasting a only few seconds. This supports Collins's (2008, pp. 14, 20) claim that the duration of violence is usually very short. Nonetheless, when individuals engage in standoffs

---

[1] While violence is the exception in all Western democracies, a look at protests in France suggests an even higher readiness for violence by police and protesters.

where rubber bullets are shot and/or stones are thrown, more people get involved, and the incidents usually last longer. Presumably this is because firing from a distance involves less direct personal confrontation and a lower inhibition to violence (R. Collins, 2008; Collins, 2009).

What causes these different violent situations to end? While instances often end quickly anyway, an exploratory outlook suggested that shouting is a factor that can stop violence, while screaming cannot. In a number of instances, people stopped using violence when others decisively shouted loud, short, and clear words or sentences. For example, during violent clashes at the protest against the FTAA meeting in Miami (see activistvideos, 2007; for the same incident recorded from a different angle, see Indymedia, 2004), confronted with violent police officers, protesters shout: "Shame! Shame! Shame!" and the officers seem to hear the shouting and stop hitting. In another instance one protester shouts very loudly at an officer clubbing other protesters: "Calm down!" This action seems to stop the officer from attacking further. It is not clear whether officers mistake the decisive short shouts for orders from superiors. However, the shouting of what sounds like orders seems to disrupt the officers' perception of emotional dominance.

Screaming does not seem to have the same effect; rather it seems to go unnoticed by the person engaged in violence. In one example in the protest against the FTAA in Miami, screaming, next to other situational dynamics, even seems to trigger violence (for visual footage, see Indymedia, 2008, min. 0:29). In this instance, two bicycle officers arrest a protester, pinning him on the ground and handcuffing him. About 20 other bicycle officers stand around their two colleagues who make the arrest. They tell a group of about 10 protesters to stand back and point their Tasers at them. The officers involved show classic signs of tension and fear: shoulders drawn up, muscles tensed, mouths stretched, eyes wide open (see Appendix B, Table B2). The protesters communicate that the arrested protester has a broken hand. A few protesters scream almost hysterically, "He's got a broken hand! What are you doing?" Another protester points out his own group's weakness unintentionally, stating several times: "You have weapons and we don't!" Officers yell: "Get back! Get back!" and get more and more agitated and tense, their voices increasingly anxious and loud. The protesters do not get back, but they do not approach either. A protester starts whining. Not even a second later, one officer tasers one of the protesters, who stands close to him and at the periphery of the protest group. After the protester falls down, the other protesters run away screaming. Although the officers' initial aim was presumably not to chase and arrest protesters but to make them step back (at which they had succeeded at this point in time), they now start running after them, and taser another protester. Not only has the short chase no clear purpose, but they also leave behind their colleagues who make the arrest. The screaming by and sudden retreat of protesters seems to have provoked the officers' immanent reaction to briefly chase them. After a short distance they stop, and the protesters flee.

In line with Randall Collins's (2008) micro-sociology of violent confrontations, it is reasonable to assume that protesters' screaming signaled situational weakness. Thus, in an inferior position, protesters' screaming and whining apparently prompted the tense officers to taser them. An explanation could be that screaming reinforces the emotional mood of a person and the impression of a weak victim who lacks self-control and calm. Screaming might add to tensions and to the perception of emotional dominance, while shouting information can imply emotional strength. It can address a perpetrator as an information-processing individual and challenge the perception that the victim is weak.

The police report on a protest in Berlin on April 12, 1968, recalls how officers burst out into a loud collective shout when they approached protesters. Their "tension gave way" in a loud roar, the report states. "The reaction of most rioters was astonishing. Surprised and confused they fled after a brief instance of resistance" (*Der Spiegel*, 1968). It seems that the tone of voice rather than the information transmitted is crucial. The tone of a voice, like the position of the body, can transmit information on dominance or weakness most instantaneously.

In summary, my analysis suggests that the interactional paths described in Chapters 4, 5, and 6 lead to specific interpretations that cause a particular emotional dynamic: situational interaction routines break down, reinterpretations take place, and this leads to an increase of tension and fear. Violence usually erupts after one side establishes emotional dominance. The breakdown of routine interactions generally occurs in the 1½ to 2½ hours after the demonstration starts and shapes the minutes and seconds of violent altercations. Interaction, interpretational, and emotional dynamics in these chaotic moments systematically lead to the eruption of violence. Yet when violence breaks out, it does not always look the same, as the Rostock and Seattle examples illustrated. Some situations bring forth very brutal and excessive violence. Such situations will be the subject of the following section.

Excessive Violence

While the outbreak of violence is the focus of this work, the following section will discuss differences in the intensity of violent behavior—in particular, how some protests become especially violent. While most violent altercations in protests show brawls and somewhat mild beatings, some take violence to another level. Violence appears excessive and particularly brutal in such protests.

Three marches in my study show this kind of particularly intense violence: the Vietnam Peace March in Washington, DC, in 1967; the Tompkins Square Park protest in New York in 1988; and, to a lesser degree, the WTO protest in Seattle in 1999. In all three cases, police riots occurred. Officers beat protesters who lie on the ground again and again, with no end in sight. Even when the person on the ground is bleeding heavily or is no longer moving, the beating continues. The police hit and kick bystanders and shop owners. They use violence that appears uncontrolled, rampant, and indiscriminate, without an apparent purpose such as making arrests or protecting a specific area.

These three protests do not represent the norm of police behavior. Like any form of physical violence among people (R. Collins, 2008), police riots emerge rarely in social movement protests in Western democracies. Accordingly, in all other protests in my study that ended in violence, protesters and police officers used less severe violence overall. However, such riots comprise insightful exceptions that help to explain how and why forms of excessive violence can emerge and how specific types of situational breakdowns can cause more severe violence.

Forward Panics

All three police riots occurred in the loss-of-control pathway, which combines spatial incursions and police mismanagement (see Chapter 4). However, these drastic forms of violence only emerged when the interactions in this pathway occurred in a very specific temporal order. Employing basic steps of sequence analysis (Abbott 1992; Abbott and Tsay, 2000; Aisenbrey and Fasang, 2010; see also Appendix B), I found a particular sequence in the protests with excessive violence. In this sequence the two conditions, spatial incursions and police mismanagement, are crucial to producing the perception of a loss of control. However, other key interactions can occur in addition: first spatial incursions occur, followed by escalation signs, police mismanagement, property damage, and lastly communication problems between protesters and police. This distinct temporal sequence seems to be responsible for the outbreak of excessive violence in the three protests.[2]

Why would this sequence matter? Collins (2008, pp. 83 ff.) shows that a unique sequence can cause people to use violence intensively and without restraint, what he calls a "forward panic." A forward panic is a two-stage sequence. The first stage is a period of prolonged tension and fear. Often frustration arises, because individuals are in a disadvantaged position and do not see or are unable to catch their "opponent." In a second stage, the disadvantage suddenly shifts to the opponent, because she or he becomes visible or gets caught. A triggering moment shifts the power balance between the opposing sides. Suddenly, one group switches from being passive to being entirely active. This atmosphere of total domination leads to a frenzied rush of destruction (R. Collins, 2008, pp. 88, 102), and the suddenly superior side enters a tunnel of violence (R. Collins, 2008, p. 94). Thus, forward panics have an "out-of-proportion" character; even assuming that violent means would be called for, the level of violence seems unfair, senseless, and excessive from a rational viewpoint (R. Collins, 2008, p. 94).

Once a forward panic is under way, it is unstoppable for the time being (R. Collins, 2008, p.94). It is a rhythmic and strongly entraining emotional dynamic, leading people within a group to synchronize their actions (see also Vetlesen, 2014). When the forward panic is over, perpetrators report classic symptoms of panic, for example, feeling detached or as if they were under water. These symptoms are connected to the very high heart rate people experience when in panic (R. Collins, 2008, pp. 46, 92; Grossman and Christensen, 2008).

Washington, DC, 1967: A 20-Minute Wait and a Moment of Surprise

What does a forward panic and use of excessive violence look like in protests? Recall the Washington, DC, march to the Pentagon: on October 21, 1967, protesters marched to the Pentagon to protest the war in Vietnam. Police units were relaxed throughout the day, waiting for the march to arrive

---

[2] In Portland, Oregon (see Appendix, table B1), police also used excessive violence against protesters after a combination of spatial incursions and police mismanagement took place. Yet this protest will not be discussed in detail here, as it is an outlier case. It is the only protest in my sample of 30 demonstrations where police superiors ordered the use of force. Police forces were later sentenced to a payment of $300,000 to 12 protesters for their use of excessive force (Busse, 2004).

at the Pentagon. Due to the low-profile police strategy, initially only 3,000 officers were on duty for the march of 30,000 protesters. Army troops were on standby, hidden inside the Pentagon. The rally had a peaceful picnic atmosphere, and marshals guarding the Pentagon relaxed throughout the day. In pictures, police and soldiers show a calm mood (U.S. Marshals Service, 2011)—they relax on the grass and appear to chat with each other. However, when protesters arrived at the Pentagon, some tried to break through the police lines, i.e., spatial incursions occurred in the form of territorial boundary crossing. Police were not able to react immediately: they had to wait 20 minutes until the Justice Department gave its approval for soldiers inside the Pentagon to be deployed outside in order to support their colleagues (see also Universal Newsreel, 2010). When approval was finally given and troops were sent outside, they arrived in a moment of surprise to a situation of chaos. They were highly emotionally charged and reacted very violently toward protesters in this suddenly advantageous situation. The violent altercations seem brutal and disproportionate.

The Vietnam protest highlights the importance of specific temporal dynamics and the sudden shift from being disadvantaged and tense to being in a dominant position. In this example, only spatial incursions and police mismanagement occurred. As discussed above, their combination is sufficient to lead to violence, as it causes a loss-of-control path. But it was the particular temporal dynamic in this protest that was decisive in precipitating a police riot: the 20-minute delay in approving officers to operate outside the building led to a drastic and prolonged increase in tension and fear on the side of the police. Officers inside were unaware of what exactly was going on outside and unable to see their presumed opponents or to react to the territorial incursion. Due to territorial invasions, their assumption was that the Pentagon was under attack and that their colleagues and soon they were in danger. They assumed that the longer this approval would take, the worse the situation outside would get. Still they had to wait and wait. Suddenly, the order was given to get outside quickly to defend the Pentagon. Finally! In officers' perception, they arrived at the last moment to support their colleagues in danger. A protester recalls (Leen, 1999): "People became frightened. [. . .] They began running every which way. At that moment, it turned into something else. A sense of chaos takes over." When units were suddenly ordered into action, they gained dominance over surprised protesters and reacted very violently. The long steady increase in tension and fear was suddenly released, which can explain the excessive outburst of violence according to Collins's (2008) forward panic concept.

New York, 1988: Chaos, No Leadership, and a Police Riot

The same pattern can be found in the Tompkins Square Park protest introduced in previous chapters. At the end of the march to the park, a riot erupted that left protesters baffled, with open wounds on the backs of their heads and blood running down their necks. Shop owners were beaten; observers and residents were battered, including elderly residents and teenagers (see, e.g., Daily Beast, 2010). Videos show an officer hitting a protester: the protester is pushed against a truck with no possibility of escape; protecting himself with his arms over his head, he screams desperately, "I'm going down! I'm going down!" With no apparent intention of making an arrest, the officer keeps clubbing him (see, e.g., Telengard, 2007). As in this scene, officers attacked people without regard to whether they posed any danger or whether they had broken the law. Their actions seem out of control, brutal, and unwarranted.

A closer look at the Tompkins Square Park clashes can illustrate the relevance of the particular temporal order of interactions for the outbreak of excessive violence. The protest runs through the whole forward panic sequence except for property damage taking place. First, spatial incursions occurred when protesters marching to the park did not disperse but decided to enter the park. Hence, police territory was invaded. Second, escalation signs occurred as helicopters flew over the protest site and fire trucks with sirens frequently entered and left the scene. Mounted police units rushed about in full gallop. Most people at the scene perceived these interactions as indicative of an escalation. Third, severe police mismanagement took place. The police were understaffed, inexperienced, and frequently without any commander in charge. The operational command was located in the middle of the protesters' assembly in the park. Hence, newly arriving units had to pass through the group of protesters before getting any information on the situation, their operation, or their assignments. The chief of operations was absent in the middle of the confrontations. Left alone by the deputy chief, the "panicky captain" issued a 10-85 call for help, which is "usually interpreted as being of an extreme emergency nature" (*New York Times*, 1988). Officers rushed to the area without being briefed about or equipped for the event. Fourth, communication problems between protesters and police occurred, and communication broke down (Purdum, 1988).

What is specific about this sequence and the way this protest unfolded is that the two interactions that drastically increase tensions—spatial incursions and escalation signs—occurred at the beginning of the sequence, yet violence did not immediately break out. Time went by, and tensions rose and rose. These two interactions alone are not sufficient to cause violence, as they do not lead to a particular interpretation by police or protesters—like a loss of control, an offense, or missing information (see Chapters 4–6). Next to police mismanagement, communication problems between protesters and police then further added to the tension, as neither group was certain about the other group's intentions or planned actions. When officers then suddenly perceived themselves to be in a dominant situation to react (e.g., when smaller clusters of protesters formed and protesters struggled or fell down), they released this tension in a violent rush.

The extent of this rush was caught on tape by the Lower East Side filmmaker Clayton Patterson, among others (Solomon and Levin, 2008). Recordings show busted heads and baffled bystanders covered in their own blood. Many victims suffered head wounds on the back of their heads, indicating that they were turning their backs, ducking, or had fallen down when being hit. Officers chased anyone on the scene, indiscriminately beating bystanders or residents coming out of bars on their way home. Four women got caught up in the police riot on their way home and were chased by police. One of the women left her stroller behind and ran with her baby in her arms. While running she was hit on the back of the head. Her friend recalls:

> What kind of cop tries to hit a woman in the head?! A woman with a baby??! I have never been in a war before, but I remember thinking right then that this is what it must be like. If you're not wearing the uniform, it doesn't matter who you are: you are a target. Nobody had a chance, and there was no time to react. [. . .] We couldn't understand why the cops were out to get four young women, and one with a baby no less. We were little New Wave nerds. [. . .] We weren't cool and never hung out with anyone famous or anything like that. And none of what just happened to us made sense. (DeRienzo, 2008)

Mayor Ed Koch later described the brutality of the events: "There were professionals there who caught much of the mayhem on camera. And it was horrible. It was terrifying" (Daily Beast, 2010). "I remember seeing cops shove their nightsticks into the spokes of passing bicyclists, and also beat and shove innocent people coming out of bars. It was an ugly, ugly night," another protester recounts (DeRienzo, 2008). The apparently senseless brutality indicates that officers seemed to have entered a tunnel of violence—an indicator of a forward panic (R. Collins, 2008)—in which they attacked anyone at the scene. A "police riot" occurred, the media later attested (*New York Times*, 1988).

Cruelty and Prolonged Fear

The two protests described here illustrate that a specific temporal dynamic of previously unplanned interactions between protesters and officers can explain the emergence of such police riots. The Seattle protest, discussed in detail in Chapter 5, shows the same temporal sequence as the Tompkins Square Park and Pentagon marches: after a buildup of tensions throughout the day, officers gained dominance over protesters in the main march when in a micro-situation and used excessive violence against mostly non-resisting protesters from there on. In these instances a prolonged increase in tension and fear is followed by a release of tensions when officers achieve sudden dominance over protesters. They enter into a violent rush in which their acts of violence appear uncontrolled and excessive.

In principle, such instances might also be an indicator of previous motivations or potentially cruel intentions of officers toward protesters. While the existence of such motivations cannot be ruled out, there is no evidence in my study that officers take part in such riots primarily due to hateful intentions toward protesters. For one, they do not riot in other protests by the same protest groups but only in few, very specific situations in which distinct temporal patterns occur. For instance, most protests that the Seattle Police Department oversaw both before and after the WTO meeting in 1999 stayed peaceful, and officers did not use excessive violence as during the WTO protest. Further, what seems to have been particular about Seattle—just as in the Vietnam War protest and Tompkins Park protests—is the sequence of interactions, the strong (even if in hindsight unjustified) fear on the side of officers and the sudden shift to dominance. These aspects, rather than prior motivations (which might be present nevertheless), seem to have led to the excessive use of violence. The brutality of officers' actions seems to be foremost a product of specific situational emotional dynamics. While these instances of excessive violence appear cruel and hate-driven, their emergence follows specific patterns that seem to be linked to the prior temporal sequence of interactions with protesters.

It is important to highlight that these remarks are not meant to justify specific police behaviors or police brutality. Officers might hold hateful emotions and cruel intentions toward protesters. I do not claim that such motivations do not exist. My analysis merely suggests that such potential hateful emotions or cruel intentions can impact but do not seem *decisive* for officers' situational actions during these protests (see also R. Collins, 2008; Collins, 2009; Klusemann, 2009). Officers' motivations (cruel or not) are too commonly present in situations that do not turn violent and—in contrast to interactional paths—they do not show a systematic pattern with regard to the outcome of violence in protests. Not only do specific situational interactions between protesters and officers and the breakdown of routines seem crucial for producing emotional dynamics that trigger violence, but the temporal order of these interactions and emotional dynamics also seems to play into the intensity of violence.

8 | How to Keep Protests Peaceful

Boredom Is the Answer

Given the insights into how situations break down and can lead to violence in demonstrations, how can we keep the peace? If strategies and motivations do not have a decisive impact on the outbreak of violence, we might adopt a pessimistic outlook and assume that we have little to no influence on the eruption of violence. To the contrary, findings show that much can be done and achieving many of the measures necessary is quite manageable.

The short answer to keeping the peace is obviously that we need to avoid the five interactions in their specific combinations and resultant situational interpretations. Yet three interactions are outstanding in their relevance for keeping protests peaceful: good police management, respect for territorial boundaries, and communication between protesters and police during the protest (see also Madensen and Knutsson, 2011). After discussing the relevance of these three aspects, a subsequent section will highlight specific measures for violence prevention.

Police Management

"Good" management can be illustrated by the march against the Group of Twenty Finance Ministers and Central Bank Governors (G20) meeting in Pittsburgh on September 25, 2009. Although violence was expected and seemed likely in this protest, efficient police management strongly contributed to keeping it peaceful: Pittsburgh police directly addressed numerous difficulties that had crippled previous operations. First, learning from the 1999 Seattle operation, among others, police were well prepared for a worst-case scenario, having developed a comprehensive plan that kept traffic flowing throughout the protest. This increased police officers' perception of being in charge of the overall situation.

Additionally, Pittsburgh police focused on communication among police units. As stated above, large-scale police operations usually involve different agencies that often lack a shared radio frequency, which renders effective communication among them nearly impossible. Consequently, units cannot call other units or the operational command for support (or for a broader assessment of the situation). In Pittsburgh, police addressed this challenge by employing the Nixle system. Using specific distribution lists for group text messaging, Nixle aims to ensure that everyone gets the information relevant for her or him. Hence, some messages are send to specific groups and some to the entire force. In Pittsburgh, using Nixle allowed communication between units, even though they did not share a frequency at the outset. This ensured that 5,700 officers could communicate and received all information relevant to them (Harding, 2009), thereby contributing to officers' feeling of safety and being in charge.

Territorial Boundaries

In addition, both police and protesters in Pittsburgh respected territorial boundaries. Protesters marched in a parade-like atmosphere. In most places officers were loosely positioned on sidewalks, many of them on bikes and without riot gear, and many observers and media watched the downtown march. From visual data the march resembles a convivial parade (e.g., G20 Peoples March, 2009; People's March Reaches Downtown Pittsburgh, 2009). Videos and pictures also suggest that police lines are loose if officers are at all visible at the scene (Jimenez, 2008; Bliss, 2009). Protesters look happy and relaxed, focusing on their own group's actions and hardly noticing the officers standing on the sidewalk. The protest routine was not interrupted, and the overall emotional mood stayed calm.

Such a parade-like atmosphere is also visible in other protests that stay peaceful, like in the City Rights protest in Hamburg, Germany, 2009, or in the protest against nuclear energy in Gorleben, Germany, 1979. The positive effect these settings can have across protests is in line with prior research: studies emphasize the strong peacekeeping effect of avoiding chaotic situations at all costs (e.g., Hylander and Granström, 2010a). The discussion in Chapters 2 through 7 has highlighted that avoiding the breakdown of situational routines can be key. Thorough organizing can provide a recognizable order in otherwise potentially confusing settings. Parade-like settings with onlookers all around can transmit a sense of importance and status to protesters, since the focus rests on the display of their claims for the public. These settings can indicate that an established situational routine of "marching to be heard" is in place that actors can rely on, making them feel safe and therefore more likely at ease.

Communication

Communication is a further factor vital for keeping the peace, protest comparisons show. The common platitude "communication is the key to a happy marriage" seems to be applicable to protests to a certain degree. Consider the protest against the NATO meeting in Kehl on April 4, 2009: protesters were hindered on their approved protest route and protesters in the front row were pushed against officers. Yet no violent altercations emerged, even though one group's territorial borders were crossed and some protesters seemed violently motivated.

In Kehl, communication between the two sides was crucial to keep individuals from overcoming their inhibition threshold for violence and keeping tension and fear at bay. Visual data show that police and protesters' loudspeakers declare several times: "Please stay calm!" (Swiola, 2009). Protesters recall, "then here was the loudspeaker van [of the police], making nonsensical announcements over and over again: 'We welcome you!' etc." (Achelpöhler, 2009). Several members of parliament talked to the police and crossed the bridge for first-hand information on what was happening on the other side. Returning to the German side, they passed their information to protesters via loudspeaker. Additionally, they conveyed and discussed the official explanation for why crossing the bridge was not possible. Police and protesters arrived at their own positions regarding the route independently. Then spokespersons for each group met, negotiated, and kept their group informed. Numerous protesters felt that the situation was about to escalate in the first half hour after spatial incursions took place, when some protesters pushed the crowd from behind. They were, however, "calmed by repeated new announcements," and the tension dissolved, a participant recalls (Achelpöhler, 2009). Videos show politicians giving long, detailed speeches about the situation. Their intonation and content indicates that their aim is not to hold a speech with the intent to motivate activists or strive for applause but that they are focused on discussing the current—otherwise potentially confusing—situation and on providing detailed information (Savkoeln, 2009).

The intensity of announcements, reiterating that negotiations were taking place and asking people to keep calm, led to several people being bored or even annoyed. An announcement—again! Yet announcements and continuous communication apparently prevented further tensions, kept rumors from spreading, and stopped one group from fearing an attack by the other. Thus, although circumstances were difficult, communication kept the emotional dynamic peaceful throughout. Such a de-escalating effect of communication can be found across cases. In another example, the Migrants' Rights March in Rostock on July 4, 2007, officers also stopped the march on the protest route. Again, tensions increased but remained manageable in large part due to constant communication between the operational command and a protest organizer's lawyer. In the end, protesters dispersed peacefully.

Communication thus seems highly relevant to keeping protests peaceful; it can reassure actors about the other side's intentions and thereby inhibit tensions and fear. Other studies underline specific aspects of communication for peacekeeping. For instance, promoting differentiated perceptions of individuals in the other group can be particularly useful and can help to educate people about the other group's heterogeneity (Reicher et al., 2004; ACPO, ACPOS, and NPIA, 2010; Hoggett and Stott, 2010). Such actions can forestall stereotyping of a group based on one member's bad behavior. If some members of a group then behave "badly," they are not seen as part of a larger homogeneous group of malicious, dangerous people. They are more likely perceived as a small fraction of a heterogeneous—largely harmless—group (Reicher et al., 2004; see also Hylander and Granström, 2010a).

Participant observation suggests that Berlin police have since 2012 focused on what is called "tactical communication": situational communication to de-escalate crowd settings. During an operation, Berlin police differentiate between "ordinance announcements" and "service announcements." Ordinance announcements are legal announcements and can therefore not be improvised. Service announcements, however, are previously specifically trained with the help of psychologists and voice analysts. Training for such announcements includes voice exercises, word choice, stress management, and specific exercises aimed to instruct speakers how to react to changing situations quickly and spontaneously. Speakers are trained to adapt announcements to the audience, sometimes using the dialect (especially when policing soccer fan crowds) or the native language of the crowd. The goal of these service announcements is to de-escalate situations by communicating in a playfully eloquent manner what is happening, what officers are doing, and why they are doing so.[1] In

---

[1] Berlin police also try to avoid the spread of rumors by updating participants at crowd events via social media.

line with research findings, such announcements may avoid police actions (such as stopping protesters on their agreed-upon protest route) being interpreted as threatening to one's safety.[2]

Expected Routines

The discussion suggests that as long as events follow a certain situational routine and meet expectations dominant in the specific cultural context, they stay peaceful. Danger lurks when the expected ritual and relied-upon situational order breaks down and tension and fear increase—in particular in the 1½ to 2½ hours after a protest starts. Protest comparisons show that officers perceiving that everything is in control, as well as constant and extensive communication between protesters and the police, can calm the collective mood. Things are all right when everything goes as expected and people can rely on their routine behaviors, police and protesters talk to each other, and the march passes by. With boredom in their eyes, officers will not feel threatened. They will not face a situation that makes them overcome their inhibition threshold to violence. When protesters roll their eyes, as in Kehl, because their own organizers and police make the millionth announcement, things are going well in terms of violence prevention. As Collins (2016c, para. 30) summarizes: "In the violent sociology of emotions, boredom is your friend." Constantly being bored throughout life might lead to frustration or anger, and in some individuals even to plans to fight. But in an actual violence-threatening instance, situational boredom seems to be a peacekeeper. The feeling of boredom underlines that things are so normal and routinized, the situation even becomes uninteresting. This feeling implies that situational routines are working and can be relied on.

Don't Forget the Batteries: Practical Guidelines

If well-functioning police management, respect for territorial boundaries, and communication are relevant for keeping the peace, two questions emerge: Why should we have an interest in keeping protests peaceful? And how exactly can police and protesters avoid violent outbreaks?

---

[2] Given that such measures are used much less in other federal states, a detailed comparison between German federal states' use of tactical communication (as well as a comparison within the United States) would be highly interesting.

If we believe that Western capitalist societies change through social movement action and that public opinion matters, it is vital that the right to protest be ensured and that claims can be made public. Given that corporate media strongly focus on violence once it occurs, the social and political positions of protesters might receive more attention if protests stay peaceful (Greer and McLaughlin, 2010; McCarthy, Clark McPhail, and Smith, 1996; Ryan, 1999; Simpson, Willer, and Feinberg, 2018). Despite corporate media often passing over peaceful protests completely, if a report on a peaceful protest is published, protesters' positions will likely be more broadly transmitted than if it turns violent. This can give protesters the chance to be more widely heard and thereby possibly change society for the better. It can also attract more participants if activists do not have to fear being in harm's way when protesting.

Even if there is no belief in societal change through social movement action or in the power of public opinion to influence policymakers, ensuring peaceful protests contributes to promoting basic human rights—freedom of speech, freedom of assembly, freedom of association, and the right to physical integrity—aiming to ensure higher standards of living and respectful treatment of human beings (United Nations, 1948).

If we see a necessity to avoid violence, how exactly can this goal be achieved? As discussed above, my study suggests that violence emerges due to a breakdown in routine interactions. We might assume that it is possible to change people's feelings of hate or their motivations for violence. But it might seem difficult at first to influence unfolding situations from becoming chaotic and emotionally charged.

This impression may in fact be misleading. Research underlines that humans have an inhibition threshold for violence and that they act boundedly rational in most situations (Blumer, 1986; R. Collins, 2008). What we need to do then to avoid violence is avoid interactions that lead to specific (boundedly rational) interpretations and foster us–them boundaries (see also Madensen and Knutsson, 2011). Otherwise, these interpretations favor specific emotional dynamics and can thereby trigger violence. Avoiding such interactions—like not invading the other's space, so the other does not feel in danger and become tense and fearful—might even be easier to achieve than changing people's ideologies (which does not mean that we should not also try to change peoples' aggressive mindsets and structural factors that might cause such mindsets). I suggest six guidelines and give examples for implementing them. These measures can be considered by policymakers, police officials, and protest organizers, as well as by individuals participating in marches.

1. *Clear and extensive communication between protesters and police can contribute to keeping protests peaceful.* Communication between protesters and police inhibits rumors and the likelihood that one group's actions will be interpreted as dangerous to the other. Communication needs to be ensured by technology, content, and willingness to communicate. It is particularly fruitful if a high-ranking person such as an operational commander or protest organizer also communicates with the other side, as in the Kehl protest (see also Reicher et al., 2004, p. 567). The above-discussed findings imply that measures to improve communication between protesters and police include the following:

    a. Equipment should facilitate communication. It should be technically possible for messages to be transmitted loudly enough so that all individuals addressed understand them acoustically.

    b. Each side should stress its intentions often and as explicitly as possible. This can guarantee that both sides are always up to date about communicated intentions from the other and can assure each group's members that their organizers are in charge and have an overview that allows them to pursue their shared goals.

    c. Each side could communicate the peaceful intentions of the other to its own group. For example, protesters could announce: "Police are here to protect us and support our right to protest." Police might stress: "Protesters are here to exercise their right to protest in an officially sanctioned and peaceful way." This could decrease perceived dangers, negative stereotyping, and rumors and thereby the likelihood that actions by one group are interpreted as dangerous (see also Hylander and Granström, 2010a).

    d. Playfully eloquent service announcements (as used by Berlin police) could be used to de-escalate situations that might otherwise be interpreted as threatening as well as creating a relaxed atmosphere from the start. In particular, announcements delivered in a down-to-earth way and with a calm voice can be helpful. In addition, speakers should try to avoid negatives (e.g., "stay peaceful" rather than "don't use violence," or "stay calm" rather than "don't be fearful") and provide extensive information about the situation if police undertake action otherwise potentially interpreted as threatening.

    e. Police could employ communication officers wearing wear yellow vests that state "communication team" instead of riot gear (e.g., Berlin police). These officers can stand next to protesters to be approachable for questions. Participant observation with Berlin police suggests these officers are often viewed as somewhere in between police and protest organizers, and protesters commonly ask them about geographical and logistical information, as well as about police actions. Their communication with protesters can further decrease tensions.

It seems vital that these officers remain accessible to protesters and do not suddenly leave when riot gear officers are brought in, as in the Rostock Migrants' Rights March. Suddenly pulling protesters' source of information can lead to even more drastic increases in tension and stronger us–them boundaries, since all protesters might suddenly feel that danger is immanent.

f. Police could mount LED panels onto their loudspeaker vans. Such pancls can be particularly useful when spoken communication is not possible (for instance, due to noise levels). Berlin police recently started using such panels to provide essential information to protesters and thereby ease tensions. For example, during participant observation with Berlin police at a protest march on May 1, 2017, LED panels were used to provide participants with a constant stream of information. One of the marches, which was part of the larger May 1 protests in Berlin-Kreuzberg, had its end point in the middle of a street block because the next intersection had to remain empty to allow visitors of a nearby street festival to be able to flee in case of a mass panic or terrorist attack. The march therefore had to end in the middle of the block and protesters had to disperse. Organizers stated that protesters were not allowed to march on and protesters could see police officers and police cars lining up in their way, blocking the entire street that would allow them to get to the next intersection. Such a situation often results in raised tension among protesters, who may worry about running into a trap. Turning into the street to see lines of officers in the middle of the road blocking them might have alarmed protesters. They could easily have assumed that the police would soon close the intersection behind them as well, trapping them with no way to escape. Compare this instance to the statement by a photojournalist at the Miami FTAA protest 2003 (see Chapter 6, "Missing Information"), who described the narrow streets and confusing setting in Miami, the sound from helicopters and the streets noise level, as well as his uneasiness in light of missing communication by police of where to go:

Yet, had the police had any sort of portable sound system, they could have announced something like this, "Attention everyone. We are not going to arrest you. We are not going to pen you up in the street. If you will turn around and look, you will see that the access to Biscayne Boulevard has been cleared." (Crespo, 2006, p. 48)

Yet, in Berlin police communicated where to go. The police loudspeaker van with an LED panel (and officers in yellow vests marked "communication teams") had accompanied the march since its beginning. The van had not made announcements so as not to interrupt the march's speakers, but its colorful, blinking LED panel had announced this place as the end of the march since its start. Thereby, protesters had no reason to assume a trap or feel threatened. Protesters merely arrived at the police lines in the middle of the street, turned around, and went back the way they came to disperse. A police official from another European country had come to see how Berlin police handle such situations and observed the march with me. Given that some of the protesters were considered radical by law enforcement, he turned to me, saying, "Wow, the Germans! They are so well behaved! They just turn around and walk back!" The findings presented in Chapters 2 to 7, however, suggest that communication via the LED panel and specific situational patterns, rather than German manners, contributed strongly to protesters' relaxed reaction.

2. *Police should focus on effective management during the protest to contribute to keeping protests peaceful.* The feeling of being in charge strongly influences police officers' perception of and behavior during protests. Concrete measures to favor effective management include the following:

   a. Communication among officers as well as continuous overview and support from the operational command should be emphasized.

   b. Police training and professionalism can maximize effective management and organization and can decrease the likelihood that officers will feel in danger. More specifically, the operational command and planning committees of police operations could consult the after-action reports of previous demonstrations more consistently, focus on compatible radio frequencies (e.g., through Nixle, as in Pittsburgh), and ensure that basic logistics work throughout. Such measures (walkie-talkie batteries, food supplies, etc.) can help minimize the risk of violence (for a similar point, see Earl and Soule, 2006). Caution should be taken against very strong expectations of things going a certain way, as this can increase tensions and fear if situations turn out differently (see Chapter 4).

3. *Respecting territorial boundaries can favor peaceful demonstrations.* Any boundary-crossing by one group into the other's assigned space will likely lead to drastic changes in emotional dynamics. Measures for avoiding territorial boundary-crossing include the following:

   a. Spaces assigned to police or protesters need very explicit definition prior to a protest. Careful organization can forestall spatial confusions. For example, loose lines of officers without riot gear on the sidewalk, with bystanders and the press watching, create a parade-like atmosphere. The emotional dynamic is likely to be calmer than in confusing settings, where neither group is certain of its territory's boundaries and feels easily affronted by the other (see also Hylander and Granström, 2010a).

   b. The problematic, potentially violent consequences of territorial boundary-crossing should be made explicit for both sides before and during a protest.

   c. During a protest, officers should make great effort to enable protesters to stick to the protest route and not hinder protesters from continuing on their sanctioned route.

   d. In some protests, showing a low police profile can contribute to de-escalation. Without police officers next to the protest route, escalation will become much less likely and some types of provocations will not occur. Similarly, using police lines to mark streets that the march is not allowed to enter (often because specific buildings that might be subject to property damage are located there) may create an incentive for territorial boundary-crossing. Depending on the march, such roads or intersections could instead be closed off by food stands, stages, or through protest organizers standing there, rather than officers.

4. *Protesters and officers should be aware of and avoid actions that the other group could potentially interpret as signs of escalation.* Avoiding escalation signs contributes to forestalling chaotic situations, which otherwise favor the emergence of violence.

Avoiding escalation signs is especially important if no communication between protesters and police exists and rumors flourish more easily.

Other studies found that disarming is a further interaction that can lead to trust building and therefore may inhibit the outbreak of violence (Hylander and Granström, 2010a, pp. 18 ff.). Examples are the black bloc stripping down at the Migrants March in Rostock, 2007, to show they are not armed and do not intend to harm officers. In the march against nuclear energy from the permanent disposal site at Gorleben to the city of Hannover in 1979, protest organizers ordered all participants—many of them farmers—to leave their pitchforks and scythes outside the city (Revista, 2009). This initiative to disarm was deliberately taken before coming across large groups of police patrolling inside the city. Disarming officers, or employing many plain-clothes bicycle officers, as in Pittsburgh, can be a further measure to promote a non-threatening atmosphere.

Practical measures should be taken to pre-empt the potential perception of escalation signs:

a. Actors should try to avoid escalations signs, such as helmets, water cannon trucks, driving around with sirens (police), or picking up stones (protesters).

b. If escalation signs cannot be avoided, actors should communicate their reasons. For instance, protesters could communicate why they mask up (frequently because they want to protect their privacy from police filming) and indicate that this does not necessarily imply that they are preparing to attack police. Police could communicate why they wear helmets (as in the Baltimore protest that stayed peaceful; see Chapter 9) and explain that this does not necessarily imply that they are preparing for attacks on protesters.

c. Police could disarm themselves (for example, by forgoing helmets or riot gear) to increase protesters' trust.

5. *Protesters aiming for a peaceful protest should particularly try to avoid, or keep in mind the potential consequences of, property damage.* The Seattle WTO protest shows how property damage increases tensions not only among police forces but also among many protesters. Protesters willing to use property damage should be aware of its consequences for escalation. This is particularly true if no communication with police forces exists.

If protesters intend to use property damage for claim-making but desire to avoid physical clashes with police, a practical measure can be particularly emphasizing in communication with police officers—especially those in the front lines—the political message or intention of these tactics and that these actions do not imply that physical harm to officers will follow or is intended. An escalating effect might nevertheless occur, since police officers tend to react to property damage as a form of unlawful behavior.

6. *Specific attention should be given to a potential increase in tension in the temporal danger zone of 1½ to 2½ hours after the start of a demonstration.* Violent outbreaks are most likely 2 hours after the start of a demonstration if tension and fear have built up due to specific interaction sequences but people have not settled into a routine mode. Across analyzed cases, violence broke out around 1½ to 2 hours after it started. If one of the three paths occurs and situations emerge in which one side perceives a slight advantage (like an opponent falling down), they are most likely to use violence around 2 hours after the start of the demonstration.

9 | Situational Breakdowns Beyond Protest Violence

I N THE FOLLOWING SECTIONS, I WILL examine whether situational breakdowns can lead to surprising outcomes in different types of events. One section will look beyond protest marches and examine uprisings after police shootings that turn violent. A second section will move beyond collective actions and violence altogether and examine failed armed store robberies.

Uprisings in the United States generally show very severe background conditions, such as symbolic and systemic racism and police racial bias, as well as a triggering event (usually the death of an African American citizen at the hands of US police) that people directly protest against (Rothstein, 2015; Moran and Waddington, 2016; Taylor, 2016). They are therefore some of the likeliest cases to feature background factors as key influences in the eruption of violence; conversely, they are some of the unlikeliest cases for the situational patterns of violence discussed in Chapters 3 to 6 to play an important role.

Robberies usually show interactions between only two people, with a very clear routine that the robber forces upon the clerk. Surprising outcomes in robberies, such as a robbery failing, are therefore unlikely to happen, and if they do we would not expect them to show similar patterns leading to collective violence. Uprisings and robberies therefore function as a "most different" case (Gerring, 2010) compared to the protests discussed earlier, making them ideal to explore the portability of the situational breakdowns argument laid out in the first chapters of this book.

Situational Breakdowns Beyond Protest Marches

A *New York Times* (2014b) video shows a citizen in a grey polo shirt standing in front of a police line at an intersection in Ferguson, Missouri, on August 13, 2014. Protesters around him hold posters reading "Excuse me . . . We need answers for Michael Brown Jr." Two small children hold placards that state "Don't shoot." The sun is shining. The citizen in the grey shirt is visibly shaken up. He points to the row of police officers blocking the street with their clubs ready in hand. "This is intimidation over there to me. And that's what this is about: Intimidation. Why can't we fix it and make a dialogue instead of that happening? Why don't [the police] come and walk with us? [*Referring to the citizens gathering*] You can't keep telling these guys: 'Be quiet. Don't curse. Pull your pants up. This, that, and the other.' This is their everyday life. And they're mad. They're mad. . . . I'm mad! (*with a broken voice, tearing up*) We should all be mad! Man, we should all be angry because of what's going on right now."

Four days earlier Michael Brown, an unarmed 18-year-old Ferguson citizen, was shot and killed by Ferguson police officer Darren Wilson. Of the 12 shots fired, 6 hit Brown, who eyewitnesses say had his hands up when being shot. Brown died at the scene. Officer Wilson is Caucasian; Brown was African American. Like after so many incidents of this nature in the United States, protesters took to the street the following days to demand answers and, ultimately, justice. In Ferguson they were soon met by police in gas masks and full military gear. Tanks drove through the city's streets, police dogs barked at protesters, and snipers pointed their rifles at citizens. Protests lasted for 17 days, with some including physical interpersonal violence between officers and protesters. The following sections will discuss the emergence of these clashes.

Uprisings[1] are similar to the left protest marches discussed in Chapters 1 to 8 in that they show people gathering in large numbers in the streets to protest a felt injustice, officers arriving to police their public claim-making, and collective violence between the two groups sometimes erupting. But

---

[1] Such events are also commonly labeled "riots." Riots are defined as "a violent disturbance of the peace by a crowd" (Oxford Dictionaries, 2018). Yet not only is this term often used in a derogatory way, but protest activities after a police shooting in the United States are also largely peaceful and not per se a "violent disturbance" (see also the discussion of the term "violence" in Chapter 1). I therefore use the word "uprising," defined as "an act of resistance or rebellion; a revolt" (Oxford Dictionaries, 2018), which is also the term commonly used by the Black Lives Matter movement, a key organizer in many recent protests against police brutality in the United States (Matthews & Noor, 2018; for a discussion, see Bates, 2015).

they also differ in meaningful ways. Among other aspects, background factors, such as systemic racism and racial tensions, play a crucial role in the emergence of uprisings after police shootings in the United States. Uprisings commonly not only address a recent police shooting, they also highlight how these shootings occur against the backdrop of racial discrimination still impacting the lives of many African Americans in the United States (e.g., Taylor, 2016). Systemic and symbolic racism are thus key factors in these events.

Second, they differ from the protests discussed in Chapters 3 to 8 in that uprisings emerging after police shootings often directly address issues of police work and accountability. Thus, tensions and us–them boundaries between protesters and police might be more salient in these uprisings from the start than in the marches discussed in previous chapters. As discussed in Chapters 3 to 6, pronounced us–them boundaries can make the eruption of violence more likely, as both groups tend to observe the other more cautiously and are more likely to perceive every action by the other group as potentially malicious and harmful.

Third, uprisings after police shootings are different in that clashes usually do not happen during marches that are organized, planned, and sanctioned well in advance. They usually take place in direct and often spontaneous response to a recent event of police brutality against a citizen of color. As a consequence, they show less established routines and might therefore not show a break in routine to be as relevant for leading to violence as it was in the protest marches discussed in Chapters 1 to 8.

As a fourth difference, physical interpersonal violence during uprisings is often not considered to be a "surprise outcome," as it is in large-scale protest marches, such as Seattle in 1999. Rather, physical interpersonal violence between protesters and police in uprisings is often understood as the default scenario (thus they are often labeled "riots," see footnote 1 in this chapter). Hence, a natural question is whether the explanations posited to lead to protest violence in this book can explain violence in uprisings as well. Are we still dealing with broken routines in police–protester clashes such as in Ferguson in 2014? Might background factors rather than situational dynamics be key to understanding these events? And could the discussed situational paths to violence only be relevant to understand the protest marches described in previous chapters?

The following sections will explore whether the same factors discussed in Chapters 3 to 6 are also at work in these events, with very different background factors and routines. They will show that while systematic and symbolic racism are key in leading to the uprisings, these factors cannot conclusively explain the outbreak of violent clashes between protesters and police. Violence in uprisings, just as in protests, is rare, and assuming that uprisings automatically lead to violent clashes can contribute to the racist stereotypes activists are protesting against.

The following sections rely on media accounts, activist accounts, reports by the Black Lives Matter movement, police reports, other scholars' accounts, as well as video recordings by citizens and the media (see Appendix C). The sections will first examine background factors such as structural aspects, and motivations, followed by a closer situational analysis of the Ferguson uprising. Subsequent sections will provide a brief look at violence during the uprisings in Baltimore in 2015, discuss how the findings may be applied to avoid violent clashes, and discuss findings in the light of the book's situational breakdown approach.

Police Shootings and (the Rarity of) Violent Uprisings

Above and beyond protesters' claims targeting police work directly, the main difference between uprisings after police brutality against African American citizens in the United States and the large-scale left protests discussed above is that uprisings occur against the backdrop of racial discrimination in the United States. Systemic and symbolic racism is the vital factor in these uprisings.

After 265 years of slavery and 90 years of segregation, African Americans in the United States gained equal rights on paper a mere 54 years ago. That systemic discrimination and racism still flourish despite these rights has been shown consistently and many times (e.g., Alexander, 2012; Anderson, 2012b; Bertocchi and Dimico, 2012; Charles, 2003; Chetty et al., 2018; Goffman, 2014; Taylor, 2016, 2014). Protest movements, most prominently the civil rights and Black Lives Matter movements, have addressed these issue since the 1960s, accomplishing major changes in legislation as well as public discourse about black lives in the United States (Taylor, 2016; Matthews and Noor, 2018). Yet systemic and individual racism, impacting the job and housing markets, education, policing, and many other aspects of social life, still abounds and forms the backdrop for the shootings of African American citizens by police in the United States.

Anderson (2012b) argues that while segregation has been abolished, the idea of the "ghetto" still prevails in today's United States. Progress since the civil rights movement has led to people of color being represented throughout society and to a large African American US middle class. Yet, although most African Americans have never set foot in "the ghetto," many in US society still associate anonymous people of color, especially men, with the icon of the ghetto: an impoverished, crime-prone urban area (Anderson, Brighenti, and Bassetti, 2007, p. 306). Blackness, as a master status characteristic, thereby creates a deficit of credibility for people of color in the United States. It is always up to the person of color to disprove the icon and to demonstrate that she or he is not part of the "ghetto," thus non-threatening, non-criminal, and non-dangerous. Yet, even if the person is able to do so, the status is often only provisional (Anderson, Brighenti, and Bassetti, 2007; Anderson, 2012a, 2012b). Patricia Hill Collins (2008) identifies a similar socially constructed icon that emerged from the slave era and that today's white US society applies specifically to black women. She shows that what she labels "controlling images" of black womanhood, such as the "mammy," "matriarch," or "welfare mother," reflect the dominant group's interest in maintaining black women's subordination and mask social relations affecting all women (P. H. Collins, 2008, pp. 76–106; see also P.H. Collins, 1986; P. H. Collins, 1993).

As a form of symbolic racism these icons thereby lead to implicit bias, open prejudice, and racial discrimination. The radicalized stereotype of the iconic ghetto can be found in many everyday events (Anderson, 2012b, 2012a, 2015), as well as in the police shootings that sparked the uprisings this section discusses. We see it, for instance, in George Zimmerman's assessment of 17-year-old Trayvon Martin, who was walking home from a candy store, as suspicious and threatening (ABC News, 2012; Anderson, 2013). Another example is the accounts of Officer Wilson of his assessment of 18-year-old Michael Brown, whom he shot and killed (ABC News, 2014).

Most studies assume background factors, in particular systemic racism and citizens' dissatisfaction with it, to be a key reason for violent clashes between protesters and police during uprisings. These studies have helped us understand how such factors can contribute to uprisings, looting, and physical violence after police brutality, be it in the 1992 Los Angeles uprisings after the Rodney King beating (and 1992 shooting of 15-year-old Latasha Harlins) or the uprisings in Ferguson in 2014 and Baltimore in 2015 (Useem, 1997; see, e.g., Bergesen and Herman, 1998; Taylor, 2016).

However, while systemic racism and societal dissatisfaction with it fundamentally shape US society and lie at the root of these clashes, this background factor does not fully explain the emergence of violence, just as background factors do not provide full explanations for violence in protest marches (Chapters 3–6). The majority of studies that discuss dissatisfaction with racism as the key factor for such clashes focus exclusively on the analysis of violent clashes[2] (Ransford, 1968; see, e.g., Bergesen and Herman, 1998). Studying only violent events, especially when interviewing protesters, can show activists' dissatisfaction with racism to be a relevant factor. Yet generally a much larger part of society is affected by and dissatisfied with such injustices than those who attend an uprising—let alone those who take part in violent clashes. A look at the overall population shows that being affected by injustices and hearing about police brutality cannot predict where uprisings take place or who participates. Many people suffer inequality and injustices in silence (Waddington, 1991, p. 288). Further, a connection between readiness for interpersonal violent action and actual participation in such an action (Ransford, 1968; Mucchielli, 2009; Sutterlüty, 2014) is not evident when systematically studying when and where violence emerges (Waddington 1991; see also Collins 2008; for a good theoretical overview, see Horowitz 2001).

When looking more closely at police shootings in the United States, a direct connection between citizens being affected by a shooting and an uprising that includes physical interpersonal violence does not seem to exist (Parry, Moyser, and Wagstaffe, 1987; Waddington, 1991). Studies on uprisings in the 1960s and 1970s show that indicators of black disadvantage could not predict the location or severity of violence (Horowitz, 2001, p. 39). The same seems true for more recent protests. For instance, while violent clashes erupted in Los Angeles after the brutal beating of Rodney King in 1992 and in Ferguson after Michael Brown was shot in 2014, this is by no means a systematic pattern. After the acquittal of George Zimmerman, the neighborhood watchman who shot and killed 17-year-old Trayvon Martin on his way home from buying candy in a store in Sanford, Florida, in 2012, violent clashes occurred in Oakland and Los Angeles, but not in Sanford itself (e.g., BBC News, 2013; Williams, 2013). In many places across the United States, protesters assembled in front of police stations after a police shooting occurred, but most of these situations remained peaceful.

That these clashes (like all physical interpersonal violence; see Collins 2008) are empirically rare is further underlined by zooming in at uprisings in which violence broke out, like Ferguson in 2014. Ferguson saw physical interpersonal violence during the 2014

---

[2] They thereby limit the analysis by sampling on the dependent variable.

uprisings, yet the majority of protest activities consisted of peaceful interactions. For instance, violence did not break out right after Brown was shot at noon on August 9, 2014. It did not emerge when Ferguson police gave a press conference and protesters assembled in front of the police department that day. Incidents like this would have been the most likely scenarios for clashes, if motivations and anger alone were key to violent outbursts. After all, protesters had just learned the news, they were understandably agitated (Associated Press, 2014). Rumors were flourishing, and police officers, seen as the cause of the immanent grievance, were trapped in the police building. Yet violence did not erupt. Violence did also not ensue after police allegedly let a dog pee on the makeshift memorial for Brown on the spot where he was shot, nor when a police car allegedly damaged the memorial. People were angry, but again, violence did not follow. The first violent clashes erupted after numerous peaceful events, on the evening of August 10.

Similarly, violence did not break out in the great majority of protest events in Baltimore from April 18 until May 3, 2015, after African American citizen Freddie Gray died due to injuries he suffered while in police custody (ABC News, 2015; Graham, 2015). During his arrest and ride to the police station, Gray sustained severe injuries that sent him into coma, including three fractured vartebrea and a spine 80% severed at his neck and later died of his injuries. But violent protests did not break out when he fell into a coma on the day of his arrest (April 12), or on the day he died (April 19). Protest activities went on peacefully for almost 10 days before larger interpersonal violence erupted at the Mondawmin Mall on the evening of April 27.

In short, much more dissatisfaction exists than violence (Horowitz, 2001, p. 467), and empirical findings contradict the idea that citizens in uprisings engage in a "violent routine" after acts of police brutality, simply because they are angry and frustrated, cannot contain themselves any longer, or have just been waiting for an excuse to be violent. Assuming violent motivations fueled by outrage and racial tensions to be the root cause for violent clashes overlooks that citizens overwhelmingly protest such issues peacefully.

What roles do such background factors then play, and what needs to occur in addition for violence to break out? I argue that systemic racism and dissatisfaction with it forms a crucial backdrop, but specific interactional patterns during uprisings play a key role in actually leading to violent clashes.

"Hands Up, Don't Shoot!"—The Ferguson Uprisings

Ferguson's Background Factors: Racial Bias, Discriminatory Intent, and Deep Mistrust

With systemic and symbolic racism affecting communities across the United States, Ferguson was still specific in 2014: Ferguson showed even more severe background conditions of police racial bias and discriminatory government actions compared to other cities in which uprisings took place (Rothstein, 2015; Moran and Waddington, 2016; Taylor, 2016). While other cities, such as Baltimore, witnessed uprisings after police brutality around the same time, Taylor (2016) shows that Ferguson faced even more pronounced racial disadvantages at the time protests erupted. It is therefore one of the likeliest cases to show that background factors are key to the eruption of violence and one of the unlikeliest cases to show the situational patterns to violence (i.e., what happened between the start of the protest and violence breaking out) discussed in Chapters 3 to 6.[3]

While the majority of Ferguson citizens in 2014 were non-white, the city was run almost exclusively by whites. In 2014, African Americans held almost no positions of political power in the city, be it on the city council, police force, or school board—let alone mayor or police chief (e.g., Taylor, 2016, pp. 75–105). In a city run by the white minority, non-white residents faced discrimination by police officers on a daily basis. A report by the US Department of Justice (2015) later highlighted that "Ferguson's police and municipal court practices both reflect and exacerbate existing racial bias, including racial stereotypes. Ferguson's own data establish clear racial disparities that adversely impact African Americans." The report even finds that "discriminatory intent is part of the reason for these disparities" (United States Department of Justice, 2015, p. 2). In this environment, Michael Brown was shot and killed by a white police officer on August 9, 2014.

The same day, protesters started to assemble in Ferguson, shouting "Hands up! Don't shoot." They demanded justice for Michael Brown and called attention to their view that Brown's death was part of a much larger problem. The emerging Black Lives Matter movement understood the incident as "a clear point of reference for what was happening to black communities everywhere" (Matthews and Noor, 2018, p. 5; Anderson,

---

[3] It therefore functions as a "most different" case (Gerring, 2010) to the protests discussed earlier, making it an ideal event to explore the range of the above-described findings about collective violence.

2014). In a recording of the protests, a resident who came out to protest police brutality after Brown was shot summarizes this point of view when talking to a journalist with frustration in his voice:

> The cops harassing me is frequently. It's all through the day, it's all through the night. When they're not beating us physically, they are doing it verbally. This has been going on before Michael Brown, before Trayvon Martin, before Emmett Till. You know this has been going on for a long time. We're just sick and tired. (*New York Times*, 2014b)

The importance of background factors for protests and clashes and protests directly addressing police behavior distinguish Ferguson from the marches discussed earlier in this book. While such differences should not be underestimated (see also Bates, 2015; Lopez, 2016; Moran and Waddington, 2016), they can still not pinpoint when and where clashes break out. In Ferguson, physical interpersonal violence is reported to have first emerged on the evening of August 10. Police deployed CS gas and smoke canisters, and some protesters threw objects at police officers (U.S. Department of Justice, COPS and IIR, 2015, pp. 14 ff.; for visual footage, see MSNBC, 2014). Although background factors were constantly present prior to this incident, violence erupted at a specific time and place. Thus, it is key to understand what led to this eruption.

Taking a closer look at what happened in the hours prior to the clashes on August 10, we find all of the factors leading to violence in protests marches discussed in Chapters 3 to 6: spatial incursions, police misman-agement, escalation signs, missing communication, and property damage increased tensions and fear and escalated events in Ferguson. As in these marches, their combination seems to have led to an increase in tensions prior to violence breaking out, us–them boundaries intensifying, reinter-pretation by involved participants, and ultimately confusing and chaotic situations in which violence occurred. In the following, I will briefly dis-cuss each situational factor introduced in Chapters 3 to 6 and its role in leading to the outbreak of violence in Ferguson.

Spatial Incursions

Spatial incursions—either police or protesters moving into the other group's space (see Chapter 4)—played a role in contributing to escalations in Ferguson on many levels. Space was important to protesters and police in Ferguson from the start. For instance, the spot where Brown was shot was contested throughout the protest events (U.S. Department of Justice, COPS and IIR, 2015, p. 8; see also New York Times, 2014). Protesters created a makeshift memorial of flowers and candles in the spot where he died, which was allegedly later invaded by a police officer who let his dog pee on it. A car then crushed the memorial, but citizens rebuilt it.

On August 10, constant struggles over space unfolded in the form of participants and observers blocking streets, police blocking intersections and dispersing protesters, and protesters trying to assemble on the streets once again. Spatial incursions happened when protesters assembled on the streets, often without being part of a registered protest, to claim space. In a recorded instance, lines of officers block off one part of the street while the other side is blocked by people looting a store (BrownBlaze, 2014). In this situation a woman walks up to an officer, asking him how she could get back to her car. He tells her "You shouldn't have come down here." "I have a right to peacefully protest," she states. "To tell me I shouldn't have come down here, that's the exact attitude that got them (presumably referring to people looting at the end of the street) doing what they are doing. That's not helpful." Their brief conversation illustrates the officers' perception that protesters should not be on the street and the protesters' perception that they have a right to do so and that negating this right was one of the causes of people looting. Both perspectives include perceptions and claims of space, also discussed in Chapter 4.[4]

Other instances prior to violence breaking out on August 10 show protesters making several attempts to "take" space, for instance, by blocking South Florissant Road by sitting on the street (U.S. Department of Justice, COPS and IIR, 2015, p. 12) or performing doughnuts on it (i.e., spinning a car in small circles; MSNBC, 2014, min. 6:50). Such actions imply that the street is theirs and they can do what they want in this space. These actions were constantly contested by police. Officers, too, had a clear spatial focus on "taking (back) space" and constantly dispersed protesters and cleared intersections (U.S. Department of Justice et al., 2015).[5] Many

---

[4] Also illustrating his perception that some property-damaging protesters speak for the entire protest group, the officer replies, "You should have known it was gonna happen. It's common sense" (BrownBlaze, 2014). He seems to perceive looting to be the default outcome and seemingly cannot contemplate other reasons for the female protester being present at the scene. This resembles closely officers' perceptions when property damage is used during the large-scale protest marches discussed in Chapter 2.

[5] At a later protest against police brutality, St. Louis officers were reportedly even shouting "Whose streets? Our streets!" when "taking back streets" (Hogan, 2017).

confrontations in Ferguson (as well as Baltimore) revolved around such instances of police dispersing protests.

In short, considering situational dynamics prior to the eruption of violent clashes in the Ferguson 2014 uprisings suggests that spatial incursions, in the form of unregistered assemblies, people blocking intersections, police dispersing protesters, and blocking off streets, were vital in changing and escalating interaction dynamics, just as they were for the protests marches discussed in Chapters 1 to 8.

Police Mismanagement

Police mismanagement refers to operational command lacking overview and/or a clear course of action during an operation or communication problems occurring among police units (see Chapter 3). Such mismanagement was more abundant in the Ferguson protest than in most of the protest marches discussed in Chapter 3 to 6, where it strongly contributed to escalations. First, police command structures were uncoordinated and incomplete during the first days of the protests in Ferguson (U.S. Department of Justice, COPS and IIR, 2015, p. xv). When a code 1000 was called on August 10 at 1:55 p.m. (U.S. Department of Justice, COPS and IIR, 2015, p. 5), the closest 25 police cars were dispatched to the scene. This code and subsequent deployment tends to complicate crowd control situations, as arriving officers usually have very different levels of experience and training and often cannot communicate with each other to form a coherent position on how to act. While working well for natural disasters, the code 1000 added to the chaotic situations on August 10 before clashes broke out (U.S. Department of Justice, COPS and IIR, 2015, p. 32).

Further, while more and more officers arrived at the scene, commanders on site were often unaware of their presence. Command directions were changing constantly, increasing officers' confusion. A report summarizes (U.S. Department of Justice, COPS and IIR, 2015, p. 36) this as follows: "Unfortunately, in the eyes of many officers and supervisors, the police response seemed like a rudderless ship because direction for officers on arrests and engaging protesters seemed to change regularly." One officer who expressed frustration about the direction and responsibilities of officers asked, "What should we be doing? How should we be doing it?" The after-action report later summarized that the resulting "lack of consistency, ambiguity, and confusing procedures led to further tensions" (U.S. Department of Justice, COPS and IIR, 2015, p. xvi). Further, logistical difficulties involved in the sudden, large operation resulted in long shifts and few breaks for officers, taking a further "emotional toll" on them (U.S. Department of Justice, COPS and IIR, 2015, pp. xix, 112).

In short, this protest seems to show similar types of police mismanagement as seen in the marches that turned violent discussed in Chapter 3. Units struggled with different levels of training and diverging approaches to policing, received conflicting orders, and faced missing coordination, a lack of effective command, and frequent changes in strategy (U.S. Department of Justice, COPS and IIR, 2015, p. 39). All of these aspects increased tensions on the part of officers in the front lines and impacted their interpretation of the operation and their interactions with protesters. Mismanagement thereby further contributed to the escalation.

Escalation Signs

A prominent picture (U.S. Department of Justice, COPS, et al., 2015, p. 57) from the Ferguson 2014 uprising shows a citizen, wearing jeans, a bright T-shirt, and a backpack, walking on the sidewalk. Five officers are approaching him. All wear military clothing, gas masks, helmets, and bulletproof vests. The citizen has his hands up. Two officers point their rifles at him. The picture looks like it was captured in a war zone. Not surprisingly, based on interviews with community members, even the U.S. Department of Justice After-Action Report (2015, p. 60) later found that equipment worn by officers and armored vehicles were "perceived to be threatening to the community" (U.S. Department of Justice, COPS and IIR, 2015, p. xvi). In other words, they were seen as clear signs of an immanent escalation.[6] In Ferguson, such escalation signs—referring to actions perceived as foreboding harmful behavior (see Chapter 5)—were a further crucial factor for escalations and the emergence of physical violence.

Throughout the entire police operation there were repeated reports of shots fired in the area and bomb threats were called in (U.S. Department of Justice, COPS and IIR, 2015, pp. 5, 91). Prior to escalation, videos further show rows of police cars with blaring sirens, officers wearing gas masks, holding sticks in their hand. Illustrating the expectation that these are clear signs of an immanent escalation, a citizen states: "We've got to get out of here. They got on gas masks. You know what that means" (BrownBlaze, 2014, min. 0:29).[7]

---

[6] That name tags were removed by some officers during operations further amplified tensions and us–them boundaries (U.S. Department of Justice, COPS, et al., 2015, p. xvii).
[7] Allegedly some police also received threats against family members throughout the protest (U.S. Department of Justice, COPS, et al., 2015, pp. viii, 78), although it is unclear how frequent these were or in what situations they occurred.

Yet the most prominent and drastic escalation signs prior to physical clashes on August 10 can be found in police use of military-grade weaponing and equipment. Police officers with sniper rifles were sitting atop military vehicles, observing the crowds through their weapon sights. This image created further tensions on the side of protesters and bystanders, wondering why police were pointing a rifle at them and whether officers might open fire. During the evening hours, red sniper lasers can be seen cutting through the smoke of stun grenades with citizens uttering apprehensively "Snipers! Snipers!!" (RT, 2014b). The after-action report (U.S. Department of Justice, COPS and IIR, 2015, p. xvii) later concluded that such sniper deployment was "inappropriate, inflamed tensions, and created fear among demonstrators."

Lastly, on numerous occasions during the operation on August 10 canines were employed, adding to tensions in two ways. First, their deployment is highly offensive at a protest against police racism, given that canines were used to intimidate civil rights protests in the US South in the 1960s. They thus invoked "powerful emotions in many observing citizens and protesters, particularly where racial tensions exist," as the Department of Justice later acknowledged (U.S. Department of Justice, COPS and IIR, 2015, p. xvi). Second, their deployment was also perceived as an escalation sign: protesters generally tend to be afraid of police dogs and often assume they will be used to disperse protesters. Police dogs thus "exacerbated tensions by unnecessarily inciting fear and anger among amassing crowds" (U.S. Department of Justice, COPS and IIR, 2015, pp. xvi, 44).

Militarization of police and use of canines also gave protesters the impression that free speech against police brutality was unwelcome. Us–them boundaries were amplified through militarization, as protesters felt their voice was suppressed. Protesters took to the streets to peacefully voice their concern about police brutality in the United States, and police in turn responded in military gear, with tanks, rifles, and canines. In a macabre irony, police pointed sniper rifles at citizens protesting police shootings. A recording of one of these instances illustrates the protesters' perception of these actions, when a female protester asks: "How can we feel like we can have free speech if there is a guy staring down a sniper rifle, as we speak?" (*New York Times*, 2014b, min.01:29). "This is harassment!" (RT, 2014b, min.0:58), another protester claims. Protesters, media, and police seem to agree that these measures only exacerbated tensions between protesters and the police (U.S. Department of Justice, COPS and IIR, 2015, p. xvi). Escalation signs thereby contributed to increasing tensions people felt in light of spatial incursions and police mismanagement in Ferguson prior to clashes.

Missing Communication

Missing communication between protesters and police, meaning an interruption of the routine flow of information between police and protesters (see Chapter 6), crucially aggravated the negative tension-increasing effects of the described escalation signs, spatial incursions and police mismanagement in Ferguson on August 10. Communication with the community did not come easy to Ferguson police from the start. The lack of police communication about what happened to Brown created an unfavorable backdrop of silence, leading to "community distrust, and media skepticism" from the beginning (*Chicago Tribune*, 2015; Moran and Waddington, 2016).

Yet, as seen in the Kehl protest discussed in Chapter 8 (see also Introduction), we can assume that such an unfavorable situation could have been turned around on the day protests occurred. The protests discussed in Chapter 6 and 8 show that extensive communication can change a tense initial situation into relaxed interactions. However, in Ferguson communication between police as a group and protesters as a group, or representative spokespersons, was either scarce or entirely absent, further aggravating the situation. In tense moments of escalation signs, police mismanagement, and spatial incursions, no or almost no communication took place. Due to the absence of a joint information center, units were unable to speak with one voice, and, as a result, officers passed on "inaccurate, sometimes conflicting and misleading information" (U.S. Department of Justice et al., 2015, p. xv; for a similar dynamic, see also the 2003 Miami protest discussed in Chapter 5). Thus, the little content that was transmitted usually did not make sense to protesters and just further amplified tensions (U.S. Department of Justice, COPS and IIR, 2015, p. xv). It bolstered us–them boundaries, which led both sides to be more alert of the other and tensions to further increase.[8]

In other instances on August 10, police asked people to disperse but did not explain what was happening or why. They frequently issued "keep moving" orders, which confused protesters, as it was often unclear what was expected of them or where they should go. It also implied that any

---

[8] Moreover, when communication was transmitted, this was often done from an LRAD device mounted on a tank. Yet the tank employment did not convey an interest in communication but was perceived as an escalation sign.

kind of assembly was forbidden, but protesters did not have notice of what law they were violating, and enforcement of the rule was often "entirely arbitrary" (U.S. Department of Justice, COPS, et al., 2015, pp. 62 ff). When citizens did not disperse, they were often not properly warned before CS gas was employed. Such dispersals violated the citizens' right to assembly and free speech (U.S. Department of Justice, COPS and IIR, 2015, pp. 63 ff).

Moreover, as most protests were rather spontaneous, activists were also lacking an organizer or a speaker van to make announcements that could provide information to other protesters, bystanders, or the police. Thus protesters, too, could not effectively communicate with police with one voice. This was amplified as, due to mismanagement taking place, community members who wanted to communicate with police had no central contact they could address (U.S. Department of Justice, COPS and IIR, 2015, p. xv).[9] This lack of communication and confusing orders seemingly further intensified tensions and mistrust during the August 10 events.

Property Damage

Property damage was a further factor amplifying tensions in Ferguson prior to physical clashes between protesters and police. Property damage refers to protesters damaging any inanimate objects, such as breaking store windows or burning cars (see Chapter 2). As in the large-scale marches discussed in Chapters 1 to 8, in Ferguson, property damage particularly amplified tensions emerging through spatial incursions and escalation signs by raising tensions on the side of officers and protesters who refrained from property damage.

On August 10, property damage started with stores being destroyed and trashcans set on fire. People then started throwing rocks at police cars driving by, and parked cars were damaged (U.S. Department of Justice, COPS and IIR, 2015, p. 18). As discussed in Chapters 3 to 6, it is common in large-scale protests that an inanimate object like a police car is attacked prior to physical violence. Cars generally enable individuals to get around confrontational tension and fear, as no face-to-face interpersonal interaction is involved (see Collins, 2018). Yet, as seen in the Rostock 2007 G8 march described in the Introduction, officers tend to perceive attacks

---

[9] In light of such missing information, police underestimated the role of social media and the "speed at which both facts and rumors were spread" (Chicago Tribune, 2015; U.S. Department of Justice, COPS and IIR, 2015, pp. xvii, 113). For a discussion of the role of rumors in escalation dynamics, see Chapter 6.

on police cars as attacks on their lives, because a colleague could have been inside the car. Hence, these instances further aggravate tensions. On August 10, destruction and looting of stores then followed. Most prominently, a QuickTip store was looted and set on fire at 8:58 p.m. While such looting may imply property damage, it looks emotionally very different from most property damage and physical violence. Videos show acts of looting in Ferguson occurring in a rather relaxed manner. Aggressions or fear seem largely absent. People seem excited and happy, rather than tense, afraid, or angry (FOX 2 St. Louis, 2014; RT, 2014a).

As in the marches discussed in Chapters 1 to 8, the majority of protesters in Ferguson did not engage in property damage. Yet a few perceived that property damage was their only way to be heard. According to one protester: "They don't hear us until we do shit, until we riot. [. . .] CNN they didn't care about Michael Brown until we rioted. . . . I understand what they did was wrong, but if Michael Brown hadn't been shot we wouldn't go through none of this" (*Time*, 2014, min. 02:50, 04:30). As in protest marches of the global justice movement (see Chapter 2), the majority of protesters using property damage in Ferguson seem to see property damage as a means of claim-making (Tilly and Tarrow, 2006)—not as an apolitical fun fest or destruction for sport. The claims, however, differ. Chapters 3 to 6 showed that protesters using property damage, for instance, by destroying a Nike store, commonly perceive it as a form of claim-making that directly targets capitalism and big corporations. Protesters who use property damage in uprisings such as Ferguson seem to commonly perceive property damage as means to be heard. After the QuickTip was looted and set on fire on August 10, a citizen journalist's video shows a Ferguson resident standing in front of his house, the burning store ablaze in the background. With resignation in his voice he states: "Frustrations just boiled over. . . . I wish they could have found a better way to express themselves, other then tearing up their neighborhood" (MSNBC, 2014). While not agreeing with the tactics of protesters using property damage, he understands its use as their "way to express themselves" and thus a their means of claim-making—in Martin Luther King Jr.'s words, as the "language of the unheard" (CBS News, 2013). Similarly, another Ferguson resident tells BBC News: "To me, I feel like it was necessary. Now we got the attention of the governor, the president, the news . . . the newscasts. So now we have been heard" (BBC News, 2014, min. 00:58). His statement illustrates some activists' assumption that such media coverage will help their cause. Because a good news story is usually notorious, consequential, or extraordinary (Ryan, 1999; see also Della Porta and Reiter,

1998b, p. 19; McCarthy, Clark McPhail, and Smith, 1996, p. 480), property damage is frequently covered by the media (see Chapter 2), and some protesters hope the reporting on property damage will lead to reporting on the protest's underlying grievances, thereby aiding their claim-making. (However, research suggests most reporting usually only centers on the property damage not the underlying grievances and may even portray property damage to delegitimize the grievance, see Chapter 2, see also Simpson, Willer, and Feinberg, 2018).

As in other uprisings, such as Los Angeles in 1992 (as well as other protests in my study discussed in Chapters 1 to 8), Ferguson police refrained from reacting to property damage in a timely matter (U.S. Department of Justice, COPS and IIR, 2015, p. 51). The resident living close to the burning store states: "They won't come down. Now they come down. That's too late now. Now they burned that bad boy to the ground," (MSNBC, 2014, p. min. 10:36). Troopers later expressed: "Peaceful protesters, residents, and even business owners were asking us, 'Why are you here if you are not going to do anything?' " (CNN, 2014, p. min.00:50; U.S. Department of Justice, COPS and IIR, 2015, p. 37). This delay—a frequent pattern—further increased tensions on the side of many officers and the large majority of protesters, who were not damaging property (for a discussion of ensuing reinterpretations, see also Chapter 2).

Paths to and Triggers of Violence

As the previous sections showed, all five interactions discussed in Chapters 3 to 6 occurred prior to violence in Ferguson on August 10, and many continued in the following days (U.S. Department of Justice, COPS and IIR, 2015; Moran and Waddington, 2016). All three paths to violence in protests discussed in Chapters 1 to 8 (each of which is sufficient to lead to violence in protest marches) also seem to have contributed to escalations in this very different type of event in Ferguson. First, a loss of control path seems to have occurred on the part of the police through a combination of spatial incursions and police mismanagement. In such a path (see Chapter 4), officers perceive that they cannot respond to spatial incursions, due to their own mismanagement issues, and tend to perceive a loss of control over the operation. This perception of the situation leads to reinterpretations of their own role and the role and possible intentions of protesters, immediately raises tensions and fear, and leads them to use violence to regain dominance when having a situational advantage (see also R. Collins, 2008; Collins, 2009). In Ferguson, a CNN report directly mentions that police perceived that the "protest got out of control" and that they therefore were attempting "to regain control of the situation" by deploying smoke canisters and using force (U.S. Department of Justice, COPS and IIR, 2015, p. 18; see also CNN, 2014). A violent outbreak in Ferguson can thus, among other dynamics, be understood in light of the effect of an accumulation of spatial incursions and police mismanagement, the relevance of control in police culture and training, and the impact of police perceiving a loss of control (for a detailed discussion, see Chapter 4).

Second, property damage together with escalation signs and missing communication seems to have been present in Ferguson prior to clashes. Such a combination generally leads protesters or police to assume an offense by the other side is taking place, which increases tensions and fears and can lead either side to use violence after gaining a situational advantage (see Chapter 5).

Third, missing communication between protesters and police, escalation signs, and spatial incursions seem to have affected protesters in a missing information path to violence (see Chapter 6). [10] In this path, the missing information about the other side's goals and intentions in the light of escalation signs and spatial incursions during the protest increases tensions and fear. This leads to rumors, increasing us–them boundaries, and tense and confusing situations that ultimately trigger violence.

Thus, prior to the first larger clashes between protesters and police on August 10, these five interactions, through three paths, led to rising tensions and mistrust between both groups, as described for protests in previous chapters: "It's been a tense situation for many hours here in Ferguson," a CNN reporter states on August 10 (CNN, 2014, min. 01:18), and a citizen journalist interviewed by MSNBC describes the tensions leading up to violent outbreaks as follows: "So you feel like something's really going to go wrong" (MSNBC, 2014). As discussed in Chapters 3 to 7, such perceptions (of losing control, an offense taking place, or missing information) lead to changes in people's interpretations of their own role, the other, and the situation they are in (Blumer 1968). Violence then breaks out after triggering moments, when people gain emotional dominance (see Chapter 7). While only a few videos show the first outbreaks of violence on August 10,[11] existing recordings show that violence does not erupt when

---

[10] At the same time, property damage further amplified officers' perception of a loss of control, and missing information amplified both sides' perception of an offense.

[11] This may be for several reasons: in contrast to large-scale marches that people attend as scheduled events and that they then also tend to film, there was nothing specific to film in these instances of

lines closely face each other; instead, most violence is carried out at a distance, when police lines advance through the streets firing stun grenades, and when protesters throw rocks at them from a distance (BrownBlaze, 2014; DeMian, 2014). Direct physical clashes seem to need a situational trigger that occurs when lines break up, smaller groups face each other, or individuals are outnumbered or are in a situationally weak position (see Chapter 7, see also Collins, 2008; Horowitz, 2001).

Black Lives Matter—Baltimore, 2015

A look at the Baltimore uprisings in 2015 suggests that situational patterns similar to those seen in Ferguson in 2014 were key to violent eruptions. In contrast to Ferguson, African Americans held some positions of power in Baltimore, such as the mayor's office, and were represented in the police force. However, as Keeanga-Yamahtta Taylor (2016) shows, this access to the political elites had changed little for the vast majority of African Americans in Baltimore as the hardship of the black middle and working class was still largely overlooked by the political elite.[12] Thus, the Baltimore uprisings occurred against a similar background of symbolic and systemic racism, discrimination and harassment, all seen as exemplified in the death of an unarmed young African American citizen in US police custody.

The violence in Baltimore erupted after Freddie Gray's death. Gray, a 25-year-old resident, was arrested on April 12, 2015, and later died from a spinal cord injury he suffered during police arrest and transport in a police van. His death was later ruled a homicide (Pérez-Peña, 2017). Protests ensued and continued peacefully for 10 days. Violence then erupted in front of the Mondawmin Mall on the day of Freddie Gray's funeral on April 27, 2015. Why did violence erupt then and there and not earlier, or elsewhere? Again, we seem to find spatial incursions (e.g., police tell protesters to disperse but cancel public transport that would allow them to do so, protesters in turn start assembling on the street and blocking it), escalation signs (police cars drive around with sirens, helicopters hovering, police and media assuming protesters are planning a "purge"),

---

spontaneous assembly on the streets in Ferguson before violence erupted. People were just milling in the streets. Further, cameras were seemingly unwanted by some actors at the scene, leading to people who were recording being insulted (MSNBC, 2014) or in one recorded instance even having their camera stolen while filming (e.g., WorthWatching, 2014).

[12] This sentiment, Taylor (2016) claims, is demonstrated in a condensed way in President Obama calling Baltimore protesters "criminals and thugs" (Feuerherd and Fredericks, 2015).

and missing communication between protesters and police (communication was absent, while it could have resolved that the rumors police heard about planned "riots" were false and that most kids present at the mall just wanted to go home but felt trapped). As in Ferguson, we see the first attacks by protesters at the Mondawmin Mall against passing police cars in struggles over space. Similar to Ferguson in 2014, protests like Los Angeles in 1992, or uprisings in US cities in the summer of 1967 (Kerner Commission, 1968, pp. 5 ff.),[13] we find an absence of police reaction to looting and the burning of buildings, which further aggravated tensions (for a discussion of police mismanagement in the first hours leading to the Los Angeles violent unrests, see Useem, 1997, pp. 362–365). As in Ferguson or the uprisings in 1967 (Kerner Commission, 1968), physical interpersonal violence does not seem to occur in Baltimore when lines closely face each other; most violence happens remotely when police lines advance through the streets firing stun grenades and protesters throw rocks at them from a distance (e.g., for videos, see FOX 10 Phoenix, 2015; Ola, 2015).

Lastly, a look at the Baltimore uprisings suggests that violence does not break out when the interactions described in Chapters 3 to 6 do not cluster. Only one day prior to the clashes at the Mondawmin Mall, including the same protest groups and police force, spatial incursions and escalation signs occurred at a downtown protest. Yet violence did not break out. This seems analogous to the violent clashes at the 2007 Rostock, Germany, G8 main march versus the tense but peaceful Rostock migrants' rights march a few days later (see Chapter 6, "Missing Information"). In the Rostock main march interactions combined in paths to violence, leaving more than 1,000 people injured, whereas only escalation signs and spatial incursions occurred during the Rostock migrant's rights march. The two interactions alone do not make up any of the three paths to violence and do not lead to a specific reinterpretation by police or protesters involved (e.g., an offense, a loss of control, or missing information). Thus, the migrants' rights march in Rostock stayed peaceful. In the Baltimore uprising we find interactions clustering in the Mondawmin Mall protest

---

[13] Asking a documentary filmmaker who covered the Ferguson uprisings what in her view led to the first clashes, she suggested looking at the 1968 Kerner Commission report on violent uprisings in the United States during the summer of 1967. "Everything here holds true for my experience in Ferguson," she stated. While research has highlighted (Gillham and Marx, 2018) how much police training and organization has changed since the Kerner Report (1968), the rarity of clashes and the relevance of the complex situational unfolding prior to the clashes mentioned in the report indeed resemble closely the here-described patterns in Ferguson and Baltimore.

that turned violent. Yet in the Baltimore downtown protest, we only find escalation signs and spatial incursions, thus no path to violence and the event stayed peaceful (e.g., Crapanzano, 2015). Similar to the Rostock migrants' rights march, the Baltimore downtown protest showed increased tensions due to these two interactions, but a specific perception of a relied-upon routine breaking down, chaos, and confusion did not take place. Like in the Rostock migrant's rights march, one vital factor there was no escalation in the downtown Baltimore protest seemed to be that protesters and police communicated extensively and officers disarmed themselves to avoid escalation signs (Crapanzano, 2015). Thus, similar to the migrants' rights march, none of the paths and thus no specific interpretations and reinterpretations took place and no increase in tensions occurred that triggered physical clashes. While the analysis of uprisings provides just a cursory look at the phenomenon, it suggest that the patterns to violence emergence identified in protest marches (specific police–protester interactions, reinterpretations, and ensuing emotional dynamics) are key to violence breaking out in uprisings as well.

Avoiding Violent Clashes?

These findings imply a positive outlook: the measures to avoid violence in protest marches (discussed in Chapter 8) may also help avoid violence in uprisings. Thus, a community that grieves in the aftermath of a shooting need not suffer additionally from violent clashes with police, as those may be avoided.

While us–them boundaries existed in Ferguson from the beginning as police actions were the immanent target of claims, comparisons suggest tensions and escalation dynamics could have been reduced or eliminated.[14] The background factors alone were not sufficient for violence to break out. As the report of the U.S. Department of Justice (2015) confirms, communicating with protesters, more carefully assigning space to protesters, or avoiding what I label mismanagement as well as escalation signs would have made a large difference during the protest in avoiding clashes. Instead, demonstrators and observers were angered by what they perceived to be a heavy-handed response by the police. With previously existing us–them boundaries between groups further intensifying, protesters yelled at and insulted police, further reinforcing us–them perceptions (see

---

[14] For a detailed discussion about how such tensions can be reduced, see Chapter 8; see also examples discussed in Hylander and Granström (2010a, 2010b).

also Drury and Reicher, 2000; Reicher, 2001). Tensions on both sides drastically increased, situations became chaotic, and both groups increasingly assumed that the other might harm them.

A comparison to the Berlin police handling of recent May 1 protests can provide useful insights into measures for violence prevention in such instances where tensions exist from the start. German officers commonly assume that some activists at May 1 protests will cause property damage and are interested in starting fights with officers—as US police officers and the mainstream media commonly assume when assessing uprisings against police brutality. Still, since the 1980s, Berlin police have managed to increasingly avoid clashes at May 1 protests—in part through conscious avoidance of escalation signs and a focus on communication during protests.

For instance, in Berlin, water cannon trucks, still used in the 1980s and '90s, are now kept out of sight. At the May 1 protests in 2017, a water cannon truck was parked 1.5 miles away from protests so that it could be brought in if needed, but it was not visible to protesters. During my participant observation (for details, see Appendix B), an officer stated: "We don't use it anymore. It just escalates the situation. I don't know when we last brought it to a protest." Berlin officers painted a similar picture regarding canines: "We hardly ever use dogs. Protesters perceive them as threatening, regardless of intentions. So we don't use them for crowd situations anymore. They just complicate things." Avoiding the deployment of tanks and similar escalation signs may therefore help avoid an increase in tensions in uprisings as well. As Chapter 8 highlighted, and as seen in the tense 2015 Baltimore downtown protest that stayed peaceful, conscious disarming by taking off helmets may be a further factor in de-escalating a tense situation—even if some people may be motivated to violence. In Ferguson, police took the opposite approach, thereby severely amplifying tensions, mistrust, and us–them boundaries.

A look at Berlin police tactics when facing May 1 protesters can also suggest measures for effective communication tactics. As discussed in Chapter 8, Berlin police distinguish between "ordinance announcements" and "service announcements" and use two different and differentiable speakers for the two types of announcement during operations. While Berlin "service announcements" are more relaxed, tend to welcome protesters to an event, and try to keep protesters informed about everything that is going on in everyday language and often local dialect, "ordinance announcements" are used for formal notifications and orders. For the latter the speaker changes so that protesters know that the type of announcement is more serious. Videos of the Baltimore protests that ultimately stayed peaceful (Crapanzano, 2015) suggest that constant informal communication with officers in the first lines also strongly decreased tensions. Yet videos suggest that in Ferguson no type of "service announcements" were made that could inform and relax both protesters as well as officers in the first lines and contribute to a more relaxed atmosphere. The few acts of communication by police in Ferguson seemingly consisted of vague and arbitrary "ordinance announcements," which amplified tensions.

While operating in very different societal and political settings, Berlin police assume they are dealing with some potentially violently motivated activists, just as Ferguson police did during the uprisings in 2014. Yet Berlin police increasingly manage to avoid clashes, in part through consciously avoiding situational escalation signs and focusing on communication when facing protesters. This comparison suggest that officers may be able to apply situational measures discussed in Chapter 8 to avoid violent clashes in uprisings.

What can citizens involved in uprisings do to avoid violence? As stated in Chapter 8, activists can try to avoid property damage and escalation signs as well as try to establish communication with police. Communication with officers seems especially crucial if spatial incursions or property damage by protesters take place, for instance by stressing why such claim-making is made and, if applicable, that it implies neither that all protesters present support such claim-making nor that attacks on officers are planned or intended when property damage is used. At the same time, it is vital to note that protesters involved in spontaneous assemblies after a police shooting are not organized to the same degree as police forces. In Ferguson, some police officials later argued that citizens failed to de-escalate the situation and media claimed the community lacked leadership and should have stopped protesters from burning stores (e.g., Rabouin, 2014; for a discussion, see Greenwald and Jones, 2015). While this narrative is hardly applied when white sports fans destruct property (who usually have a clear leadership as they are part of an organization; see Greenwald and Jones, 2015), it is also not the job of a citizen to go out at night and tell looting protesters to stop. This is what police are for. The expectations of police can and should be different, as police are paid by the citizens to protect their neighborhood, property, and physical well-being as well as to protect their fundamental rights, such as their right to assembly and free speech. Police are paid to manage and de-escalate situations such as spontaneous gatherings in Ferguson that may turn into unrest. And case comparisons suggest it is in their power to do so.

Further, when discussing what protesters could have done to avoid clashes, it needs to be stressed that without police harassment, discriminatory intent, and racism in in the police force (United States Department of Justice, 2015) and the killing of Michael Brown, the uprisings that ended in clashes in Ferguson in 2014 would not have taken place. Thus, if police officers in some US cities frequently harass people of color and then ask citizens to police themselves in uprisings against such harassment, this may further lead to an erosion of trust in police and thus complicate future police–protester interactions (see also Anderson, 2014).

In short, the relevance of communication and a clear situational order seem vital for promoting peaceful interactions in uprisings just as in large-scale protest marches.[15] Numerous lessons discussed in Chapter 8 may therefore apply even when police accountability is the target of gatherings, even if background factors and us–them boundaries are pronounced from the beginning, and even if police expect some participants to be motivated for violence. Future research needs to take a more systematic look at situational dynamics across larger numbers of uprisings to determine how physically violent clashes between protesters and police can be avoided. The here-discussed findings provide but a cursory outlook.

Violent Uprisings as Routine Breaks

This chapter's look at uprisings suggests that the above-discussed dynamics to the outbreak of protest violence (Chapters 1–8) may also be present in police–protester clashes beyond protest marches. Although the specific words may differ, the basic syntax of the process seems to be similar in many ways.

Ferguson is just one case, but it is one where the assumption that background factors were crucial for what happened is prominent. Still, evidence suggests that neither a background of systemic and symbolic racism nor the event of a police shooting was sufficient to bring about the eruption of violence in Ferguson. Even with such prominent background factors present and even after police shootings, collective violence rarely breaks out. Yet, as in protest marches, violence breaks out in moments of tension, confusion, and fear in which the routines people usually rely upon have collapsed. Assuming an automatic violent reaction, a type of "violent

---

[15] This aspect is also emphasized in Horowitz's (2001) ethnic riots study, in Bramsen's (2018) analysis of protest violence in authoritarian regimes, and in Hylander's and Granström's (2010a) study of how to avoid hooligan violence.

routine," in uprisings after police shootings is thus empirically doubtful. Rather, the logic of routine breakdowns seems to apply.

Moreover, assuming a "violent routine" is also normatively problematic. It can reproduce racist stereotypes, as it is overwhelmingly applied to activism by people of color. US mainstream media (e.g., Schweber, 2011; Simpson, 2011) generally refrain from labeling as "rioters" white people who destroy parts of their city and attack officers—be it after a Pumpkin Festival, because their baseball team won, or because of the firing of a football coach after a child sex abuse scandal (Greenwald and Jones, 2015). Rather, they are commonly dubbed passionate young people or sports fans a bit out of control (Simpson, 2011; Schweber, 2011; for discussion, see Bates, 2015; Greenwald and Jones, 2015). Thus, violent eruptions by majority white crowds are usually not seen as the "routine," and being violent is usually not attributed to all attendees at such an event. In these events the public discourse assumes that a commonly peaceful routine is broken.

Yet, US mainstream media commonly do label non-white citizens who use property damage and clash with police when protesting racism "rioters." Violent clashes with police are often portrayed as the "routine" outcome in uprisings such as Ferguson in 2014 or Baltimore in 2015 (Schneider, 2014; Bates, 2015). However, as previously discussed, violent clashes in uprisings after a police shooting follow the same logic of a peaceful protest break in routine as marches. Violence rarely breaks out in uprisings, and if it does, only few protesters participate and specific situational dynamics preceded the event. While some citizens in uprisings— like protesters or officers in the protest marches discussed in Chapters 3 to 6—may just wait for an excuse to use violence against others, a cultural narrative associating uprisings with violence distracts from the overwhelmingly peaceful manner in which citizens express their grief, anger, and dismay at racist discrimination in the United States (Inwood, Tyner, and Alderman, 2014).

Moreover, this narrative often implies that activists involved in these protests are unable to protest peacefully (Schneider, 2014). Such accounts not only depoliticized these protests but quickly go hand in hand with labeling protesters "criminals and thugs," (as did President Obama; see Feuerherd and Fredericks, 2015),[16] "offenders," or "gang members" (media accounts; see Greenwald and Jones, 2015). They thereby reproduce racist narratives of the "iconic ghetto" (Anderson, 2012b) that

---

[16] Or "scum," as French president Sarkozy called protesters damaging property in the 2005 Paris uprisings (Rieff, 2007).

contribute directly to what activists are protesting against. Failing to see that violence in uprisings against police brutality and systemic racism is an empirical rarity perpetuates a narrative that discredits such protests entirely. It distracts from identifying situational measures that can help prevent violent clashes and from acknowledging and addressing the reasons for such uprisings: the reality of racism in the United States.

Situational Breakdowns Beyond Violence

A masked person enters a store and points a gun at the clerk: this is a robbery. An implicit interaction ritual prescribes that the clerk hand over money in exchange for not being hurt or killed (Luckenbill, 1981, p. 31). This ritual is understood universally, and clear scripts exist in people's minds regarding what needs to be done and how to behave. Even clerks who have never been in a robbery understand what is going on when someone pulls out a gun and points it at them. It is clear what a clerk is supposed to do and how the situation should evolve. A surprising outcome in this scenario is not the use of violence but if an armed robber fails to get the money from the clerk despite this clear ritual and situation of dominance.

The following section will discuss such surprising outcomes. They will show that a detailed look at what happens during robberies reveals that situational dynamics can lead to situational breakdowns and surprising outcomes in these events, just as in large-scale protest marches and uprisings. If routines in robberies break down, surprising outcomes emerge, such as robbers leaving empty-handed despite being armed and motivated to rob an unarmed clerk. [17]

Convenience store robberies are highly interesting events with which to study surprising outcomes because they are unlikely to show patterns similar to the protests discussed in Chapters 3 to 6. First, they involve only a few individuals (usually one robber and one victim). They thus

---

[17] As in previous chapters, I will provide numerous case descriptions to discuss the findings of my analysis and illustrate the rich detail visual data can provide. In these descriptions I focus on the coded movements, actions, verbal accounts, and emotions by perpetrator(s) and victim(s). Further information (e.g., date, location) can be found in Appendix D and when watching the footage referenced there (e.g., clothing, bystander behavior). The examples discussed in the text were chosen to illustrate core ideas as well as variations in the patterns identified in my analysis. While YouTube links may change, many of the links provided in this book have been stable over many years. If links change, a YouTube search using keywords on the event (date and location of the robbery) can usually identify other uploads of the same footage.

feature individual interactions quite different from the collective behavior exhibited by thousands of people in protest marches. Second, convenience store robberies are unlikely to show similar patterns because they, in contrast to the protest marches described in previous chapters, entail a clear distribution of dominance, with one party forcing a routine upon the other. There is thus little leeway for the people involved for structuring interactions on the fly. It seems unlikely that robbery rituals would break down due to situational interactions, reinterpretations, and emotional dynamics. Instead, prior motivations and strategies seem bound to prevail.

To study whether findings discussed in Chapters 3 to 6 apply to these types of events, I compared 20 store robberies in the United States as well as 4 comparative cases in the United Kingdom (see Appendix D). Today, CCTV footage enables us to look into the black box of what happened once a robber entered the store: Which individual did what and at what time? What movements or facial and bodily expressions did they display? CCTV recordings allow examination of these complex and at times chaotic events in slow motion, frame by frame, and in numerous replays. They allow studying whether situational dynamics and breaks in routines might play a role in such surprising outcomes or whether situational dynamics show no patterns and instead background factors, such as perpetrators' or clerks' experience levels in such situations, may play a key role in these instances.

"Creating" a Robbery

How do robberies unfold? In a way, all robberies are a type of situational bluff; robbers are usually not motivated to shoot someone, otherwise they could enter a store, shoot the clerk, and take the cash. Yet what appears to matter to most robbers is not to shoot someone but to make believable the threat that they will shoot someone if they do not comply (Luckenbill, 1981). This means that robberies follow a ritual that establishes a threat by a perpetrator, which the victim perceives as real. What does this look like?

Consider a robbery that took place in Los Angeles, California. The video was uploaded by the Los Angeles Police Department in 2011 (see case A2, Appendix D, Table D1). Three men casually enter a small convenience store. All of them wear everyday clothes. The clerk is sitting behind the counter, leaning back. Two of the perpetrators walk directly to the back of the store. They pretend to be customers, but presumably check if anyone else is in the store. Their partner stands in front of the counter near the exit, waiting for them. The clerk gets up from his chair to attend to the customers and stands with a relaxed body posture. His shoulders are down; he is not paying much attention to the perpetrator standing in front of the counter. The latter briefly talks to his partners. He then turns and looks at the clerk's face for the first time since entering the store. The perpetrator's facial expressions indicate anger and aggression when he pulls a firearm (min. 0:34–0:36). He points the weapon at the clerk, his arm straight. The clerk flinches and displays bodily expressions of being frightened; he moves backward a little, his shoulders tighten and go up, he raises his hands and holds them up high. He nods at the perpetrators. He seems to understand what is about to happen and what is expected of him. While the second perpetrator jumps the counter, the clerk already opens the cash register. The clerk's legs appear tense, his body posture is immobile. Once the register is open, the perpetrator shoves aside the clerk with ease. The clerk shows no resistance, low emotional energy (e.g., passivity and shrinking postures; Collins, 2008; Klusemann 2009, p. 9), and stumbles sideways. The second perpetrator takes the money from the register, while the first one stands in front of the counter pointing his gun. After his partner collects the money, he moves to the side so the former can jump back over the counter. They flee with the money 44 seconds after entering the store.

These instances reflect the majority of successful robberies; they are brief and show high-frequency interactions (Petrosino, Fellow, and Brensilber, 1997, p. 415; Faulkner, Landsittel, and Hendricks, 2001, p. 708). They also show that in successful robberies the perpetrator and victim display distinct behaviors that we would commonly expect during this ritual: the perpetrators "play" the criminal (Luckenbill, 1980, 1981) by appearing highly motivated and capable of hurting the clerk seriously in case of non-compliance. Perpetrators in successful robberies often use a moment of surprise to ensure that clerks realize that the situation changed drastically and that they, the robbers, are now in charge.[18] They show that they will decide which behaviors are, from now on, acceptable and what will happen next. Luckenbill (1981, p. 29) found that in 65 percent of cases, offenders displayed normal appearances and then started the offense. In other robberies, perpetrators started their offense immediately; they entered the store displaying their gun with an angry look on their

---

[18] Although extant studies suggest that perpetrators may use violence to establish dominance at the beginning of a robbery (Luckenbill 1981, p. 32), only one of the cases in this study, B12, showed this pattern, further suggesting violence is empirically rare and generally avoided (Collins, 2008). Because uploads of violent behaviors can be found across YouTube and LiveLeak, it is unlikely that preselection took place that excluded such cases from being uploaded.

face (see also Mosselman, Weenink, and Lindegaard, 2018). Either way, perpetrators show their counterpart that this is a robbery and they are in charge from now on. To indicate the robbery has begun, they usually display strong body postures and make themselves big, looking angry and capable of violent actions.

Meanwhile, clerks in these robberies engage in submissive behaviors and display that they are fearful for their life. They show indicators of fear, like shoulders drawn up, flinching, moving backward, and complying with demands and thus display characteristics of being the "victim." If a clerk's face is visible during a robbery in which perpetrators were successful in getting the money, it usually shows a frightened look.[19] This display is not surprising, as clerks are usually scared that perpetrators might harm or kill them. Their mental health commonly suffers long-term from these encounters (Bobic, Pavicevic, and Gomzi 2007).

We would assume that robberies always take place as just described, given that one person is armed and could kill the other and given that all participants generally seem to know how to behave in such a situation to "make it work." We would assume situational breakdowns as described in previous chapters to be very unlikely, if possible at all, because the ritual is so clear; we are only dealing with two to a handful of participants, usually one who threatens harm, who is prepared and motivated to commit the crime, and one who complies in order to survive. Prior motivations and strategies seem bound to prevail, as people seem unlikely to change their interpretations of what is going on and unlikely to display unexpected behaviors during such encounters. Yet we find that even in these situations, rituals can break down and surprising outcomes can occur; the robbery can fail even though the robber has a gun and could kill the clerk. As in protest dynamics, we find clear patterns of situational breakdowns leading to surprising outcomes in robberies.

Situational Breakdowns in Armed Store Robberies

Consider the example of a robbery attempt in a store in California in 2013 (see case B8, Appendix D, Table D1).[20] A robber enters the store,

---

[19] CCTV cameras are frequently mounted behind a clerk. In numerous cases I therefore relied on body postures to code emotion expressions (see also Nassauer, 2018b).

[20] While this recording is uncut and includes sound, it is part of a compilation of videos uploaded online. Such compilation videos need to be treated with caution to ensure that natural behavior is captured (Nassauer and Legewie, 2018). Further, the commentary of the uploader needs to be muted or ignored during the analysis.

his face covered. He points a gun at the clerk. The clerk is standing behind the counter, speaking on a landline phone. A transparent screen of bulletproof glass separates the counter from the remainder of the store. The clerk moves forward and puts both hands on the counter, the phone squeezed between her shoulder and ear. The robber apparently wears a mask, which makes his words hard to understand. The clerk asks, "Is that real?," referring to his handgun. "Yes," he mumbles. She moves back and slightly sideways, as if she believes him and tries to get some distance between herself and the gun. She says in a skeptical tone, "That's real. Why would that be real and you point it at me?" She puts the phone receiver between her other shoulder and ear. Her posture is relaxed; she moves freely and stands up straight. Her question seems to confuse the perpetrator. His posture becomes stiffer. After a pause, he mumbles, "Thirty seconds!," and then repeats it louder. "Huuuh?," she says, leaning forward. "C'mon, thirty seconds," he states more forcefully. "For what?," she replies. He continues responding to her questions: "The change!," he says slightly annoyed and with less force in his voice, while pointing toward the cash register with his gun. "I ain't got no money," she replies and shakes her head. "C'mon, ma," the robber replies. His voice now sounds querulous and slightly frustrated. He puts his gun down. "I ain't got no money," she repeats. "Open that up!," he shouts. "I ain't got no money." "Open that up!" "I ain't got no money." "Open that up!" She pauses (1 second) before she replies, "I ain't got no money!" "Open that up," he tries again. "I'm on the phone with somebody right now," she tells him casually and slightly annoyed, as if speaking to a rude customer. He reacts by pushing the gun barrel through the service hatch to point it at her. Immediately, she grabs the barrel with one hand, trying to point it away from her. With the other hand, she now puts the phone receiver down. While the conversation continues, she manages to pull his gun toward her and turns his hand on her side of the service hatch. He asks her to let go, but she confidently shakes her head and calmly responds, "I ain't let go shit." She manages to get the gun and he runs off.

The situation has completely switched. Although the clerk surely feels protected by the glass initially (other clerks in the robberies I studied do not have this advantage), it is remarkable that she does not, or at least pretends not to, understand the fact that she is now the victim in a robbery and might be killed. The robber could still shoot her through the service hatch, yet she begins by questioning whether the gun is real and early on she makes the offender respond to her questions. When the perpetrator says, "30 seconds!" she replies "For what?," not accepting the obvious ritual that is to take place. He plays along by telling her what he wants from her—"The change!"—even though the problem was presumably not that she did not understand. This allows her to increasingly get the upper hand during the encounter although he is armed and threatening her life. Yet he is not deciding what will happen, she is. She asks, he responds. Instead of being startled or showing fear, she states casually that she has no money but feels no need to show him an empty cash register, or to put her phone away, until 40 seconds into the robbery. Numerous times she blocks his attempts to make the situation a robbery. Soon he tells her, "C'mon ma!," begging for her compliance rather then forcing it. Completely out of character for a robber, his body posture and tone of voice now remind of a person asking someone for a favor; he displays low energy and his voice is querulous. Her tone becomes increasingly unfazed.

Both then repeat the same sentence several times and in the same manner. Micro-sociological research suggests that this makes it more difficult for a person to establish dominance. When the emotional level remains stable, boredom sets in, which counteracts dominance (Collins 2008, 2009, pp. 571 ff.). The last time they repeat their sentences, she pauses before she replies with emphasis, "I ain't got no money!" Collins (2005a) and Klusemann (2009, p. 7) pointed out that such pauses dramatize power stratification since they let the listener experience unease and show that the interaction will continue when the speaker wants it to. She is thereby indicating that she is the one dominating the ritual. When the perpetrator states his request one more time, she responds "I'm on the phone with somebody right now!," which reaffirms that she is not following the typical script for victims in a store robbery. The content of the sentence, her body posture, and tone of voice convey that she is busy. She treats him like a rude customer instead of a potentially lethal criminal. In the end she obtains his gun and he runs off, the robbery a complete failure, the outcome certainly surprising.

While a rather drastic example, the failed California robbery illustrates a pattern found across my dataset. Although the distribution of physical dominance and the ritual about to happen seem clear to all involved, the ritual can fail at the micro-level because of seemingly minor hiccups that, on paper, should not change the power balance or ritual. Perpetrators have decided to rob a store, obtained a weapon to do so, decided on a place and time, sometimes cover their faces, bring a bag for the stolen goods, and then enter the store with the intent to carry out the crime. Yet, despite distinct motivations and strategies, how a situation unfolds can override these strategies and the motivations with which people enter into it. Situations can break down, and the robber may end up being treated like a child, although he stills holds the gun and managed initially to scare the clerk. A similar pattern of situational breakdowns leading to unexpected and uncommon outcomes was visible in protests and uprisings.

But through which interaction dynamics and situational patterns do robberies break down? Why do clerks behave in such a way that could potentially cost them their lives? Comparisons suggest that the syntax of these breakdowns is the same as in protests, while the specific words differ. A detailed look at successful and failed robberies suggests that specific situational interactions, reinterpretations, and emotional dynamics that unfold during the robbery matter in surprising outcomes in robberies, just as they do in surprising outcomes in protest marches and uprisings. Due to specific interaction dynamics, people reinterpret the situation, as well as the other person's and their own role in the interaction (see also Blumer, 1986). Such reinterpretations lead to changing emotional dynamics, the failure to establish dominance, and failure of the robbery. Similar to surprising outcomes in protest movements and uprisings, we find specific interactions that systematically change people's interpretations and trigger surprising outcomes: the use of space, management and coordination among individuals, communication, and signs of incompetence. Further, we find certain emotional dynamics to be key for routine breakdowns and surprising outcomes in robberies. Each of these aspects will be discussed in turn.

Interaction Dynamics: Space and Coordination, Signs of Incompetence, and Communication

Several interactions systematically play a role in leading to surprising outcomes in robberies. Somewhat analogous to spatial incursions and police mismanagement leading to surprise outcomes in protests and uprisings, the use of space and the coordination of robbers among themselves are vital elements in leading to surprise outcomes in robberies. Moreover, similar to escalation signs in protests and uprisings, the interpretation of the other's actions as a sign of their trustworthiness also plays a role in robberies. In robberies signs of incompetence (on side of the perpetrator) matter for the unfolding of the robbery, and surprising outcomes to occur. Lastly, verbal and non-verbal communication are vital in sustaining or breaking the robbery ritual.[21]

---

[21] As this section provides an exploratory outlook, these findings are not exhaustive and further patterns might be identified in future research.

First, case comparisons show that a timid use of space and bad coordination among perpetrators can systematically disrupt the robber's script and lead to surprising outcomes in robberies, meaning the robber does not get the money. Robberies in which robbers confidently use space and coordinate well among themselves (if several perpetrators are involved) generally convey a threat successfully. The example of the successful Los Angeles robbery in 2011 illustrated that clerks stand stiff and still in such instances, while the robbers take up space in the store, move freely and coordinate themselves well: for example, one perpetrator is moving to the side so the other can jump the counter with the cash register in hand and they flee shortly after with the money.

Coordination and the use of space look different in failed robberies. Take the example of a robbery in Birmingham, United Kingdom (see case UK B2, Appendix D, Table D1): three perpetrators enter a store on January 29 at 7:29:22 p.m., brandishing their weapons. They carry a machete, a hammer, and a stick. The clerk is sitting in his chair, speaking on the phone. Although the counter is narrow, all of them stay close to each other in front of it, almost in each other's way. They wildly wave their weapons up in the air. One perpetrator holds on to another's shoulder. The clerk remains seated for a full 10 seconds after the perpetrators have entered. The perpetrators stand in each other's space and swing their weapons in the air, while the clerk continues to speak on the phone for the first 5 seconds after they entered. Like the mumbling robber in California, the self-crowding robbers do not manage to scare the clerk. After 10 seconds of having the machete swung in front of his face, he looks at the robbers angrily and stands up with a confident body posture. One of the perpetrators grabs the cash register but immediately lets go of it when the clerk pulls the cord that connects the register with the counter. The cash register falls down and the clerk pulls it back towards him. The perpetrators run away hectically—16 seconds after entering. The clerk takes a baseball bat from behind the counter and slowly goes after them, with a strong physical presence, displaying confidence and making himself large.

The Birmingham perpetrators break character and routine in two ways: they do not use space confidently and they struggle to coordinate themselves. As a result, their use of space does not suggest that they are in charge: they stand very close to each other, indicating apprehensiveness, rather than dominance. Comparisons suggest that controlling space is part of the script of the "dangerous robber." Failing to do so during an unfolding robbery fosters situational breakdowns. Even clerks who are scared initially may change their interpretation of the perpetrator, their own role as a scared victim, and the ritual itself, if no longer seeing the situation as a robbery, due to the perpetrators' timid use of space. A similar robbery with three perpetrators using non-firearm weapons in the United Kingdom (see case UK A1, Appendix D, Table D1) shows that interactions evolve quite differently if space is used confidently and robbers coordinate themselves just as in the successful Los Angeles robbery described above (see case A2, Appendix D, Table D1).

Second, robberies may break down when robbers show slight signs of incompetence, such as stumbling, moving sluggishly, or bringing an uncommon, unwieldy, or impractical weapon. Both immediately change the clerk's perception and reactions to the situation. As a symbol of dominance, a weapon is essential for impressing and scaring a victim (Wright and Decker, 1997; Collins, 2009, p. 574). Yet, bringing a weapon and being motivated to commit a robbery is no guarantee of success. To the contrary, weapons illustrate how fragile these rituals can be and how strongly they are connected to perpetrators' and victims' expectations and situational unfoldings. Clerks start behaving unexpectedly if they perceive perpetrators' weapons out of place. Although still being armed and able to harm the clerk, robbers systematically become confused and ill at ease as the ritual collapses. In some cases, armed robbers even flee from unarmed clerks. In a store in Riverbank (CA), the robbers enter with an AK47 assault rifle (see case B2, Appendix D, Table D1). Yet the elderly store clerk approaches them from the back of the store in a relaxed manner laughing. He finds the rifle absurdly big for his small store, as he later states in an interview (Fox40 News, 2012). His reaction in turn seems to change the robbers' interpretation of the situation, impacts their emotional state, and shifts the interaction dynamic (see case B4, Appendix D, Table D1). Mishaps, such as walking in the wrong direction, stumbling or falling, seem to have the same effect as unexpected weapons in breaking the routine (see cases B5 and B7, Appendix D, Table D1; see also Nassauer, 2018b). They set in motion reinterpretations by individuals involved, which leads them to adapt their behavior: Clerks no longer interpret the other to be a threatening offender, no longer see themselves as the victim, and are thus no longer scared. They show upright, energetic body postures and react confidently, as illustrated by the clerks in California and Birmingham. Such actions interpreted as signs of incompetence on the part of perpetrators lead to situational breakdowns and surprising outcomes across robberies caught on CCTV.

Lastly, verbal and non-verbal communication seems to heavily influence situational breakdowns in robberies. The analysis of protests and uprisings underlined the role of verbal and non-verbal communication in changing interaction dynamics and leading to subsequent surprising outcomes. In robberies, verbal and non-verbal communication also seems to be a vital component of routines. The discussion of the failed California robbery, where the clerk was on the phone (see case B8, Appendix D, Table D1), illustrated the relevance of verbal communication, specifically content, pauses, intonation, and repetition, among other speech features for situational dynamics. Both individuals in this event adapted their verbal communication to each other in tone and content, thereby moving more and more out of character and ritual. At one point this cumulated in the clerk saying "I'm on the phone with somebody right now!," a statement completely out of place during a robbery and out of character for a robbery victim.

Looking at non-verbal communication, a striking feature in several failed robberies is so-called mimicking behavior. Take the example of a case in Westhoughton, Greater Manchester, United Kingdom (see case UK B1, Appendix D, Table D1): two robbers enter the store, one carrying a knife. They first briefly walk in the wrong direction (i.e., signs of incompetence). When changing direction to walk toward the cash register, the robbers are confronted by an employee. One robber and the employee go back and forth, trying to stab (robber) and hit (employee) each other. When moving around, both seem entrained in the same rhythm and mirror each other's movements. When the clerk bends down briefly to pick something up (he quickly slips of his shoe to use it as a weapon), the perpetrator bends down milliseconds later. He is unintentionally mimicking the clerk's behavior. He seems to realize there is no need for him to bend down, and moves back up. Only seconds later, the clerk bends down again (this time to pick up a grocery item he might throw), and again the perpetrator bends down milliseconds after the clerk's movement. Again he seems to realize shortly after there is no need to bend down and moves back up (for further examples, see Nassauer, 2018b).

Such mimicking behavior can be explained by a human tendency to fall into shared rhythms in conversational turn-taking and behavioral dynamics (Collins, 2005a, pp. 76 ff., see Collins, 2009, p. 569). So-called rhythmic entrainment (Collins, 2009, p. 569) seems to occur: humans tend to automatically mimic and synchronize movements with each other and thereby converge emotionally (Hatfield, Cacioppo, and Rapson, 1993; Collins, 2005a). While one person tries to dominate the other in a robbery, falling into shared rhythms and converging in such a way counteracts the establishment of dominance. Thus, although one person is armed and threatening to kill the other, unfolding verbal and non-verbal communication during the encounter can still foil a robber's plans.[22]

Emotional Dynamics and Routine Breaks in Criminal Behavior

Emotion display and recognition are further vital components to sustaining or breaking a robbery ritual. A display of adequate (i.e., expected) emotions by perpetrators and clerks generally favors success in store robberies. In robberies where perpetrators were successful in getting the money, clerks showed not only submissive behaviors but also displays of fear and/or low emotional energy (i.e., avoiding gaze): raised eyebrows, raised upper eyelids, tense lower eyelids, and mouths stretched back (Ekman, 2003, pp. 160 ff.). Other videos show shrinking body postures, leaning away, and hands touching or covering face, eyes, or mouth. Across successful cases, clerks stood immobile, looked left to right, and showed drawn-up shoulders, tense legs, leaning backward, and hands up over the head or defensively in front of the chest.

In the protests described in earlier chapters, we saw how crucial emotional dynamics were in leading to surprising outcomes. Fear indicates that norms have broken down, since the default emotion is happiness or boredom displayed by either group or anger displayed by protesters when shouting claims. Fears surge once routines break down. What role does the display of fear play in robberies? Fear is a natural reaction when someone is threatening to harm or murder you, so perpetrators expect clerks to express this emotion. Therefore fear (displayed by the clerk) is a fundamental part of a robbery interaction ritual. When clerks do not display fear during a robbery, this indicates that the routine is going wrong and things may go south. Clerks' uncommon emotions seem to confuse the perpetrator and usually cause them to display signs of fear only 0.5 seconds after seeing that their victim is unafraid. Such uncommon emotion display by clerks can break the routine and can catch even experienced robbers off guard.

Perpetrators' emotion display, too, can influence the unfolding of a robbery. Perpetrators in successful robberies display strong body postures and confidence, to which the clerks respond with fear.[23] Robberies fail

---

[22] Consider also a robbery in Florida, in which the robbers' conflicting orders and hectic body language fail to turn the situation into a robbery from the start (see case B11, see Appendix D, Table D1).

[23] While anger is displayed in the majority of successful robberies, an outlier case indicates that anger does not necessarily need to be present to establish dominance. In this robbery in a convenience store in Seattle, Washington (see case A3, Appendix D, Table D1), the perpetrator is very calm and polite. After pulling his gun, he asks "Could you do me a favor?" and then states calmly but firmly "I'm robbing you, sir." He displays confidence in his words, a strong body posture, and determined voice. Although the perpetrator is polite (even apologizing several times for robbing

if perpetrators display a lack of confidence or anger or if they display emotions unexpected during a robbery. Perpetrators might, for example, display happiness when pulling a gun (see cases B3 and B7, Appendix D, Table D1), which makes clerks drop out of character as the victim and resist. Consider a robbery in Burke County, Georgia (see case B9, Appendix D, Table D1): when pretending to pay, a customer suddenly pulls a gun on a clerk. He is displaying micro-expressions of happiness by smirking and smiling. The clerk apparently notices these expressions. Upon seeing the gun, she is initially startled and moves backward. However, when she looks up and sees the perpetrator's face, she moves forward again and displays facial expressions that indicate anger. The perpetrator displays fear when she shoves his firearm away, and he shows fear and sadness when she starts struggling with him. When he tries to reach over the counter to grab the money, she hits him several times on the back of the head with the cash register drawer until he runs away. Upon seeing the emotion expression on the perpetrator's face, her behavior indicates that she did not believe him any more. She did not play the role of the victim because she was unafraid of the smirking offender. Instead, she got angry and resisted.[24]

The perpetrator's tone of voice also transmits emotions and can therefore influence whether or not a robbery is successful. In successful cases, perpetrators displayed dominance partly through a calm and decisive voice. In contrast, the voice of the robber in California (see case B8, Appendix D, Table D1) contradicted the display of dominance and threat when stating "C'mon, ma!" in a soft, querulous tone. In a further case, a robbery in Broward County, Florida, on July 23, 2010 (see case B6, Appendix D, Table D1), the perpetrator shows indicators of sadness in his voice from the start. After some small talk with the clerk about the phone contracts she sells, he pulls his gun, sadly stating, "I really hate to do this, but. . . ." She initially complies and moves over to the cash register. "I hate doing this. I am embarrassed by it," he says sadly. He looks down almost the entire conversation, avoiding direct eye contact, while she starts

---

the clerk), he transmits dominance and decisiveness. The clerk breathes heavily and shows fear and sadness in his facial expressions. While this suggests that anger does not need to be a part of the perpetrator's display, anger expressions can most directly imply that the perpetrator is willing to use his weapon.

[24] The clerk rationalizes this behavior in an interview with the TV station that aired the footage (see Appendix D). While she claims in one interview that she "called his bluff" when he drew the gun, in another she claims that his body language before entering, which she observed on her surveillance camera, already tipped her off. Such hindsight rationalizations should not be taken at face value (see Appendix A), but the perpetrator's body language and related emotion expression seem to have been a main indicator for the clerk's assessment of the situation.

talking in an uplifting tone, speaking with compassion. His body postures are increasingly shrinking, and he speaks with a soft voice. He interrupts himself, sighs, and touches his mouth and face numerous times. She then moves forward, turns her head sideways and down, as if cheering someone up. She looks into his eyes and says to him "You know what? You [*unintelligible*], you have a beautiful life." He moves slightly backward, visibly shaken up. He turns his head to the side up and down again, stating in a depressed voice and with low energy: "Talk about making it harder!" The 5-minute robbery attempt continues with her praising Jesus numerous times, both realizing they know the same pastor, and discussing possible solutions to his financial problems. At the end he repeats that he is sorry and leaves without the money.

The cross-case comparison of armed store robberies caught on CCTV suggests that the voice can be a vital part of displaying emotions and staying in character. Previous chapters (e.g., Chapter 7) have shown that it impacts protest encounters when people scream or shout information. In a robbery, when a perpetrator shouts decisive orders at a clerk, the clerk is more likely to be quiet, stand still, and show fear. Yet, when perpetrators' emotional displays, through facial expressions, body postures, and voice, indicate, even unwillingly, that they are sad about committing the crime, the clerk may start trying to cheer them up. When a perpetrator appears undecided, the clerk might talk to him in a decisive tone, and when a perpetrator displays that he is happy and proud, the a clerk might get angry or ignore him.

Key Dynamics at the Micro-level of Crime?

Criminal events unfold in micro-situations, and how the situation unfolds matters for a successful crime to take place. An analysis of robberies now observable via CCTV shows that situational breakdowns can occur even in instances with only two persons involved and clear routines of what is about to happen. Patterns of success versus failure in robberies apply both to male and female clerks (all of the perpetrators in the sample are male); they seem to apply regardless of whether the clerk is much younger or much older than the perpetrator or looks stronger or weaker. Not physical but emotional dominance seems to be key for these crimes to be successful. As in protest marches, specific interactions can lead to confusion, fear, and surprising outcomes in such instances.

Analyses also show that people expect certain behaviors. If these are not met, they adapt and may switch to another routine that makes more sense in light of the situational dynamics (see also Blumer, 1986; Garfinkel, 2005). In robberies, just as in the protests and uprisings discussed in earlier chapters, one side adapts to the other side's emotions and actions and changes their interpretation of the situation and behavior accordingly. Factors similar to those in protests and uprisings are vital to these surprising outcomes: people's use of space and their coordination among themselves, signs of incompetence, and verbal and non-verbal communication, as well as emotion expression.

What does this finding tell us about peoples' motivations and strategies for criminal behavior? If personality traits and motivations were essential, resisting clerks would be likely to instantly resist and/or reach for their own weapons. We would presumably see some clerks react very differently from the start. However, most clerks in the sample comply when robbers show behavior commonly associated with a robbery and only resist (either passively or actively by using their own weapons) after specific situational patterns happen in which a perpetrator acts out of character and breaks the routine. From the outside, breaking character does not change the perpetrators' physical or tactical advantage, or the clerk's situation. The clerk is still in a robbery situation and confronted with an armed perpetrator. Rather it derails routine scripts and changes interpretative and emotional dynamics. CCTV footage shows several clerks initially complying but then resisting after they perceive the perpetrator to be out of character. They seem to take the perpetrator less seriously and accordingly do not continue behaving like a victim.

This is in line with findings on the role of situations versus motivations in changing protest dynamics: if motivations alone were enough, police or protesters would immediately use violence against the other group at the start of a protest—at least they would do so from time to time. Yet, it usually takes 1½ hours and a specific set of situational dynamics before violence occurs (see Chapters 4–7). If motivations alone were key in robberies, rather than the situational unfolding, we would see robbers being successful regardless of their weapon being uncommon, the rhythms they establish with clerks, or the way they communicate or take space. Yet, findings suggest situational dynamics have stronger relevance than personality traits and motivations in leading to social phenomena and to surprising outcomes in particular (see also Collins, 2016c).

In short, while the cultural expectations we hold about a situation shape our interpretations, findings suggest that culture alone, just like a perpetrator's motivations, experience, strategies, or expectations, is not enough to lead to surprising outcomes—neither in crime nor in protests or uprisings. While culture shapes our actions by influencing what people expect, perceive, and want (Swidler, 1986), how interactions during the event play out, as well as the interpretations and emotional dynamics they provoke, seem to fundamentally impact the outcome.

The situation itself seems to be highly important for robbers to actually obtain the money and for clerks to comply or show resistance—just as for a protest or uprising to stay peaceful or become violent. Cases suggest that surprising outcomes occur because of situational breakdowns in which confusion arises after routines people rely on collapse. The situational unfolding thus seems to be a crucial factor in causing what manifests as two different types of crimes: a "robbery" or an "attempted robbery." Failed robberies stem from routine interactions breaking down.

Conclusion

SITUATIONAL BREAKDOWNS—SURPRISING OUTCOMES IN PROTESTS AND BEYOND

In a Nutshell

This book examined surprising social outcomes. It discussed how these outcomes, such as violence during generally peaceful marches, violence during uprisings, or the failure of armed robberies, do not occur due to people's motivations or strategies but because of situational collapses—moments of emotionally charged chaos during which communication is poor, misunderstandings arise, and people's perceptions of their roles, that of others', and the encounter change drastically. The book maintains that similar dynamics are common across various types of individual and collective violence and other puzzling outcomes such as failed crimes.

Chapters 1 to 6 examined instances of collective behaviors. They traced interactions during protests that alter interpretations and emotional dynamics and trigger the emergence of physical violence. They compared the influence of situational dynamics to the influence of background factors, such as motivations, strategies, police or protesters' cultures. These chapters showed that situational dynamics during protests provide comprehensive explanations for violent altercations. More specifically, findings suggest that that it is not police strategies but police mismanagement during protests that influences the emergence of violence; not the media or participants' expectations of violence, but escalation signs during the protest; not the presence and motivations of black bloc activists or other violently motivated protesters, but property damage committed by protesters during a demonstration. Communication problems between protesters and police during an event and incursions by one group into another group's territory are further vital factors that contribute to eruptions of violence.

Case discussions illustrated that five interactions—spatial incursions, police mismanagement, escalation signs, property damage, and communication problems between protesters and police—lead to violence if they occur in specific combinations by triggering reinterpretations of events. Officers perceive a loss of control if police mismanagement combines with spatial incursions. Either group (i.e., protesters or police) perceives an offense if spatial incursions combine with escalation signs and property damage. Either group perceives a lack of information as dangerous if communication problems between protesters and police coincide with spatial incursions and escalation signs.

All three paths lead to interpretations that raise tension and fear since either officers perceive they lost control over the operation, one group perceives an offense by the other, or missing information about the other group's goals and intentions is perceived. An increase in tension and fear leads to violent outbreaks if one side gains emotional dominance over the other (e.g., when a person falls, is outnumbered, or turns her back). With this finding, this book adds a vital aspect to the explanation of protest events, violence, and other surprising outcomes; emotional dynamics that disrupt routine interactions stem from situational dynamics during the same event. Relational mechanisms and paths can be identified on the micro-level of protest events. Situational reinterpretations (Blumer, 1986; Drury and Reicher, 2000; Stott and Drury, 2000; Reicher, 2001) are vital components in these dynamics and need to be connected with relational (Tilly and Tarrow, 2006) and emotional (R. Collins, 2008) explanations. These findings may allow us to move toward a more comprehensive situational approach to surprising outcomes and human action.

These situational paths can also be employed to avoid violence. Measures to keep protests peaceful include (1) clear, extensive communication between protesters and police, (2) a police focus on effective management during a protest, (3) respect for territorial boundaries, (4) awareness and avoidance of actions that another group might interpret as signs of escalation, and (5) awareness of the consequences of property damage. Attention should be paid to potential increases in tension in the temporal danger zone of 1½ to 2½ hours after a demonstration begins.

Chapter 9 discussed the relevance of situational breakdowns in other types of surprising outcomes. It focused on other forms of protest to study surprising outcomes beyond marches and on non-violent interactions to study situational breakdowns beyond violence. It discussed that systemic and symbolic racism are key factors leading to uprisings. Yet these factors cannot fully explain when and why violence breaks out. While uprisings after police shootings in the United States are often assumed to end in physical clashes by default, we see only a few end in violence, and if they do, dynamics at the micro-level are present prior to a violent outbreak. As protest marches, they show spatial incursions, property damage, police mismanagement, missing communication, and escalation signs increasing tension and distrust on both sides.

The second part of Chapter 9 examined non-violent surprising outcomes, focusing on an interaction ritual that is usually very clear, rigid, and non-negotiable—armed store robberies. The discussion showed that in these contexts, surprising outcomes (the armed robber not getting the money from the clerk) occur due to micro-level dynamics and breaks in routine as well. The implicit routines are overly clear, but although one person enforces the robbery ritual onto another, and despite a clear situation of dominance (i.e., one person is armed, the other fearing for her or his life), these routines can break down. Unexpected interactions or emotion expression can cause robbers to become confused, afraid, and unable to obtain a store's cash or valuables. These findings point to situational mechanisms that appear essential to a variety of surprising social outcomes.

External Validity

We find situational breakdowns not only in protest marches but also in violent uprisings and armed store robberies. What about events beyond these cases? Can a situational approach also explain more drastic types of violence? In the following, I will briefly examine findings on events ranging from fistfights to rampage shootings and atrocities.

The straightforward micro-perspective applied in this book to explain physical interpersonal violence might seem counterintuitive, since there is a common belief that violence is planned, intended, or ordered and hence occurs due to motivations, strategies, or other background factors. Yet numerous recent insights from various disciplines on outcomes in different cultural contexts buttress the micro-perspective as promising. Looking just at the last couple of years, more and more studies have found evidence for the crucial role situational dynamics play in leading to various types of violence.

Most prominently, Randall Collins (2008, 2009) shows that, contrary to conventional assumptions, violence is not easy. Across different types of violence, people overcome their inhibition threshold through one of five situational pathways (Collins, 2009, p. 570): attacking the weak (discussed as a key emotional dynamic in causing violence in generally peaceful protests, produced by the three interactional paths identified in Chapters 5–7); avoiding confrontation through audience-oriented staged or controlled fights (such as boxing); confrontation avoiding remote violence (such as snipers, drones, or throwing objects in protests); through deception (such as suicide attacks); or through absorption in technique (e.g., snipers showing a strong focus on the technical aspects of their gear, distracting themselves from the actual event of killing another person).

Recent research on fistfights and brawls supports the crucial role of dynamics on the micro-level in violence. For instance, in his analysis of poor inner-city African American communities in the United States, Elijah Anderson (2000) shows how for most people the "code of the street" is a front, employed specifically to avoid violent confrontations. While observers might think that the code of the street implies a readiness for violent behavior, the opposite seems to be the case, and people seem focused on avoiding violence, even in scenarios in which they seem ready for it.

Studying affluent white youths based on ethnographic fieldwork and a dataset of 189 violent encounters, Curtis Jackson-Jacobs (2013) arrives at similar results. In his study the youths often set out to get into fights. Yet, they hardly ever do actually fight. Rather, they avoid violence in most circumstances. Despite being motivated to use violence, they are faced with confrontational tension and fear. In order to be able to fight, they must accomplish specific situational patterns and reinterpretations of an "urgent 'last chance' crisis—one requiring violence right now" (Jackson-Jacobs, 2013, p. 25). Jackson-Jacobs's study shows that not their motivations but situational dynamics are key to violence (see also Felson, 1984). Since only very specific situational dynamics cause violence to break out, these fights are overall rare.

Further supporting the role of situational dynamics in physical violence, Harel Shapira's (2016) ethnographic study of gun ranges in Texas indicates that gun schools focus heavily on situational dynamics to enable individuals to use their gun (i.e. violence). He shows that gun courses train people to generate fear more easily. Tension and fear of the "other" can be a first step to violence, as discussed in Chapters 1 to 8, and gun courses promote participants' situational tension and fear. The second key lesson in gun school courses is training in tactics, which seems to draw heavily on the establishment of situational emotional dominance (Shapira, 2016), equivalent to what Collins (2008) describes. Effectively, participants are taught good and bad situational techniques, which will enable them to use their gun more readily. Gun courses thereby seem to provide participants with two toolkits that make it more likely that the gun will be used: increasing tensions and fear and techniques to establish dominance.

A study on brawls in front of UK nightclubs by social psychologists Levine, Taylor, and Best (2011) underlines that situational dynamics are also key in achieving the opposite—stopping aggression from turning violent (see also Madensen and Eck, 2008). And researchers Hylander and Granstöm (2010a) found that a recognizable situational order can avoid violence by European soccer hooligans, as it makes it difficult for violently motivated fans to create the situational chaos that generally facilitates violent outbreaks (see also Madensen and Knutsson, 2011). These results are in line with findings discussed in the early chapters: if the situational order leads to chaos and confusion, if groups break up and individuals are isolated, violence is more likely to erupt. In contrast, a clear situational order and the feeling of boredom support peaceful events. Given that violence is not easy, surprising outcomes, such as the eruption of violence, usually follow the breakdown of situational routines.

Studies suggest that even people who are highly committed to using violence—such as rampage shooters—need such situational dynamics. While background factors, such as bullying, mental illness, or gun access, matter in rampage shootings (Leary et al., 2003; Newman et al., 2005; Langman, 2009; Kalish and Kimmel, 2010; Sommer, Leuschner, and Scheithauer, 2014), situational dynamics can add a further explanatory variable. Despite a strong motivation for the shooting and often months-long planning, it seems many shooters actively avoid confrontational tension and fear and actively seek to establish emotional energy to be able to carry out their plans. Collins (2014) showed that shooters avoid confrontational tension and fear through absorption in technique, focusing on technical aspects of the weapon rather than the actual killing of people. Furthermore, shooters often use earplugs, sunglasses, or black wardrobe to increase their own feeling of dominance and to create a surreal experience that distracts them from killing other humans (Collins, 2014, p. 417). Many shooters also seem to target weak victims in particular, who ran away or turned their backs to the shooter(s). This deprives them of a valuable "weapon" in that situation: their face (Collins, 2014). Thus, it seems even rampage school shooters, the "deeply disturbed young men who are willing to contemplate horrific acts" (Gladwell, 2015), need to create a favorable micro-situation to be able to overcome situational confrontational tension and fear and carry out violence.

Lastly, evidence pointing to the crucial explanatory factors on the micro-level of violent incidents can also be found when looking at atrocities. Studies that take a closer look at what happened in the specific situational dynamics before the outbreak of large-scale violence were able to challenge long-held convictions on their key triggers and causes. One example is Martin McCleery's (2016) study of the Bloody Sunday shooting. In this incident, on January 30, 1972, British soldiers shot and killed 26 unarmed civilians who were part of a protest march against internment in the city of Derry, Northern Ireland. McCleery shows that the situational dynamics building up to the shooting throughout the day indicate that a forward panic (see also Chapter 7) took place that led to the shooting. He finds that a prolonged period of tension and fear occurred on the side of the soldiers who later fired the shots and thereby contests explanations centering on actors' motivations or strategies being key.

Klusemann's (2009; see also Klusemann, 2012) acclaimed study of the 1995 Srebrenica massacre in Bosnia-Herzegovina is another example that highlights the crucial role of situational dynamics in leading to large-scale violence, such as atrocities. Klusemann shows that micro-situational dynamics in the meeting between Serbian general Mladić and UN commander Karremans constitute a key turning point for the subsequent massacre that left thousands of Muslim Bosniaks dead. His findings thereby challenge prevalent approaches in the study of war and atrocities that focus on background factors as key explanatory variables. They suggest that, just as in other outcomes like brawls, hooligan violence, or rampages, which are often measured on the macro-level and attributed to aggregate level variables, atrocities seem to be determined by situational dynamics.[1]

What about revolutionary settings in non-democratic countries, where we find strong background factors favoring violence? While research on situational aspects in such instances is still scarce, a study on the topic by Isabel Bramsen (2018) suggests that situational dynamics matter for the outbreak of violence in non-democratic countries as well. In 2010 the world witnessed a wave of protests and political turmoil across parts of the Arab world. Beginning with the Tunisian revolution, uprisings followed

---

[1] Interestingly, in contrast to the other studies discussed here, Klusemann (2009) does not trace the seconds and minutes right before the violent outbreak. He focuses on the analyses of situational dynamics in the negotiations, which then caused the micro-structural situation that led to the massacre starting the next day. The analyzed situation thus created the *context* that led to the massacre. Klusemann's findings highlight that situational dynamics shape each further context. Without Klusemann explicitly discussing it, his findings illustrate a feedback loop between the micro-level and macro-level and show that each new "context" is the product of a previous micro-situation.

in Egypt, Syria, Libya, Yemen, and Bahrain. Mass protests also occurred across many other countries, such as Algeria or Kuwait. While some protests remained peaceful, in many cases violent altercations erupted. In her study, Bramsen (2018) suggests that situational dynamics were also vital in many of these eruptions of violence.[2] She shows that in the videotaped instances she analyzed, emotional dominance is gained by attacking from afar or above, within vehicles, or at night, or by attacking the outnumbered. Her findings indicate that violence is avoided when victims face their potential attackers. In line with Randall Collins's theory (2008, p. 82) and findings on protest violence discussed in Chapters 1 to 8, her findings suggest that situational dynamics are vital even in these revolutionary circumstances in authoritarian regimes, in which violent motivations are presumably much greater and routines are generally more violent than in the marches discussed in this book.

In short, various findings suggest that a closer look at what happens in situations before violence breaks out can challenge long-held convictions on the causes of various violent events (see also Hoebel, 2014; Snow and Moss, 2014; Equit, Groenemeyer, and Schmidt, 2016; Sutterlüty, 2017), such as the Bloody Sunday killings in Northern Ireland in 1972 (McCleery, 2016), the Srebrenica massacre in Bosnia-Herzegovina in 1995 (Klusemann, 2009), or the violent revolutions in Bahrain and Tunesia in 2011 (Bramsen, 2018).

Theoretical Implications

Findings provide a variety of implications for social science theory, including the role of motivations, emotions, and rationality, reinterpretations, expectations, and culture, as well as a human inhibition threshold to violence.

Motivations Versus Situations, Emotion Versus Rationality

Findings suggest motivations and strategies must pass through the bottleneck of a situation to lead to an intended outcome—in large-scale interactions, such as protest marches, or small-scale interactions, such as

---

[2] Studying violence in Rwanda, political scientist Lee Ann Fuji (2011) suggests that it was not prior strategies or motivations of the actors that were key to the violence but relations and networks between people. How these are re-enacted and how violence in Rwanda emerged situationally can be a vital subject for future research.

robberies. Surprising outcomes show prior situational patterns of broken-down routine interactions. Cases discussed throughout this book suggest that situations can override prior motivations and interactions can override prior strategies. Although one obvious assumption would be that we act irrationally when situations override our motivations and strategies, cases demonstrate that this is not the case; emotions and rational thinking are not mutually exclusive during these situational processes. Yet they have a joint influence on surprising outcomes. People seem to act boundedly rational in these instances, meaning they reflect rationally, but their rationality is bounded by their knowledge of the situation, others' intentions, and the possible consequences of their actions (Blumer, 1986; R. Collins, 1993). Simultaneously, findings suggest that emotions affect a person's actions, with fear particularly influencing situations that turn violent. However, fear does not "take over." Consider the protest events described in Chapters 4 through 6, or the uprisings and robberies analyzed in Chapter 9: it is precisely the actors' rational interpretation of events (in the light of the limited overview they have during a situation) that leads them to emotional reactions, which trigger unexpected outcomes.

In hindsight, many police and protesters involved during demonstrations, activists and police involved in uprisings, or robbers in convenience stores might not have been in real danger that would justify high degrees of tension and fear. Yet their perception of being in danger was rational, given the limited information they had during the situation. For instance, some incidents led people to reasonably perceive an offense during a protest, which caused them to become afraid. Similarly, aspects of their counterpart's posture, micro-expressions, and/or actions led robbers to perceive that something was off about a clerk, which made them anxious. Although research traditionally conceptualizes emotions and rational thinking as mutually exclusive, findings suggest that rationality and emotions are inseparable and their interplay can explain actor's reactions (see also Goodwin and Jasper, 2006).

Collective and Individual Reinterpretations

Findings discussed in this book suggest that interpretations by groups (e.g., police or protesters) or individuals (e.g., a robber or a clerk) lead to emotional dynamics that trigger surprise outcomes, and these interpretations emerge in light of situational interactions. Looking at collective interpretations, three dynamics seem particularly relevant theoretically: interpretations of in-group behaviors, interpretations of out-group behaviors, and reinterpretations. Looking at individual interpretations, the analysis of robberies suggests that interpretations of routine versus out-of-script behaviors and reinterpretations of one's role are highly relevant.

First, findings highlight that collective actors' interpretations of in-group interactions change protest dynamics. People might, for example, interpret interactions by their own group, such as putting on gas masks or picking up stones, as preparing for trouble, and this might make them worry and become fearful. Next to such actions, people also interpret emotions of other in-group members due to their "tendency to automatically mimic and synchronize facial expressions, vocalizations, postures, and movements with those of another person" (Hatfield, Cacioppo, and Rapson, 1993, p. 5). Studies show that group members thereby converge emotionally, and such entrainment leads participants to get caught up in each others' rhythms (see robberies discussed in Chapter 9, as well as Collins, 2005a, p. 47). Yet, through mutual gaze among in-group's members, protesters might also realize that other protesters are afraid and thus become afraid themselves. This dynamic was at work in the Rostock 2007 protest example. Protesters increasingly noticed a spreading atmosphere of concern and became fearful themselves. Such negative emotional contagion can spread across a group even if the interaction triggering it was not observed: not knowing why someone else is afraid can make a person worry even more.

Mutual gaze not only increases emotional contagion, it can also increase solidarity among in-group members (e.g., Drury and Reicher, 2000; Reicher, 2001; Hatfield, Carpenter, and Rapson, 2014; Hatfield et al., 2014). During protests, shared emotions usually create positive emotions toward insiders, shared emotions toward the state of the world, and negative emotions toward a threat or opponent (Jasper, 2006, p. 26). People's perceptions of the interactions and emotions of their in-group thereby influence their emotional states, and emotional states influence their further interpretations and feelings of solidarity. Interpreting the actions and emotion expressions of the in-group thereby shapes collective interactions.

Second, people interpret an out-group's actions, which can also produce shared emotions. For example, people may interpret actions by an out-group as threatening: running into another group's space might be interpreted as the other breaking an agreement, and this action by the out-group can thus generate fear in the in-group. If groups are unable to communicate and are therefore unaware of each other's plans and intentions, they might see the other group doing strange and unexpected things without knowing why, and this can unsettle them even more (Reicher et al., 2007,

p. 410). The interpretation of the out-group actions thereby impacts sub-sequent interactions.

Third, such interpretations not only cause emotional dynamics to shift, intensify, challenge, and reinforce in-group and out-group perceptions, they can also cause actors to fundamentally reinterpret their own roles. Officers might, for example, define themselves as doing their jobs at the beginning of a march. After 1½ hours of interactions with protesters in which officers perceive protesters' actions as an indicator of group hostility, their interpretation can change: officers perceive the out-group as increasingly homogeneous, and they adapt their self-definition to the re-interpretation of the other. For instance, faced with a perceived homogeneous, threatening out-group, they might define themselves as defending their physical integrity against a hostile group of protesters.

Research suggests that the more a collection of individuals is perceived and treated as a homogeneous group by an out-group, the more it identifies as a homogeneous group itself (Stott and Reicher, 1998; Reicher, 2001). Studying protests in the United Kingdom, Drury and Reicher (2000) found the following:

> Initially, for some at least, to be a campaign participant is to be a respon-sible citizen exercising his or her democratic right to protest, both able to take advantage of those rights and bound by the responsibilities such rights incur. Later, to be a campaign participant is to stand in opposition to police and authorities, and hence both able to protest only through radical action and bound to challenge the illegitimacy of the system. (p. 29)

A protester's statements at the march against the IMF meeting in Washington, DC in 2000 illustrates this development in the US and German protests studied. The protester was initially against the presence of the black bloc, as she did not condone their tactics. But after harsh police reactions, she saw herself and the black bloc as part of a coherent group of protesters and opposed to the police: "In this moment I have total solidarity. There are no more questions of tactics or style or guidelines, we are simply there together, facing the same threat, making the same stand, facing the same fear" (Starhawk, 2002). Her statement exemplifies how crucial interpretations of situational interactions are to the understanding and perception of the self, the context, and the other. Such reinterpretations are essential to explaining the emergence of violence.

Fourth, the discussion of robberies shows that mutual gaze, rhythmic entrainment, and mimicking behaviors also influence situational dynamics during encounters between two people or small groups. Cases show that people notice even the subtlest of actions or emotional expressions of others, since perpetrators and clerks tend to become entrained with each other's rhythms. Due to such entrainment, perpetrators can be unable to establish dominance, and robberies can fail. Further, if actors (perpetrators or victims) during such an encounter interpret the role of the other to have changed (e.g., "the robber" becoming "the customer"), their own roles also shift (e.g., "the victim" becoming "the clerk"). Thus, when a perpetrator shouts decisive orders at a clerk, the clerk is more likely to be quiet, stand still, and show fear. When a perpetrator's emotional display indicates, even unwillingly, that he is too sad to commit the crime, the clerk might start trying to cheer him up. When a perpetrator seems undecided, the clerk might take the dominant role. When a perpetrator displays that he is happy the clerk might get angry, when he seems proud of himself the clerk might ignore him. Across robberies, perpetrators and clerks try to make sense of these new situations by adapting their behaviors and changed roles and react accordingly. In short, the book discusses that situational reinterpretation by collective and individual actors influences subsequent actions heavily and shapes situational emotions and unexpected outcomes.

Expectations, Culture, and Violence

The discussion highlights that situational interaction, interpretation, and emotion are crucial to situational breakdowns that cause surprising outcomes. If emotions change due to interpretations of interactions, the question is: Where do interpretations of interactions come from? This brings us back to the role of culture. Yet, by *culture* I do not refer to the monolithic sense of a US or German national culture, or a police culture or organization that breeds strategies that cause violence. My analysis suggests that situational patterns to protest violence are similar in the national context of the United States and Germany. They also look similar across decades, with disparate dominant policing styles or with different protest groups participating. If national or protest cultures were essential, violence would be more common across protests of this culture. Yet the same national or protest cultures exist during most protests that remain peaceful in Western democracies and in the few that turn violent.

However, culture seems to matter in that it appears to operate at the micro-level through situational interactions, interpretations, and emotions (DiMaggio, 1997). Findings suggest that people see things through their cultural lens, and, depending on the cultural context, they expect certain behaviors and actions when attending a protest (Jasper, 2009) or when being a perpetrator or a victim during a robbery. The loss of control path in particular illustrates the cultural component of situational interpretations. Officers in Western democracies expect to be in control of a situation during all types of operations. If officers perceive themselves as losing control during a protest, they do so due to a specific police culture, meaning due to established and reinforced interpretative schemata that they use to evaluate information (DiMaggio, 1997). They interpret their own roles, the situation, and the actions of others through cultural expectations, and this interpretation influences social outcomes.

Robbers also expect to be in control of the situation, and they expect a victim to comply; they have a gun and could kill the clerk. Victims expect robbers to be dominant, confident, and in charge of the situation—to be dangerous criminals. If robbers act against cultural expectations and stumble or fall, are sad or insecure, interactional routines break down, established schemata no longer hold, and victims return to responding to what seems like more adequate schemata—for example, clerk–customer or cheering-sad-person-up routines (see Chapter 9). If a perpetrator's actions do not culturally reflect expected scripts in terms of robbery behaviors or emotion expressions, clerks adapt their roles to the changed situation and do not comply.

Findings show that culture shapes (strategies of) action by influencing what people expect, perceive, and want (Swidler, 1986). Yet, when Randall Collins (2005b, p. 1) stated in an interview, "Culture in general does nothing," he underlined that static values, motivations, and toolkits do not explain actions (see also Swidler, 1986, p. 274). A protest organized by non-violent organizers, or taking place during a soft protest policing culture, does not automatically mean that the protest remains peaceful, and a black bloc presence or harsh police strategy does not automatically mean that it will turn violent. As Chapter 9 showed, protesters and police facing each other during uprisings after a police shooting in the United States does not indicate that violent clashes will follow—even if background factors such as systemic racism and frustrations with these factors are high. Being a motivated armed criminal does not automatically lead to a successful robbery. Instead, this book suggests that we need to focus on actions, interpretations, and emotions during such situations. A crucial part of a society's culture—which Collins (2005b, p. 1) suggests implicitly—is the interpretations and emotions that arise when individuals and groups confront situations that are or are not part of their expectations, routines, and rituals. In this sense, this book's findings accord with arguments from cultural sociologists such as DiMaggio (1997) and Swidler (1986). Findings suggest that culture impacts situations, but they also show that the micro-level shapes culture through situational routines (Anderson, Brighenti, and Bassetti, 2007; Collins, Walby, and Spencer, 2010). In short, how culture plays out in *situations* seems essential to a variety of unexpected social outcomes.

Are We Violent . . . or Peaceful?

Although this book focuses on surprising outcomes, such as protest violence, violent uprisings, and failed armed robberies, findings also have implications for a theoretical discussion of humanity's violent and non-violent nature. Several arguments discussed throughout this book suggest that violence is difficult and rare and does not come easy to people. One indicator is that routine interactions during protests and elsewhere in Western democracies are overwhelmingly peaceful, even though people could use violence against each other at any time. Chapters 1 through 8 show that specific situational patterns must occur to break routines so that violence erupts, even if people might be motivated to use physical violence. Case comparisons demonstrate that violence does not occur easily. Even several escalating interactions occurring together do not lead to violence (for instance, spatial incursions and escalation signs, as during the migrants' rights protest in Rostock in 2007, discussed in Chapter 3) unless they combine into one of the paths described. To increase tension and fear to a point at which actors overcome their threshold and violence occurs, a combination of interactions is required. Such combinations lead people to conclude that interaction rituals have broken down. If violence emerges, it is usually used against a situationally weak opponent, since an inhibition threshold for violence is more easily overcome toward people who appear weak (see Chapter 7, see also R. Collins, 2008, 2009).

Another indicator for a threshold to violence is that actors in the protest marches studied never arrived at a protest and started fighting immediately. Usually about 1½ hours passed before violence broke out, and it always followed combinations of interactions accumulating during these hours. Thus, contrary to common belief, violence does not break out at these protests whenever opportunities arise. Violently motivated individuals—police officers or protesters—fail to engage in violence most of the time. Findings suggest that if protesters motivated to use violence attend, something more than mere motivation must prompt them to use violence.

It seems that although "background factors" (like social rejection, a bad childhood, or social grievances in the face of systemic racism) play a role in leading to violence, humans still experience an inhibition toward violence and need to interpret situations in a specific way to overcome their threshold and actually use physical violence (see also Athens, 1980; Felson and Steadman, 1983; Felson and Tedeschi, 1993). Sociologist Jack Katz (1988; see also Felson and Boba, 2010) points out that "something causally essential happens in the very moments" in which people commit a crime or use violence:

> Although a criminal's economic status, peer group relations, Oedipal conflicts, genetic makeup, internalized machismo, history of child abuse etc. usually remain unchanged, the person must suddenly become propelled to commit the crime in a specific situation, in contrast to most other moments of her or his life. (Katz, 1988, p. 4)

Research from other disciplines supports the notion that violence does not come easy to humans but that we need to overcome an inhibition to be violent—even if motivated (Nassauer, 2018a). From an anthropological standpoint, it makes little sense for humans to fight, since solidary group interactions offer more security and the costs of fighting usually outweigh potential gains. Studies suggest that a human inhibition for violence exists as a product of humans' necessity to live within a group or larger society in order to be well supplied and protected (Eisenberger and Lieberman, 2004; Bauer, 2011). Supporting this notion, studies in neurobiology show that aggression, like fear, is reactive and not an immanent human urge. Solidary actions release positive neurotransmitters and can therefore count as human "urges" (Rilling et al., 2002; Tabibnia, Satpute, and Lieberman, 2008; Siegel and Victoroff, 2009). This neurological need for solidary actions might be explained by findings in anthropology and primatology that being part of a group helped the first hominins to survive (Silverberg and Gray, 1992, p. 2; Sousa and Casanova, 2006). Further, neurological studies underline that aggression rarely leads to actual violence and that when violence happens, humans usually do not gain from it; positive neurotransmitters are generally not released if mentally healthy humans use physical violence against each other (for an overview, see Bauer, 2011).

In short, findings from various research fields show that humans exhibit an inhibition threshold toward violence. Findings across disciplines suggest that people's violent nature, which some researchers (e.g., Reemtsma,

2008; Theweleit, 2015) and mainstream media illustrate with gory detail, is an intellectual predilection and part of media sensationalism rather than empirical fact.

The discussed findings can explain why the situational dynamic is key for humans to act against their seemingly peaceful nature, be it in protests, fistfights, atrocities, or rampages. An innately peaceful nature might explain why violence tends to occur only after routines break down.

Research Implications

Studies might further examine and test the findings discussed in this volume and identify additional micro-situational patterns to surprising social outcomes. Studies that examine situational dynamics across a larger set of cases would be especially helpful in analyzing whether explanatory patterns on the micro-level exist systematically. The following sections discuss four aspects particularly interesting for future research.

Protest Policing and Protest Violence

One interesting line of future research would be to re-examine the role police strategies play during the emergence of protest violence in Western democracies. Numerous researchers explain a higher or lower level of protest violence during certain periods using dominant policing strategies and tactics (see, e.g., G. T. Marx 2006; McPhail and McCarthy 2005), suggesting that more violence occurs when escalated force is the predominant strategy (e.g., McPhail, Schweingruber, and McCarthy, 1998). Although the dominant policing strategy in a country changes over time, which influences various aspects of social movements, my findings suggest that the influence of policing strategies and tactics on protest violence needs to be reconsidered and re-examined.

Results suggest that situational dynamics offer an alternative explanation for increases or decreases in protest violence across time periods. For instance, some scholars report increasing violence at large-scale transnational protests of the global justice movement (Della Porta, Peterson, and Reiter 2006). Future studies could analyze whether such an increase can also be explained by a greater likelihood of the occurrence of interactions discussed in this book. Since global justice protests are often located at global summit sites, which are widely closed off, spatial incursions are more attractive to protesters and more likely. Another reason for higher levels of violence during global justice movement protests compared to the 1980s could be a greater likelihood of police mismanagement due to many officers being employed at these large-scale marches, which complicates management. A decrease in violence from the 1960s to the 1980s might be explained by paths to violence becoming less likely overall: Due to increased police training and professionalism, police mismanagement and communication problems between protesters and police might have declined in the 1980s. Due to a change in protester tactics, spatial incursions and property damage could have become less frequent than during the 1960s.

In short, the combination of interactions during a protest might offer an alternative explanation for increasing levels of violence at global justice movement protests and the decrease in violence from 1960s movements to the new social movements. Described paths to violence might also explain why most protests, even those with repressive, rigid policing strategies, remain peaceful: while some of the interactions might be more likely during specific time periods, the interactions rarely emerge in the specific combinations that foster violence.

Structural and Individual Aspects of Forward Panics

Future research could examine cases of high-intensity violence more systematically. The temporal dynamics of police riots presented here comprise only a cursory look at the phenomenon. Additional systematic research should comparatively analyze a larger sample of police riots and investigate the exact duration of interactions during a protest, covering, for example, temporal overlaps or intermissions between interactions and employing sequence analysis (Abbott, 1995; Aisenbrey and Fasang, 2010) together with video data analysis (Nassauer and Legewie, 2018). Cross-country comparisons of potential differences in forward panics due to diverging protest groups, political opportunities, and police structures should also be assessed. Such a comparative perspective would shed light on the link or disjuncture between structural conditions and micro-situations in explanations of violence.

Regarding forward panics, future research should focus on why some group members—in my study, police officers, in Randall Collins's (2008) study, soldiers, among others—undergo a forward panic while some seem immune to this emotional dynamic and do not participate in acts of excessive violence (Kersten, 2012, p. 291; see also Fujii, 2013, p. 415). Are some people better at establishing dominance and consequently get into a forward panic more easily? Such studies could also consider the hormonal levels of individuals during analysis, as Mazur (2009) suggests, to explain differences in officers' reactions to a perceived loss of control. Combined with methods, such as sequence analysis, qualitative comparative analysis, and video data analysis (see also Appendix B), such a disciplinary combination of bio-sociology with crowd psychology and sociology might further our understanding of instances of excessive violence.

Expanding to Further Outcomes, Countries, and Protests

Another question is whether findings on violence during demonstration marches apply to other types of protests or to marches in other countries. Bramsen's (2018) research on situational dynamics of protest violence during the Arab Spring suggests that micro-situational dynamics are essential in leading to protest violence in non-democratic regimes as well. Future research should verify findings and expand this comparative effort. Can similar interactional dynamics be found, for instance, during protests in countries in Asia, Central and South America, Africa, and Australia? While Chapter 9 discusses spontaneous protest assemblies and uprisings, what role do combinations of interactions and emotional dynamics play in violence during other types of protests, such as sit-ins?

Moreover, analyses of emotional dynamics and emotional dominance should be expanded to further unexpected outcomes. Among many other phenomena, it would be interesting to conduct systematic analyses of emotional dynamics during sports games with unexpected outcomes. Researchers could code athletes' emotion expressions to study their effects on actions. It would be particularly useful to study emotional turning points, which might cause a losing team to gain emotional momentum, turn the tide, and win. A closer look at rhythms and mimicking behaviors in leading to surprising outcomes in sports may also prove fruitful. One example of shifting momentum can be found in Game 1 of the 1995 NBA Eastern Conference semifinals. The New York Knicks led the Indiana Pacers 105 to 99 at Madison Square Garden with 18.7 seconds remaining. Yet, the Pacers managed to score an improbable 8 points in only 9 seconds in one of the biggest late-game upsets in the NBA. Another example would be studying emotional dynamics such as the soccer World Cup qualifier match between Germany and Sweden in Berlin in October 2013. Although Germany was a heavy favorite and up 4 to 0 after one hour of play, Sweden managed to turn things around, scoring 4 goals in only 30 minutes and resulting in a 4-to-4 final score. It would be particularly interesting to study whether emotional dynamics, mutual gazes, and emotional entrainments (Mazur et al., 1980; Hatfield, Cacioppo, and Rapson, 1993; Collins, 2005a; Hatfield et al., 2014) could systematically produce situational turning points that cause unexpected outcomes in sports events.

Roots of Inhibition to Violence

More research is also needed on a potential inhibition threshold to violence. Findings on cases across decades, countries, and types of violence suggest the key to physical violence eruption can be found on the micro-level. If this is the case, the question emerges: Why would situations be needed for eruptions of violence across such varying types of altercations as well as historical, political, and cultural contexts? Randall Collins (2008) suggests situational dynamics are key, since we have an inhibition toward violence that needs to be overcome in the situation. Does this inhibition mean we are inherently peaceful? Broadening the view to neuroscientific studies, anthropology, and primatology might help answer this question and provide further evidence for the argument that the micro-level is needed for violence emergence. Numerous findings in these disciplines suggest an innately peaceful human nature and may thereby provide evidence why situational routines need to be disrupted for violence to emerge (Nassauer, 2018a).

If such a threshold to violence exists, an open question is whether it is socialized and cultural or an innate, genetic human trait? One way to explore this question would be to study situational patterns of violence in humans' direct ancestors. Finding similarities and differences in exploratory studies on human and non-human primates' violent behaviors could help explore the source of human inhibition to violence. If we assume primates are a window into humans' past and help us understand human nature (Sousa and Casanova, 2006, p. 93; see also Peterson and Wrangham, 1997; Mazur, 2009; Sussman and Marshack, 2010), studying their situational patterns to violence more closely might be highly fruitful (Nassauer, 2018a). If non-human great apes do not show similar situational patterns as humans, this finding could suggest that a threshold developed through civilization processes and may be a cultural trait. If we find similar patterns among non-human great apes and humans, the threshold could be a biological feature that we may have inherited from our ancestors (Nassauer, 2018a). The recent increase in visual data collection on behaviors of great apes in their natural habitat is especially promising to study situational patterns to violence in non-human great apes (Diane Fossey Gorilla Fund

International, 2016). Studies could, for instance, employ these data to examine in which situations other great apes' aggressions shift to physical violence. Do great apes primarily physically attack situationally weak victims, or from a distance? Are similar ratios systematically visible in great ape severe violence, as in severe human violence (3:1 or 7:1; see also Nassauer, 2018a)? Findings suggest that studies on biological, psychological, cultural, anthropological, and educational factors can strongly complement recent research on violence in sociology, criminology, political sciences, and social psychology (Nassauer, 2016, 2018a, 2018c). Connecting a micro-situational perspective with evolutionary theory, as requested by numerous researchers (Laitin, 2008, p. 444; see also Mazur, 2009), can thus be a highly promising avenue for future research.

Concluding Remarks: Everyday Life and Fear of Violence

Beyond the scientific and practical implications of the findings, this study also has societal implications. Why is it relevant to society that such outcomes are a result of interaction routines that have broken down and of situations of emotionally charged chaos during which people are confused and afraid?

The findings suggest that the micro-level plays a crucial role in determining social outcomes. This can allow us to make changes at the micro-level that are much more easily applied than trying to change macro-level structures or people's motivations. That micro-level changes have strong influences on social outcomes and on macro-level phenomena, such as collective and individual violence, and crime rates makes micro-sociology an optimistic discipline. It implies that major changes are possible by targeting the micro-level, by avoiding specific patterns of interactions, reinterpretations, and emotional dynamics. Findings on the role of situational dynamics suggest that small changes may show big impacts.

Further, the finding that surprising outcomes are the result of situational breakdowns and that violence commonly occurs due to confusion and helplessness, tension, and fear point to a human inhibition threshold to violence. Although many people believe, and are encouraged to do so by mainstream media, that levels of violence and crime are rising and that life is becoming increasingly unsafe (Glassner, 2010), empirical studies show that violence and crime have greatly decreased. Many assume that people are inherently violent and cruel, and although many people act and vote according to this conviction, empirical insights point in another direction. Researchers report that violence rates have never been as low as they are today (R. Collins, 2008; Pinker, 2012; Ferguson, 2013; Gramlich, 2018).

In line with such research, my study suggests that most people do not tend to use violence during protests out of cruelty but due to breakdowns in routine interactions, leading to confusion, distress, uncertainty, anxiety, and fear. Violence does not simply break out of people as part of a violent nature. To the contrary: violence is difficult, even for those protesters or police officers who are motivated and plan on using it. Findings also show that criminal actors, like most people, rely on situational routines that offer comfort and assurance. If robbers see a victim not playing along, their default option is not cold-blooded violence but rather to become afraid of the unknown situation they are in and run. Findings from store robberies show how people match their role to that of the other, causing robbers to apologize to victims or clerks to cheer the robbers up. Findings suggest that people tend to become entrained with each other rather than dominate each other or use physical violence.

These findings provide a positive outlook. If physical violence is empirically rare and humans must overcome a threshold to use violence, this can have implications for people's well-being. Fear of peoples' cruel nature and violence lurking around every corner perpetuate everyday actions, voting behaviors, and policymaking guided by worst-case scenarios that are unlikely to happen (Glassner, 2010). Psychologists stress that fear leads people to make the worst decisions (e.g., Keinan, Friedland, and Ben-Porath, 1987). An inhibition to violence and a tendency to create a safe, reliable situational micro-order through interactions counter the idea that people need elaborate protection from each other on a personal level. Findings suggest that most industrialized countries do not need severe security to prevent violence and crime, which not only costs public funds but also often entails curtailing civil and human rights (e.g., privacy, free speech, and free movement, right of asylum). An inhibition to violence might mean that people can worry, fear, consume, and hoard less and instead enjoy society, be in solidarity with others, and share more. We might even spend some of the time we invest in protecting ourselves from others in helping people in need or protesting on their behalf.

APPENDIX A | Studying Situational Dynamics in the Twenty-First Century

F OR A LONG TIME A specific analysis of the situational dynamics in protests, uprisings, robberies, and other events was difficult to conduct, simply because extremely detailed data on such events did not exist. For instance, if a researcher were to go to a protest to observe it first-hand, she or he would not have a detailed retrospective overview of who was where, doing what when: When exactly did actors get tense? What did they do before that? What did they see? Participating, a researcher could only look at one or two protesters interacting but could not observe the people standing opposite them or all around them and thus would be unable to remember the emotion expressions of various actors' faces at each point in time. In many other surprising outcomes, such as armed store robberies, participating in order to obtain situational information on what happened is next to impossible.

Due to such shortcomings in participant observation, other scholars instead relied on interviews with protest participants or officers, criminal offenders or victims. This technique, however, removes them even further from what took place: it would be impossible for the interviewee to remember every detail of what happened, where she or he was, what emotions others displayed, exactly how many other people were there, and how they seemed to feel during each moment of the interaction. This is not surprising, given that studies show that our memory for detail tends to fade quickly. For instance, in one experiment participants were interviewed directly after leaving a restaurant. They were asked to give information on the waiters' clothes and did so in great detail. They did not recall that no waiters had been working in the restaurant (Bernard et al., 1984). Similar experiments support the finding that we remember selectively and have a hard time remembering situational dynamics in great detail. How should participants remember situational dynamics of an event in the kind of detail given for the Rostock protest described in the Introduction? Remembering situational detail gets even more difficult when dealing with violent or emotionally stressful events such as a potentially life-threatening robbery situation or an escalating protest or unrest (see also Fujii, 2010). First, individuals involved in violent clashes or criminal events tend to portray themselves as either perpetrators or victims and tend to dramatize or rationalize the action in hindsight. Second, people who fear for their safety—or even their life—during protests, uprisings, or criminal events tend to experience feeling as if under water, or report a tunnel view, due to the strong bodily effects of fear (Grossman and Christensen, 2008; see, e.g., R. Collins, 2008). Many victims suffer long-term psychological consequences after being robbed (Gale and Coupe, 2005; Bobic, Pavicevic, and Gomzi, 2007). Participants can therefore usually not remember clearly the details of what happened. This leads to retrospective accounts of participants being a poor primary source for studies of what happened and why (Bernard et al., 1984, p. 509; Vrij, Hope, and Fisher, 2014).

Videos of such situations, in contrast, can show in detail what happened with certain actors at what time and place, frame by frame. They can allow us to look at highly chaotic and complex events in slow motion, over and over again, and thereby avoid relying on the memories of people present who might be unable to keep track or may be too emotional to recall what happened. Therefore, videos can have a drastic advantage over observer accounts or interviews in reconstructing situational dynamics, creating an "incomparably richer record" of what happened (Jordan and Henderson, 1995, p. 52; see also Nassauer and Legewie, 2018). With technology making real-life interactions more available than ever before, we might therefore be "entering the Golden Age of visual sociology" (Collins, 2016b, p. 93). Researchers are likely to increasingly rely on videos to gain information on a variety of social phenomena.

An example illustrating the strong advantage of visual data over first-hand accounts to reconstruct what happened during emotional and threatening situations is the terrorist attack on the Westgate Mall in Nairobi, Kenya, in 2013. The terrorists' siege of the mall lasted four days, with 67 dead and 175 injured. Shoppers who managed to flee the mall while the siege was underway all told a coherent story to media and security forces about the attackers who were still killing people and keeping hostages inside: there were 10 to 15 attackers, multi-ethnic, one of them a British woman, and one fled with escaping shoppers. While media reported this first-hand information for weeks, the evaluation of CCTV after the siege had ended showed that even though victims and onlookers had a high interest in helping police end the siege (sometimes their friends or relatives were still in the mall), the key information they provided was not correct: only four attackers had stormed the Mall, all were Somali, all were male, and none had fled (Gatehouse, 2013; Krulwich and Abumrad, 2015).

This example drastically illustrates that what humans *think* happened in highly chaotic, emotional instances they were part of and what *actually* happened can be fundamentally different. This makes accounts by observers, participants, media, or bystanders less reliable in studying what happened in detail than CCTV or other visual data that record an entire event of interest. If ethical concerns are taken into consideration (Legewie and Nassauer, 2018), a researcher aims for optimal capture and the recording shows untainted, unstaged behavior (Nassauer and Legewie, 2018), video data can have a crucial advantage over other types of data to reconstruct the unfolding of events.

Only very recently have advances in technology allowed researchers to obtain systematic, extremely detailed insights into violence-threatening and violence-emerging, as well as criminal and mundane everyday situations. Novel visual and multimedia data, like cell phone recordings uploaded online, provide an immense and daily increasing data pool. For instance, more than 300 hours of new content are uploaded on YouTube every minute (as of 2018, see also Mahler, 2014), many documenting real-life social situations and interactions. Visual data on natural behavior increases by the minute through filming drones, smartphones, GoPro cameras, and body cameras (such as used by some police units), among other devices. They record events from births to funerals, from concerts to mass panics, from religious ceremonies to sexual intercourse, from public harassment to police shootings of unarmed civilians. The year 2017 witnessed the first instances of people live-streaming committing a murder. In short, recordings capture mundane as well as exceptional human behavior in steadily increasing numbers (Nassauer and Legewie, 2018).

In addition, more than 245 million closed-circuit television (CCTV) cameras installed worldwide capture situations in public and private places (Lien and Dave, 2016). They record ordinary behavior, such as people standing in line or entering the subway, as well as extraordinary behavior, such as people fighting in front of a pub (Levine et al., 2011) or reacting to an earthquake. Online video platforms such as LiveLeak prominently feature CCTV footage, making such data pieces on human behavior globally available for every person with Internet access and allowing researchers to share their data with interested readers and researchers around the globe (see Chapter 9).

This pool of video data on various events grows by the minute and can provide insights into how protests unfold. More than 5,700 videos existed as of July 2017, for instance, on YouTube about the June 2007 Rostock protest alone. They allow tracking who was where when, doing what, and responding with what consequences (see Appendix B). Some recordings are only a few seconds long; others last hours. Some cover only a specific situation; others are shots of the whole march passing by. Some were recorded by police, protesters, and bystanders; others originated from the media or professional filmmakers. Recordings by documentary filmmakers, activists, observers, and journalists uploaded online can also provide details on how uprisings evolve and what actions and interactions police and protesters engage in prior to violence breaking out.

CCTV recordings of robberies uploaded on Internet platforms such as YouTube or LiveLeak allow a researcher to get first-hand insights into the black box of situational criminal behavior. On YouTube 143,000 videos could be found as of July 2017 when looking for "robbery CCTV," with LiveLeak showing similar numbers. While researchers need to ensure that no relevant situations are cut from the recordings (which can be possible for example through checking the time indicated in the CCTV recording) and that uploaded videos display natural behavior and are not in any way staged (through, for instance, checking the reliablity of uploaders and favoring reliable sources, such as the Los Angeles Police Department or the *Guardian*), these data allow researchers to gain invaluable new insights into situational dynamics, interaction, and emotions during criminal events (for further details, see Nassauer, 2018b).

In particular, when studying chaotic and emotional events, like violence or events with various actors, but also when particularly interested in second-by-second dynamics, visual data can be key to determining what happened during an event. They allow analysis of what the visual captures about situational dynamics of human social life (Nassauer and Legewie, 2018) and can be used to trace situations or events step by step regarding aspects such as persons' movements, field of vision, and exchange of glances or gestures, as well as people's emotion expressions and body postures in order to explain a specific process or outcome. The vast advantage of visual data is further increased when used together with other types of data for reconstructing and analyzing events (Nassauer and Legewie, 2018). For example, when studying protest events, several videos can show the same situation from various angles; documents can further back up what happened. Triangulation might complete a situational analysis; police radio traffic transcriptions might show which police unit knew what, at which time and place, and give vital insights into interpretations by officers. Document data might also provide evidence on background factors of an event, for instance, which police strategy was planned (see also Appendix B).

While video data uploaded online can be widely shared and favors high transparency, ethical concerns apply (Legewie and Nassauer, 2018). Since people filmed in most videos uploaded online could not consent to the footage being used for research purposes (in some cases not even to the recording being uploaded), researchers need to weigh the ethical risks and benefits of using footage for a study. Relevant aspects are potential harm to study subjects, potential benefits to research, whether the events captured and the online platforms they were uploaded to are public or private, and the role of transparency in the research process (for details, see Legewie and Nassauer, 2018; see also Fujii, 2012; Unger, Narimani, and M´Bayo, 2014).

Through analysis of recently available visual data that capture situations as they happened and a triangulation with various types of document data (as well as participant observation and interviews), this book provides an account of how and why violence can erupt even in marches for peace, takes a close-up look at how violence emerges in uprisings in the United States, and describes how robberies unfold and may fail against all odds.

APPENDIX B | Methodological Notes on Studying Protest Violence

H OW AND WHY DOES PROTEST violence emerge? Which roles do situational dynamics versus background factors play in their emergence? To analyze the emergence of protest violence, I formulated a working hypothesis based on the in-depth analysis of four cases (see Table B1): *The emergence of violence in protests can be explained consistently and comprehensively by the situational unfolding of the protest (from its beginning to end).* More specifically, I assume that interactions between protesters and police officers that emerge during demonstrations provide a consistent and comprehensive explanation of the emergence of protest violence. These interactions operate as mechanisms[1] of violence, and combinations of interactions operate as paths (or processes[2]) to violence by leading to a reinterpretation of the event, one's own role, and the role of the other group. They thereby raise tension and fear sharply, and violence emerges when one side establishes emotional dominance over the other. People do not plan these specific combinations of mechanisms, but they emerge in the interaction dynamic. This assumption is supported in the analysis if: (1) interactions relevant to the outcome in multiple case studies are identified; (2) an analysis of these interactions reveals paths for the emergence of violence across a random sample of demonstrations that explain the outcome consistently and comprehensively; (3) subsequent re-analysis of the cases untangles the mechanisms that connect interactions and their combinations with the emergence of violence; and (4) an analysis of background factors shows no systematic connection to the outcome.

I examined my working hypothesis based on a systematic comparison of randomly selected cases. I employed a variety of data sources and analytic techniques to

---

[1] A mechanism is a "delimited class of events that alter relations among specified sets of elements in identical or closely similar ways over a variety of situations" (Tilly and Tarrow, 2006, p.24). Mechanisms can compound into processes.

[2] Processes are "regular combinations and sequences of mechanisms that produce similar transformations of those elements" (Tilly and Tarrow, 2006, p.24).

TABLE B1 Protests Studied

NO.	VIOLENCE (1, YES; —, NO)	UNITED STATES (PROTEST ISSUE, CITY, YEAR)	NO.	VIOLENCE (1, YES; —, NO)	GERMANY (PROTEST ISSUE, CITY, YEAR)
Initial case	1	World Trade Organization (WTO) meeting, Seattle, 1999	Initial case	1	Group of Eight (G8) meeting, Rostock, 2007
Initial case	1	Free Trade of the Americas meeting, Miami, 2003	Initial case	1	Asia-Europe meeting (ASEM), Hamburg, 2007
01	1	Rutgers University, New Brunswick, NJ, 1995	14	1	Nuclear power plant, Wilstermarsch, 1981
02	0	Washington Peace March, Washington, DC, 1971	15	1	US Cambodia invasion, Berlin, 1970
03	1	Tompkins curfew and gentrification, New York City, 1988	16	0	City politics and gentrification, Hamburg, 2009
04	0	Iraq Invasion, Washington, DC, 2002	17	0	North Atlantic Treaty Organization (NATO), Kehl, 2009
05	0	Group of 20 (G20), Pittsburgh, 2009	18	0	Migrant's rights, Rostock, 2007
06	1	International Monetary Fund (IMF) and WTO, Washington, DC, 2000	19	1	Education policies, Hannover, 2008
07	1	IMF, Washington DC, 2003	20	1	Education fees, Frankfurt, 2008
08	1	Republican National Convention (RNC), Saint Paul, MN, 2008	21	1	NATO, Munich, 2003
09	0	Iraq War, San Francisco, 2003	22	1	Social service cuts, Frankfurt, 2007
10	0	RNC, New York City, 2004	23	0	Education policies, Frankfurt, 2009
11	1	Bush administration, Portland, 2002	24	1	Springer Press and Vietnam War, Berlin, 1968
12	0	Iraq War, Washington, DC, 2007	25	0	Emergency laws, Bonn, 1968
13	1	Vietnam War, Washington, DC, 1967	26	0	Gorleben nuclear power plant, Hannover, 1979

study background factors for violence, such as police strategy, attendance of violently motivated protesters, or expectations of violence, as well as situational dynamics, i.e., what happened between the beginning of the march and the end.

Case Selection and Sampling

I focus on an unlikely case of protest violence: demonstration marches of left protest groups in two Western democracies (Germany and the United States) from the 1960s through 2010. The outcome of violence in these cases is unlikely in several regards: (1) violence is generally unlikely (Collins, 2008); (2) traditionally, social movements are *the* peaceful form of claim-making (Tilly and Tarrow, 2006); (3) protest marches are even more unlikely to turn violent than more confrontational social movement performances such as squatting or sit-ins; and (4) left social movement protests in the United States and Germany are, with regard to protest policing as well as protest repertoire, generally more peaceful than in other countries. This makes the eruption of violence in these marches all the more surprising.

Graham and Gurr (1969, p. 789) remark that modern protests are unlikely to become violent, since the associational form gives the group better control over its actions and allows it to show force without using physical violence. Protesters have alternatives—of which violence leads in the fewest cases to success and is therefore a last resort (Graham and Gurr, 1969). In terms of the empirical frequency of violent demonstrations, Della Porta (1995, p. 216) stresses that violent protest events in Western democracies are by far outnumbered by non-violent protest events. As an example, Fillieule and Jobard (1998, p. 70) report that in the 1990s in France, only about 5 percent of all demonstrations became violent "in the form of destruction of public/ private property or attacks to other persons." Further, protest violence in Germany and the United States is less frequent than in France or Italy, let alone non-Western democracies. In the United States injuries or property damage occurred in only 2 percent of protests from 1970 to 2000 (McAdam, Tarrow, and Tilly, 2001, p. 9). If we apply my definition of violence as including only physical attacks on other persons, these numbers drop further (see Chapter 1). Moreover, protest marches are less likely to turn violent than more confrontational protest techniques, and protests by moderate protests groups are less likely to turn violent than protests by radical groups (Fyfe, 1991; Marx, 1998; Waddington, 1998). Still, there are incidents where violence does occur. These instances therefore comprise a puzzling exception to the rule. They are meaningful because they may be caused by mechanisms that are especially powerful in leading to violence even in these "unfavorable" settings.[3] In more technical terms, studying large-scale marches in Western democracies comprises "deviant cases" (i.e., cases showing a "surprising value," here violence). Deviant cases are well suited for developing new explanations for an outcome such as violence (see Gerring, 2010, p. 647).

Within this sample, I compared the United States and Germany as two "most-similar" cases. A most-similar case selection design is common in exploratory analyses or initial

---

[3] Future analyses of protest marches in contexts more favorable to the emergence of violence may be highly fruitful, since they may reveal additional relevant factors.

stages of research (Gerring, 2010, p. 667), such as in my study: identifying novel situational patterns for surprising social outcomes. A most-similar design limits variation in factors outside the analytic focus: in my study, the political system, i.e., Western democratic countries; protesters repertoires, i.e., marches; and police organization, i.e., rather decentralized police forces in Germany and the United States. Simultaneously a most-similar design incorporates variation in outcome and relevant factors (e.g., attending protest groups, claims, policing, situational factors). Among protests in the United States and Germany, I sampled cases from 1960 through 2010 to study the influence of different policing strategies and protest claims in different time periods. I included only demonstration marches that were sanctioned (either prior or ad hoc) in the analysis. I compared large-scale protest marches of movements that occurred simultaneously in the United States and Germany (e.g., student movement, hippie movement, environmentalist movement, global justice movement), while movements specific to one country (e.g., protests taking place in the German Democratic Republic, 1949–1990, and civil rights protests in the United States in the 1960s and 1970s) were not included in the analysis due to my scope conditions.

For protests in Germany and the United States, I used a combination of case selection and sampling techniques to conduct both initial in-depth case studies to identify interactions and systematic cross-case comparisons to study my working hypothesis. I used two samples. I first selected four protests with the greatest data availability to ensure a maximum depth of insight into interaction dynamics (Blatter, 2012). I used these four cases to identify interactions that both influenced emotional dynamics and occurred systematically prior to the emergence of violence during demonstrations. The first sample of cases was thus used to develop concepts of situational factors relevant to violence grounded in the data (Corbin and Strauss, 1990).

To study whether my working hypothesis holds and whether interactions identified in the first sample provide a consistent and comprehensive explanation of violence during demonstrations, I then employed random sampling of a larger Excel-based database. Each row in the spreadsheet represented one demonstration march and had the same probability of being selected. This procedure was not meant to produce a representative sample of a larger population of cases. Instead, the idea was to examine my working hypothesis based on cases that were monitored only regarding scope conditions prior to the analysis. The random sample was drawn from two media archive databases and two datasets and yielded 109 demonstration marches. I employed Lexis Nexis and Factiva, the PRODAT dataset (Wissenschaftszentrum Berlin für Sozialforschung, 2011), and The Dynamics of Collective Action dataset (Stanford University, 2009). From this pool of potential candidates for analysis, I randomly selected 26 cases. The full sample was 30 protests: 18 violent and 12 peaceful, 15 per country (see Table B1). The peaceful cases serve as a comparison group; if factors occur in both positive and negative cases, they are likely to have little explanatory value. I selected a medium-N sample of 30 cases to allow a very detailed in-depth analysis of each case, while also allowing a systematic comparison of similarities and differences across cases (see Ragin, 1994).

Video Data Analysis

To reconstruct and analyze protest events, I employed video data analysis (VDA; Nassauer and Legewie, 2018). VDA relies on visual data that capture events in order to trace situations or events step by step to explain a process or outcome. The approach focuses on aspects such as people's actions and interactions, movements, exchanges of glances or gestures, facial expressions, and body postures.

The outcome in my study, physical interpersonal violence, was defined as a physical action that injures or kills a person. I coded a protest as violent if I found visuals or accounts of actors injuring or killing another person by (1) throwing an object, (2) using harmful devices (e.g., tear gas or Taser), or (3) hitting or kicking another person. The focus is not on isolated incidents but rather on *situations* turning violent, that is, numerous acts of physical violence in the sense of more than 10 people hitting or kicking each other during a protest. Empirical cases of these protest groups usually either show no or very isolated instances of individuals shoving each other or large-scale violence with many more than 10 people involved. This narrow concept of physical violence facilitates a clearer, more nuanced analysis. For instance, it allows studying whether other types of actions commonly labeled "violent," such as property damage, influence the emergence of physical interpersonal violence.

In the first step of analysis, I used VDA in the first sample of four initial cases to identify interactions and develop concepts grounded in the data that would later be translated as conditions into qualitative comparative analysis (see below). All factors that could impact a violent outcome were only coded as potential factors if they occurred before violence broke out.

Video Data and Triangulation

Testing the explanatory potential of situational dynamics for protest violence and comparing them to potentially relevant background factors places strong demands on data, which must be very detailed to allow reconstructions of protest events and provide context on events. They must provide undistorted information regarding interactions as they occurred during demonstrations and on emotional states people experienced at various times during the event. They must safeguard against observer bias and both post-event omissions and embellishment from participants (Nassauer and Legewie, 2018). Standard data for detailed case reconstructions would include interviews, media accounts, and participant observations (see, e.g., Drury and Reicher, 2000; Fernandez, 2005; Gillham and Noakes, 2007). Yet these data do not capture the information needed for the research question examined here (see Appendix A). Most importantly, they do not provide the extensive information on emotional and interactional dynamics of all situations during a protest necessary for the analysis. As discussed throughout the book, videos and pictures allow studying interactions by preserving the essence of how they occurred (Knoblauch et al., 2006, p. 11; Luckmann, 2006, p. 31). If they show people's faces and body postures, they can also provide information on their emotional states.

To analyze situational dynamics of events, Collins (2016b, p. 82) suggests that in the current state of visual research, "it is best to collect everything possible, all images available from all sources." In addition, I found it useful to triangulate not only visual data, but all data available on an event that could help reconstruct how it unfolded in meticulous detail. Triangulating visual data (i.e., photographs and videos recorded by journalists, police, protesters, bystanders, and documentarians) and document data is ideal for a detailed reconstruction of events in which instances need to be confirmed by various sources to balance potential bias of single sources (Nassauer and Legewie, 2018).

Data triangulation can provide a safeguard against potential observer (i.e., recorder) bias. Thus, I used a great number of sources for visual footage, offering the opportunity to observe the same situation from various angles. For each case I then supplemented visual data with a variety of other types of data: (1) court data that reconstructs an event due to alleged violent attacks; (2) police reports on and (if available) transcripts of police radio communication during protest operations; (3) official statements of protest groups and participants' reports; (4) media content such as news reports and articles; (5) reconstructions from other scientists; and (6) information from photographers and videographers regarding events they recorded. These data types are especially relevant in cases prior to the 1990s, where visual data are less abundant. Videos, pictures, and accounts from police, protesters, media, and other observers on every point in time cross-validated each other. By assembling visual and other data like a puzzle, I could determine the unfolding of events in detail (see Figure 2, Introduction).

For the four initial cases, I analyzed an average of 50 visual data pieces and 50 document data pieces in order to filter interactions and emotion expressions crucial for the emergence of protest violence. For the additional 16 cases, I examined an average of 15 pieces of document data and 20 pieces of visual data. In none of the cases did fewer than 10 pieces of data exist. For all coding of video and document data, the software atlas.ti was employed.

To assemble video data, I drew heavily on Internet sources such as YouTube and Flickr, open-access websites to which anyone can upload videos or pictures. A researcher can easily find data from a variety of authors regarding an event since users entitle, describe, and tag their videos and pictures. Data collection using the Internet is not only time efficient, it also offers a growing pool of visual data due to increasing dissemination and use of recording technologies (Nassauer and Legewie, 2018; see also Legewie and Nassauer, 2018).

Analytic Procedure

Following my working hypothesis, key to identifying relevant interactions was to determine if and when an emotional change occurred and then work my way back from these changes to see what interactions prompted them. Employing video data analysis, I reconstructed each protest march in great detail, constructing a tempo-spatial matrix for each event from beginning to end or until violence erupted. In a later step, I examined whether the identified interactions impacted a violent outcome regardless of emotional dynamics (see qualitative comparative analysis).

For each of the four initial cases, I reconstructed interactions and emotional dynamics in meticulous detail, asking who was when where, doing what, and with what consequences. Figure B1 illustrates such a case reconstruction for the Rostock G8 protest, 2007: Throughout the protest I coded place and time of interactions and emotional dynamics, to then be able to systematically analyze if I find patterns across a randomly sampled set of cases.

In the four initial cases, a first focus was to determine when an emotional change occurred in accordance with Collins's (2008) micro-sociology of violent confrontations.

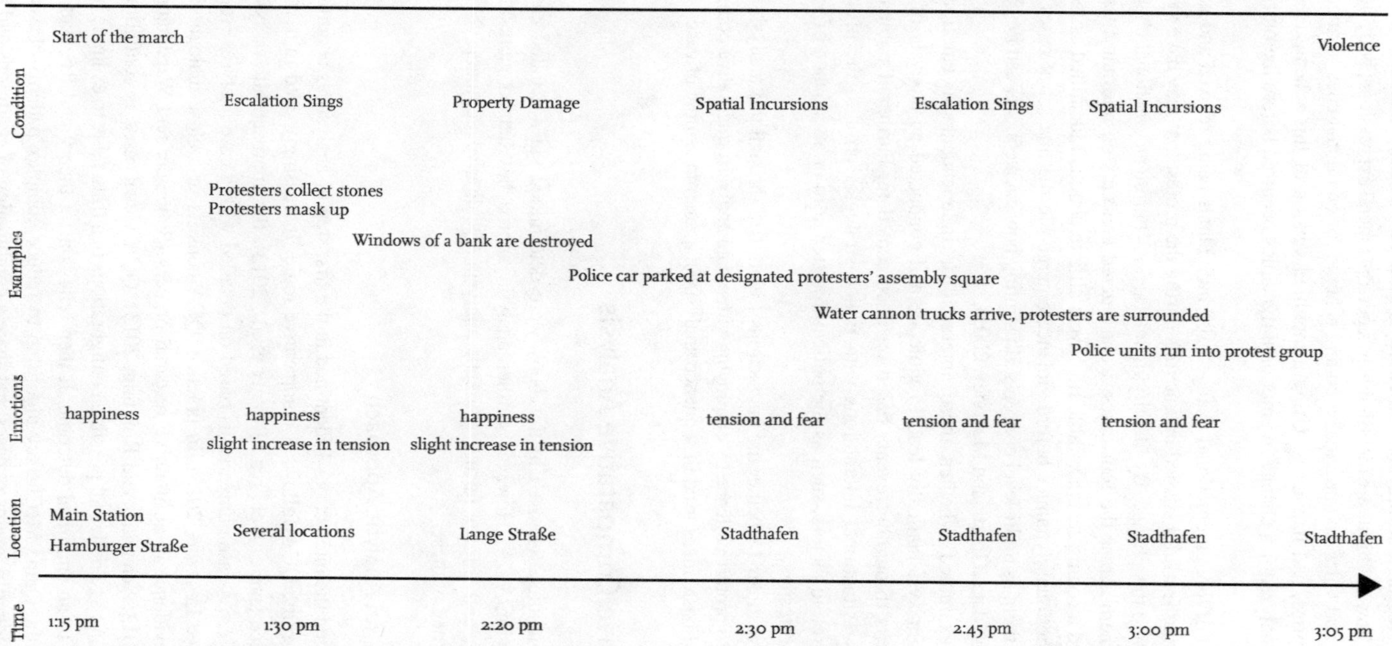

Condition	Start of the march	Escalation Sings	Property Damage	Spatial Incursions	Escalation Sings	Spatial Incursions	Violence
Examples		Protesters collect stones / Protesters mask up	Windows of a bank are destroyed	Police car parked at designated protesters' assembly square	Water cannon trucks arrive, protesters are surrounded	Police units run into protest group	
Emotions	happiness	happiness / slight increase in tension	happiness / slight increase in tension	tension and fear	tension and fear	tension and fear	
Location	Main Station / Hamburger Straße	Several locations	Lange Straße	Stadthafen	Stadthafen	Stadthafen	Stadthafen
Time	1:15 pm	1:30 pm	2:20 pm	2:30 pm	2:45 pm	3:00 pm	3:05 pm

FIGURE B1. Case Reconstruction Example, Rostock G8 Protest, 2007

I relied on Klusemann's (2009) coding scheme the author adapted from Ekman et al.'s (1972, 2003) research on universal emotions to code emotion expression. Ekman et al. (1972) show how emotions are identifiable in a person's facial expressions, body postures, movements, and voice and provides a coding scheme for emotional cues of anger, fear, sadness, surprise, and happiness. Using a modified version of this scheme (see Table B2), I first analyzed if a change in emotional dynamics occurred before the outbreak of violence.

After identifying an emotional change from individuals being relaxed and happy to being tense and fearful, I studied interactions during the protest that may have systematically prompted this change. By identifying interactions before an emotional change and comparing them across the four cases, I constructed concepts on relevant interactions and produced a coding scheme. Table B3 covers all interactions I identified as factors in changing emotional dynamics before violence emerged in the first set of cases. Figure B2 displays them as multi-level concepts, illustrating how each concept can be observed directly in the data (Goertz and Mahoney, 2005).

I then examined whether these interactions, independent of emotional dynamics, might systematically lead to violence and conducted an analysis of actors' interpretations throughout events based on document data. Further, I compared the role of these situational interactions with police strategies prior to the protest and other background factors, such as the police:protester ratio or attendance of violently motivated protesters.

I later investigated whether the interactions I identified through this analysis systematically led to protest violence by employing video data analysis, qualitative comparative analysis, and basic ideas used in sequence analysis in a random sample of cases.

Qualitative Comparative Analysis

The key dynamics discussed in this book were determined via a detailed case analysis employing VDA. However, further analytic approaches helped gain additional perspectives and inform further in-depth analysis. Qualitative comparative analysis (QCA) was one of these.

QCA as an Analytic Approach

I translated the interactions I identified in the first step of analysis as conditions into QCA. Generally, QCA follows a comparative logic. Increasingly used in a variety of social science studies (see, e.g., Rihoux et al., 2013), the approach allows systematic, formalized, cross-case comparisons based on detailed within-case analyses (for a good overview, see Legewie, 2013). In practice, QCA consists of a close dialogue between ideas and evidence in an iterative research process (Schneider and Wagemann, 2012; Legewie, 2013; Schneider and Rohlfing, 2013). QCA views cases as configurations of conditions and assembles all possible configurations in a truth table to examine how they correspond to an empirical outcome. It then relies on set theory and Boolean algebra, employing the Quine-McCluskey algorithm to reduce complex patterns of association in data and identify groups of cases that share a combination of conditions and agree on

TABLE B2 Coding Scheme on Emotion Expression

EMOTION EXPRESSION	SPECIFICATION	CODING EXAMPLES	CODING RULES
Anger	Facial and bodily expressions and/or voice indicate that the person is angry toward/about someone or something.	*Face and Body Language:* Brows lowered and drawn together; tensed upper and lower lids; direct hard gaze; lips firmly pressed together or open and tensed; clenched fists; moving firmly.	Anger can be distinguished from fear and sadness, as it is visibly a more active emotional state. Anger can overlap with acting confidently (and from a strong power position); can be distinguished based on context information.
Fear	Facial and bodily expressions and/or voice indicate person is fearful toward/about someone or something.	*Face and Body Language:* brows raised and drawn together; wrinkles in center of forehead; raised upper eyelids; raised and tense lower eyelids; open mouth; drawn back, tensed, or stretched lips; avoiding gaze (head down or turned to side, lowering and closing eyes); struggle for control; hand touches or covers face, eyes, mouth; postures and movements shrinking; fumbling (fingering of the clothing; twisting of the fingers).	Fear can be distinguished from anger and happiness, as it is visibly a more passive emotional state. Fear can be distinguished from sadness based on context information and body movements: in sadness the body is less tense, and usually less hectic movements occur than in fear.
Sadness	Facial and bodily expressions and/or voice indicate that the person is sad about someone or something.	*Body Language, Face:* Inner corners of eyebrows are drawn up; upper eyelid corner is raised; corners of the lips are down or the lip is trembling; shrinking body posture; struggle for control; hand touches or covers face or eyes.	Sadness can be distinguished from anger and happiness, as it is visibly a more passive emotional state. Sadness can be distinguished from fear based on context information and body movements. In sadness the body is less tense and usually less hectic movements occur than in fear.
Surprise	Facial and bodily expressions and/or voice indicate that the person is surprised about someone or something.	*Face:* Raised brows (curved and high); skin below the brow is stretched; horizontal wrinkles across the forehead; eyelids opened (no tenseness); jaw drops open so that lips and teeth are parted but no tension or stretching of mouth as in fear.	Surprise can be distinguished from fear and sadness, as it is visibly a more active emotional state. To differentiate surprise from fear, I rely on context information and body movements: fear tends to go hand in hand with shrinking body postures, or struggle for control.
Happiness	Facial and bodily expressions and/or voice indicate that the person is happy about someone or something.	*Body Language:* Moving closer to each other; group laughter; body contact; relaxed body posture. *Face:* mutual eye contact (no gaze aversion); lip corners raised diagonally; muscles around the eyes tightened; wrinkles around the eyes; cheeks raised.	Happiness can be distinguished from fear and sadness, as it is visibly a more active emotional state. Happiness can be differentiated from surprise and fear relying on context information. The actors' facial expressions are more relaxed.

TABLE B3 Coding Scheme on Interactions

INTERACTION	SPECIFICATION	CODING EXAMPLES	CODING RULES
Communication Problems	No regularly functioning communication between police and protesters due to: – technical problems (interrupted or acoustically not clearly understandable) or – content problems (unclear information and orders)	– "Unfortunately we currently have no contact with the police" (announcement from demonstration organizers at rally main stage, Rostock) – Orders to disperse not understandable (Miami)	One of two aspects has to be present before the outbreak of violence for the factor to be coded as present. It has to be indicated that communication was interrupted or seriously delayed at some point between the start of the demonstration and the emergence of violence or the end of the demonstration.
Property Damage	Protesters damage property	– Windows of a bank are smashed (Rostock, Seattle) – Stores are destroyed (Seattle)	Data has to show property damage by protesters during the demonstration before the outbreak of violence for the factor to be coded as present. Different from escalation signs in that protesters not only prepare for such actions but actually cause damage
Spatial Incursions	One side: – loses control over the space that was assigned to them – advances into the space which is assigned / perceived to be the space of the other group	– Police "lose control of the area" (Seattle) – Police run into protesters' assembly space (Rostock) – Protesters try to enter the "no-protest zone" (Miami)	One of the aspects has to be present before the outbreak of violence for the factor to be coded as present. Different from property damage as no property damage occurs, but spaces are physically occupied, for the factor to be coded as present. Different from escalation signs as spatial struggles are excluded from the condition.

| Police Mismanagement | A) Poor planning and leadership 1) Officers in the field note that they do not get sufficient support from leading staff, in terms of:
– logistics and satisfaction of basic needs (food, rest)

– support in conducting the operation (no supporting units are sent, officers are not allowed to search protesters for weapons, etc.)

2) Operational command:
– lacks strategy and overview over operation
– does not know where to deploy officers as it is not up to speed with recent developments

B) Communication problems among police. No regularly functioning communication of the police, due to:
– technical problems (interrupted or acoustically not clearly understandable)
or
– content problems (unclear information and orders) | – No backup strategy, no adequate planning; "we have no strategy" (field officer, Seattle)
– "There is no unified command" (field officer, Miami)
– Units are surprised to meet other units in certain parts of the city (Rostock)
– Average working time of 16–22 hours; average time to rest: 4–6 hours; lunchboxes have to suffice for 16 hours (Rostock)
– No information that CS gas is mixed into water tank's water, so that units could have put on gas masks (Rostock)

– Technical problems with communication: too much radio traffic (Seattle), announcements are acoustically difficult to understand (Rostock), communication breakdown (Seattle), or only half of the agencies have the same radio frequency (Miami)

– No information on general situation or development of the situation by leadership (Tompkins)
– No communication about how to proceed (Rostock) | One of the two secondary-level aspects has to be present in the data before the outbreak of violence for the factor to be coded as present.

It has to be noted that management problems occurred, communication was interrupted or suffered notable time delays at some point between the start of the demonstration and the emergence of violence/end of the protest. |

(continued)

TABLE B3 Continued

INTERACTION	SPECIFICATION	CODING EXAMPLES	CODING RULES
Escalation Signs	One side receives knowledge about actions of the other side, which are interpreted as indicating an escalation. – police officers perceive actions of protesters as preparation for breaking the law or for a physical attack – protesters perceive actions of police officers as preparations for arrests or for a physical attack	– Police observe protesters collecting stones, masking up, and carrying steel poles (Rostock, Seattle) – Police hear rumors of protesters preparing for trouble (Seattle) – Protesters observe police masking up (Rostock) – Protesters see police quickly approaching them for no apparent reason (Rostock)	One of the two secondary-level aspects has to be present in the data before the outbreak of violence for the factor to be coded as present. Different from spatial incursions as they are not included in this condition. Different from communication problems between protesters and police (where the absence of knowledge might also lead to the assumption of an escalation) in terms of getting certain knowledge, which then leads to the conclusion that the situation escalates. Different from property damage as the assumed preparation for property damage, or a different action, is coded as a sign for escalation. If property damage occurs, it is coded as such and not as escalation sign.

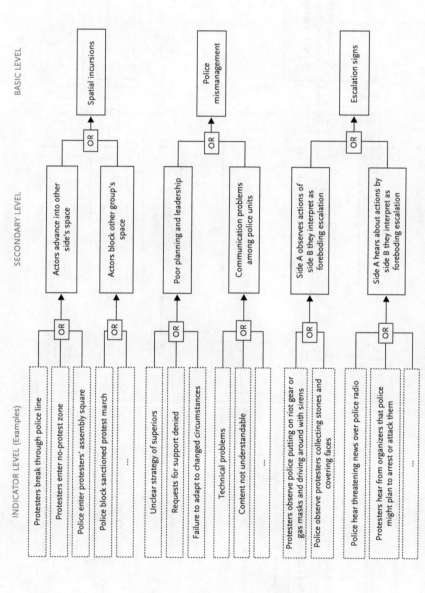

FIGURE B2. Schematic Representation of Two-Level Concepts of Interactions

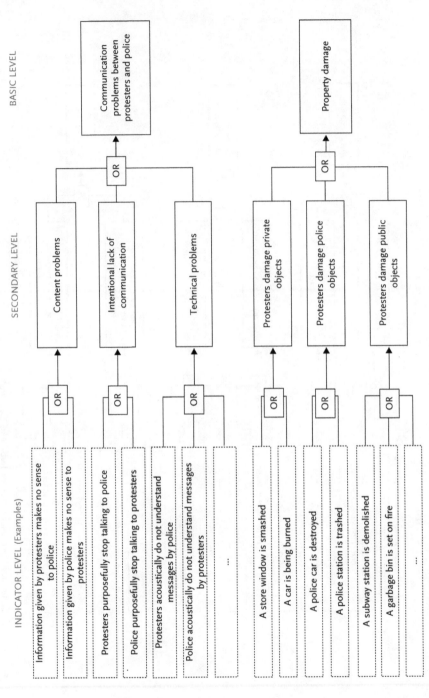

Figure B2. (Continued)

outcomes.[4] Employing anchored calibration in QCA (Legewie, 2017) can help researchers formulate explicit concept structures and coding rules. Anchored calibration relies on conceptualizing conditions and outcome(s) in a systematic framework, anchoring this framework with empirical data pieces, and using the anchored framework to assign membership scores to cases—a crucial research step in QCA studies (see Legewie, 2017).

QCA is uniquely suited to examine my working hypothesis. First, it identifies patterns in medium-sized data sets in the form of combinations of conditions sufficient for an outcome. This allows moving beyond analysis of single interactions between protesters and police officers to focus on whether interactions combine to produce an outcome. Second, QCA allows analyzing whether interactions consistently and comprehensively explain the emergence of violence. It offers formal tests of the consistency with which a combination of conditions produces an outcome and examines associations in terms of necessary and sufficient causes. Consistency is calculated as the proportion of cases with outcome Y present that are consistent with condition X being sufficient for Y. Consistency drops below 1.0 if any case in the data set deviates from a combination of interactions being sufficient for an outcome (for a broader discussion, see A. Marx, 2006; Rihoux, 2009, p. 375). I regarded any value below perfect consistency for one or more combinations of interactions as insufficient to support my working hypothesis.

Comprehensiveness was measured using the coverage of cases. QCA provides a formal test to assess how many cases are explained by a combination of conditions. A combined coverage score below 1 for the combinations of interactions identified by QCA would mean one or more cases were not explained through interactions, rejecting my hypothesis that interactional dynamics can systematically explain the outcome (Schneider and Wagemann, 2007).

I used dichotomous crisp set QCA (Ragin, 1987, 2008) to test my working hypothesis and identify combinations of interactions that inform subsequent within-case analyses in the third step of analysis. Crisp sets are more useful for this study than fuzzy sets, since I am not interested in the intensity of violence. The research question is about distinction in kind, not degree; does violence emerge (1) or does it not (0)? As fuzzy logic of violence introduces theoretical assumptions irrelevant to this research question, a crisp logic promises to produce sharper and clearer results in my study. I employed anchored calibration (Legewie, 2017) to carve out and reflect on potential grey areas between the presence and absence of a condition and formulate transparent coding rules (see also Winter and Kron, 2009).

Selected QCA Results on Protest Violence

Results of the QCA analysis suggest that three combinations of the five interactions (so-called conditions) form alternative paths to violence. These paths were identified in the QCA of 26 random cases and remained stable when running QCA on all 30 cases. This

---

[4] Lucas and Szatrowski (2014) claim that QCA produces a high rate of false positives. Other scholars question this critique (Fiss, Marx, and Rihoux, 2014; Ragin, 2014; Vaisey, 2014), arguing that the authors fail to grasp essential aspects of QCA. Yet Lucas and Szatrowski refer to studies in which researchers do not revisit the cases for a qualitative analysis of the QCA results. Since this reassessment of the cases forms a crucial part of the analysis in this paper, the issue does not apply to this study.

TABLE B4 QCA Paths to Violence

PATHWAYS TO VIOLENCE		CASES COVERED (RAW COVERAGE)	CASES EXPLAINABLE BY PATHWAY ONLY (UNIQUE COVERAGE)	CONSISTENCY
Spatial Incursions and Police Mismanagement		78%	28%	1.0
Spatial Incursions and Escalation Signs and Property Damage		50%	07%	1.0
Spatial Incursions and Escalation Signs and Communication Problems		42%	14%	1.0
Solution Consistency	1.0			
Solution Coverage	1.0			

finding was confirmed in subsequent in-depth case analysis: (1) a loss of control path in which spatial incursions and police mismanagement combine; (2) a missing information path in which spatial incursions lead to violence when combined with escalation signs and communication problems between protesters and police; and (3) an offense path in which spatial incursions combine with escalation signs and property damage. A comparison of the two countries shows that the same conditions and paths operate in both countries.

Table B4 summarizes the QCA results. It shows tests for consistency and coverage of the three paths. All three paths are perfectly consistent with sufficiency for the outcome. This indicates that the conditions in these cases are systematically related to the emergence of violence, no cases deviate from the three paths, and the interactions identified in the first phase of the case analysis produce a consistent explanation of the outcome. None of the three paths suggest contradictions (see solution consistency of 1 in Table B4), and the combined coverage of 1 for the three paths (i.e., the solution coverage in Table B4) demonstrates that the five interactions account for the emergence of violence in all cases in the sample. These findings support my working hypothesis.

The analysis shows that a combination of police mismanagement and spatial incursions in the loss of control path is the most common path to violence in my sample. The path explains the emergence of violence in 78 percent of cases. The second path explains 50 percent, and the third 42 percent (see Table B4).[5] Twenty-eight percent of the cases are explained uniquely by the first path (i.e., they cannot be explained by a path other than the first), 7 percent are uniquely explained by the second, and 14 percent by the third. In short, QCA provides strong support for my working hypothesis. Using QCA's strength of combining formalized cross-case comparisons with in-depth case studies (Legewie, 2013), results can help uncover how these three paths and their component interactions lead to violent confrontations.

---

[5] Adding percentages of the single paths, total coverage exceeds 100 percent because some cases can be explained by more than one path. Paths overlapped, and in several cases the emergence of

Identifying Mechanisms and Processes to Violence

While QCA thus helped identify patterns, the findings are largely based on qualitative in-depth analysis using video data analysis (Nassauer and Legewie, 2018). After employing QCA, I used subsequent case analysis to determine whether the identified combinations of interactions provide a convincing and comprehensive explanation of the violent cases in my dataset. Together with analytic approaches such as qualitative content analysis (Mayring, 2007), process tracing (Gerring and Thomas, 2006; Blatter, 2012), and video data analysis (Nassauer and Legewie, 2018), QCA results can be used to unravel causal mechanisms and processes that systematically lead to an outcome (Legewie, 2013). The identification of turning points and "smoking-gun observations" can buttress the claim of a causal connection, while causality always needs to rest on the underlying theories used by a researcher (Blatter, 2012; Collins, 2016b; Nassauer and Legewie, 2018).

The third step of analysis identified these five interactions to be mechanisms and their combinations to be processes to protest violence. In these processes different combinations of mechanisms interactively determine the outcome. In all cases with the outcome (violence), one of the three combinations systematically changed interpretations and increased tensions and fear, as described throughout Chapters 3 to 6.

Sequence Analysis

Further, I drew on notions of sequence analysis (Abbott, 1992; see Abbott and Tsay, 2000; Aisenbrey and Fasang, 2010) to study if specific temporal sequences of interactions can systematically produce violence. Sequence analysis is a method to explore what sequence regularities can tell us about social life (Abbott, 1995, p. 109). I created empirical sequence types and assigned a sequence to every violently ending case. I isolated sequence types in which the general order of conditions is kept (i.e., conditions could drop out but the order had to remain the same). By forming sequence types, I was able to look for similarities and differences within and across the resulting groups of sequences. This analysis allowed studying if the temporal order of identified combinations of conditions influences a violent outcome. I did not employ optimal matching and cluster analysis, as would be the case in a full-blown sequence analysis. Yet such an analysis, based on larger numbers of cases, could be highly fruitful to further explore the role of sequential patterns in protest events and other surprising outcomes.

Participant Observation and Interviews

As further sources of information, I relied on interviews and participant observation. I interviewed protesters, journalists, and protest observers about specific protest events.

---

violence can be explained by multiple paths, as the Seattle 1999 protest illustrated. This clustering of conditions in cases is a common phenomenon (Ragin, 2008, p. 147), indicating cases are overdetermined and several dynamics operate in a single case.

I contacted activists who had uploaded footage on YouTube and residents who had uploaded pictures on Flickr, asking them for additional assessments on the protests they captured. I interviewed a member of a German human rights organization via phone on her assessment of the Rostock G8 events and contacted organizers, journalists and documentary film makers to gain additional information on specific incidents.

To gain further insights into police planning and implementation of protest operations, I conducted participant observation with Berlin police in spring of 2017. I observed operation planning at the highest level of Berlin crowd policing forces (the operations department, "Direktion Einsatz") as well as implementation during several operations. I observed officers' daily routines over the course of two weeks in March 2017 and accompanied Berlin police to two protests that were said to have a high risk of turning violent in April and May. I revisited the department in 2018. During participant observation, I conducted open qualitative interviews with officers on the highest level of planning, officers employed in the front rows at crowd policing operations, unit leaders, personnel managers, officers planning operations on the communication side, and officers employed in "communication teams," among others. While Berlin police cannot be regarded as representative of German police, these insights served as background information to provide a deeper understanding of police structure and practices as well as the police's view on protest dynamics.

APPENDIX C | Methodological Notes on Studying Uprisings

W HILE I APPLIED MY ANALYTIC PROCEDURE of video data analysis (Nassauer and Legewie, 2018; see also Appendix B) to study the emergence of violence in uprisings in Ferguson and Baltimore, my analysis of these events should be understood as a first outlook on uprisings from a situational perspective, not an exhaustive analysis of the phenomenon. Further systematic research needs to analyze the role of situational versus background factors in uprisings in the United States and other countries.

Case Selection

Among potential uprisings to select, I chose Ferguson and Baltimore for several reasons. First, since they took place rather recently, much more video data are available on these instances than on uprisings in the United States in the 1960s or even the 1990s. Such videos were vital to take a detailed look at situational dynamics. Second, I compared Baltimore and Ferguson because they are two of the most prominently discussed uprisings in which the idea prevails that violent clashes were caused by background factors (racial injustice) and an event trigger (the killings of Michael Brown and Freddie Gray by US police), making them unlikely to show the situational patterns I identified. Uprisings thereby function as a "most different" case (Gerring, 2010) to the protests discussed above, making them ideal to explore the portability of the situational breakdowns argument. Further, the Ferguson and Baltimore uprisings differ in aspects of racial discrimination: in Ferguson racial discrimination was even more severe than in Baltimore (Taylor, 2016). This variation can thereby provide further insights into the role of background factors in leading to violence in uprisings.

Data and Analysis

I relied heavily on video data by protesters, media, police, and bystanders to reconstruct events, as well as media reports, protesters accounts, and documents by police[1] to gain information on the role of situational dynamics and background factors to violence. I contacted activists present at the events and documentary filmmakers filming the day of the protest, one of which answered questions via email.

Based on a triangulation of data, I employed video data analysis (Nassauer and Legewie, 2018) to reconstruct what happened throughout the event. A specific focus lay on whether interactions discussed in Chapters 1 through 8 were present or not in these instances, which emotions were displayed in facial expressions, voice, and body language, whether or not the unfolding of events mattered for a violent outcome, and what role background factors played. Yet, as these protests are usually more spontaneous than the marches discussed in Chapters 1 to 8, their beginning, end point, and spatial extent could not be grasped as clearly as in most marches. My analysis therefore provides but a cursory outlook.

Due to these events being greatly shaped by racial discrimination against people of color in the United States and my being a white person from Germany, I relied heavily on the work of my US colleagues on the topic and accounts of protesters and observers present at the events (see references in Chapter 9, see also Black Lives Matter, 2017). I reconstructed the uprisings based on these accounts, and I am thankful to Elijah Anderson and Lee Ann Fuji in particular for our talks on race and racism in the United States.

---

[1] Police reports are especially useful for assessing police mismanagment and escalations signs on the side of police. In the Ferguson uprising even the police report (U.S. Department of Justice, COPS and IIR, 2015), assessed mismanagement and escalation signs by officers. Since neither protesters nor police usually aim critique at their own group, these reports provide strong evidence for their relevance.

APPENDIX D | Methodological Notes on Studying Robberies

YouTube and CCTV Data on Crime

What happens once actors are in a criminal incident remained a black box for decades. This means their incident's internal workings were not understood since it was impossible to observe such crimes in great detail. Although commonly used data types such as participant observations and interviews with perpetrators, bystanders, and victims of crimes provided meaningful insights into criminal behavior (e.g., Athens, 1980; Wright and Decker, 1997; Lindegaard, Bernasco, and Jacques, 2015), witnesses face difficulties when it comes to recalling situational dynamics (see Appendix A). First, people have problems remembering details of everyday situations (Bernard et al., 1984, p. 509), and more so when it comes to highly emotional events (Grossman and Christensen, 2008; R. Collins, 2008). Second, interview data and document data cannot provide micro-situational details on how events unfolded second by second (LeCompte and Goetz, 1982; Bernard et al., 1984; Vrij, Hope, and Fisher, 2014, see also Appendix A).

However, in recent years many crimes have been caught on CCTV, showing how events unfold. Further, visual data have recently and increasingly been uploaded to Internet platforms such as YouTube and LiveLeak and are thus easily accessible to researchers. In contrast to CCTV obtained by police or courts, data uploaded online represent a collective good. Researchers can provide links to recordings that have been analyzed, and viewers worldwide can access the data freely. Such CCTV footage uploaded online thus allows us to observe criminal incidents first-hand. Their access via online platforms strongly favors transparency and the replicability of research findings (Nassauer and Legewie, 2018; however, see Legewie and Nassauer, 2018).

CCTV footage uploaded online allows researchers to unravel the micro-situational dynamics that underlie criminal behavior by providing frame-by-frame evidence of emotions, interactions, timing, and actors' movements in space. They thereby enable us to open the black box of crime in the making and help refine existing theories on crime by emphasizing the situational component. Because they can be shared with interested readers across the globe, online data sources allow other researchers to reproduce and verify findings, thus ensuring high levels of transparency and reproducibility.

Conducting an analysis of visual data to examine store robberies, a researcher needs to ensure the validity of the data regarding two criteria. First, researchers need to reflect whether videos show natural behavior, meaning behavior that is natural in a given situation and that would also occur if a camera were absent (Nassauer and Legewie, 2018). This is important for the present analysis, since online video platforms might feature more spectacular or unusual cases than are the "norm," or uploaded videos might show behavior that is staged. While this cannot be ruled out, many of the videos analyzed were uploaded by police departments, or police gave them to TV channels, who broadcast the tapes in order to identify the perpetrator(s) or to report on local news (for a full list of uploaders, see Table D1). Recordings are therefore unlikely to show staged events. In addition, analysis suggests that the cases do not display complete outliers of human behavior, since specific patterns in situational dynamics of the successful cases versus unsuccessful cases were found.

Second, to ensure validity, researchers conducting VDA need to strive for optimal capture of the event of interest so that no essential details determining the encounter are missing (Nassauer and Legewie, 2018). Generally, CCTV recordings of convenience store robberies provide information on the whole crime, taking place in a confined space. They presumably even capture the entirety of the time the actors spend together during their lives. If these criteria are ensured, and ethical aspects are considered (Legewie and Nassauer, 2018), YouTube and LiveLeak can be valuable data sources for criminological and sociological research. They allow analyzing a daily increasing number of recorded crimes. This opportunity for valid, transparent, and reproducible research holds a promising future for studying crime caught on camera.

Case Selection and Sampling

The sample of my robbery study consists of 20 convenience store robberies in the United States and 4 cases in the United Kingdom caught on CCTV (see Table D1). Comparing cases within the United States, we can assume actors' behavior is comparable in several regards. First, all perpetrators in these cases know that they are likely to be filmed. Further, perpetrators and victims have similar understandings and expectations of robberies that they rely on when interacting in a robbery: although variations exist within the United States, perpetrators have comparably similar access to firearms and can expect similar legal consequences when caught. Lastly, actors are likely to display similar emotional dialects, which favors the comparison of emotion expression (Elfenbein and Ambady, 2003; see also Ekman, 2003; von Scheve, 2012). UK cases serve as a comparative outlook. The United Kingdom has a great many CCTV cameras in convenience stores and public places (hence, robbers can assume they will be filmed) but much lower numbers of firearms than the United States (making it possible to study the role of firearm weapons in situational scripts).

As Table D1 illustrates, I comparatively analyzed 5 successful cases and 15 failed cases, plus 4 UK robberies. The focus is on failed cases: examining what breaks rituals can help in understanding how they normally work (Garfinkel, 2005). Theoretical

TABLE D1 Sample of Robberies Studied

CASE	CASE ID	WHERE	WHEN	PERPETRATOR:CLERK RATIO	UPLOADER/PROVIDER	LINK
1	A1	Modesto, CA	12/12/2011	4-1	ModestoNews.org	https://www.youtube.com/watch?v=bLhXAQijoUk
2	A2	Newton, CA	2011*	3-1	LAPD Online	https://www.youtube.com/watch?v=0JUnGTtuKyw
3	A3	Seattle, WA	2011*	1-1	CBS	https://www.youtube.com/watch?v=QgWUsCAiCmI
4	A4	Dallas, TX	4/18/2011	2-1	Dallas Police Department	https://www.youtube.com/watch?v=UzmLJcLh_XU
5	A5	Hillsborough County, FL	2010*	1-2	Hillsborough County Sheriff	https://www.youtube.com/watch?v=Yeea8B3PhK4
6	B1	New York, NY	2013*	1-1	The Guardian	https://www.youtube.com/watch?v=z0HH59xCA1E
7	B2	Riverbank, CA	Jan. 2012	2-2	Fox40 News	https://www.youtube.com/watch?v=BG-vEAGeMWM
8	B3	Davis, CA	2011*	1-1	Individual	https://www.youtube.com/watch?v=GXILVPwAQW8
9	B4	Manasses, VA	12/28/2010	1-1	Individual	https://www.youtube.com/watch?v=ZqpB8VifxAE
10	B5	Lexington, KY	2/27/2015	2-1	ABC News	https://www.youtube.com/watch?v=VF40Q_ouaao
11	B6	Broward Country, FL	7/23/2010	1-1	New York Post	https://www.youtube.com/watch?v=KqsTz75Dio8
12	B7	Fresno, CA	6/27/2014	2-1	Individual	https://www.youtube.com/watch?v=QbV5YWgNjCU

(continued)

TABLE D1   Continued

CASE	CASE ID	WHERE	WHEN	PERPETRATOR:CLERK RATIO	UPLOADER/PROVIDER	LINK
13	B8	California	2013*	1-1	YouTube channel "Ministry of CCTV"	https://www.youtube.com/watch?v=l5werq8tlTU
14	B9	Burge County, GA	2016*	1-1	WSB-TV (ABC News)	https://www.youtube.com/watch?v=gYtA1ohgHFc
15	B10	Ambridge, PA	2013*	1-1	ABC 4-WTAE TV Pittsburgh	https://www.youtube.com/watch?v=HvY-50M3NZQ
16	B11	Oakland Park, FL	2015*	1-1	Broward Sheriff's Office	https://www.liveleak.com/view?t=041_1461181267
17	B12	Dallas, TX	10/8/2011	2-2	Individual	https://www.youtube.com/watch?v=Hi7_uiAUEa4
18	B13	Seffner, FL	4/27/2015	1-1	Hillsborough County Sheriff's Office (HCSO)	http://www.liveleak.com/view?i=414_1462376149
19	B14	Philadelphia, PA	1/16/2016	2-2	Philadelphia Police Department	https://www.youtube.com/watch?v=GBY0kfOkAyo
20	B15	Eureka, CA	3/14/2014	1-1	Individual	http://www.liveleak.com/view?i=661_1458072424
21	UK A1	Oldham (UK)	3/22/2003	3-1	The Telegraph	https://www.youtube.com/watch?v=Ojw3gZq02YQ
22	UK B1	Weshoughton (UK)	0/14/2013	2-1	Mail Online	https://www.youtube.com/watch?v=oD7TAHduZww
23	UK B2	Birmingham (UK)	1/29/2014	3-1	IAmBirmingham	https://www.youtube.com/watch?v=VbU9wDLfRbM
24	UK B3	London (UK)	Dec. 2010	3-2	Individual	https://www.youtube.com/watch?v=B5WNNdoUvy4&feature=youtu.be

NOTE. * indicates the year of the upload, since the date of event is not indicated by the uploader. All cases with an A case ID are successful robberies, cases with a B case ID are failed robberies. Five of the 20 US CCTV videos include the original sound, 15 videos include no sound. One of the 4 UK CCTV videos includes sound. Several of the US cases include comments by journalists, uploaders, or music. These comments were put on mute for the analysis. Two of the US videos in the analysis were edited, visibly omitting seconds of footage (B2, B5). In some of the cases the clerk cannot be seen the entire time. While links may change, most links are stable over time. Further, most videos are uploaded by several providers on YouTube and/or LiveLeak. Thus, if a video is no longer available under the specified link, readers can usually find the same video uploaded by another user by searching for time, place, and characteristics of the event described.

sampling (Corbin and Strauss, 1990) was used to select cases. This sampling procedure stems from grounded theory (Corbin and Strauss, 1990): cases are selected based on minimum and maximum difference from cases already included in the research project. The goal of this procedure is to build theories grounded in the data.

The 20 US cases examined occurred from 2010 until 2016, across 9 US states, involving a total of 45 robbers and clerks. The 4 UK cases occurred from 2010 until 2014 and involve a total of 16 robbers and clerks. Perpetrator numbers ranged from 1 to 4 per robbery, with a total of 32 perpetrators involved in the 20 US cases and 11 perpetrators in the 4 UK cases. Perpetrators and clerks ranged in age from approximately 18 to approximately 60 years. Some covered their faces before entering, with others not wearing disguises. In all cases, the perpetrators were male. Of the clerks in the 20 US cases, 18 were male and 8 female: in the 5 successful robberies 5 of the 6 clerks were male, 1 female. In the 15 failed robberies, 13 of the 20 clerks involved were male, 7 female.

Analyzing Actions, Movement, and Emotions

I coded all 20 robberies using atlas.ti software for qualitative data analysis. Among other things, atlas.ti provides tools to assign codes freely to every point in time in a video. Codes were developed to be mutually exclusive. For each frame during the robbery, one code was assigned to each person visible in the recording. I then comparatively analyzed the sequence of codes per case (frequencies of behaviors and emotions, who initiated actions and who reacted, speed of changes in behavior and emotions as well as rhythms of action and reaction, etc.). One type of code refers to behaviors, such as movements (moving forward, backward, standing still) or action (hands up, picking something up). Other types of codes refer to universal emotions identifiable in a person's facial expressions, body postures, movements, and voice (Birdwhistell, 1970; Ekman et al., 1972; Ekman, 2003; see coding scheme, Appendix B, Table B2). Applying video data analysis (Nassauer and Legewie, 2018), I observed a person's movements, field of vision, use of space, interactions, exchange of glances and gestures, facial expressions, and body postures to decipher the syntax of situational dynamics. Detailed observations on each instant of the recording helped trace the unfolding of the crime step by step and made it possible to identify distinct patterns in successful versus failed robberies.

BIBLIOGRAPHY

Abbott, A. (1992) "From Causes to Events Notes on Narrative Positivism," *Sociological Methods & Research*, 20(4), pp. 428–455.

Abbott, A. (1995) "Sequence Analysis: New Methods for Old Ideas," *Annual Review of Sociology*, 21, pp. 93–113.

Abbott, A., and Tsay, A. (2000) "Sequence Analysis and Optimal Matching Methods in Sociology. Review and Prospect," *Sociological Methods & Research*, 29(1), pp. 3–33.

ABC News (2012) *Trayvon Shooter Told Cops Teen Went for His Gun*. ABC News. Available at: https://abcnews.go.com/US/trayvon-martin-shooter-teenager-gun/story?id=16000239 (Accessed August 1, 2018).

ABC News (2014) *Officer Darren Wilson Says He Struggled with Brown, Feared for His Life*. Available at: https://www.youtube.com/watch?v=YVVmn14NnII (Accessed August 1, 2018).

ABC News (2015) "Freddie Gray's Death Ruled a Homicide, Officers Face Charges," *ABC News*, September 2. Available at: https://abcnews.go.com/US/freddie-grays-death-ruled-homicide-states-attorney/story?id=30728026 (Accessed August 15, 2018).

Achelpöhler, W. (2009) *Demonstration in Kehl—ein paar Eindrücke*. Grüne Linke. Available at: http://www.gruene-linke.de/2009/04/05/eindrucke-von-der-no-to-nato-demo-in-kehl/ (Accessed August 16, 2017).

ACPO, ACPOS, and NPIA (2010) *Manual of Guidance on Keeping the Peace*. London: National Policing Improvement Agency.

activistvideos (2007) *Miami FTAA Protest Footage*. Available at: http://www.youtube.com/watch?v=tIbQ1shTK8o&feature=youtube_gdata_player (Accessed March 18, 2018).

Aisenbrey, S., and Fasang, A. E. (2010) "New Life for Old Ideas: The 'Second Wave' of Sequence Analysis Bringing the 'Course' Back into the Life Course," *Sociological Methods & Research*, 38(3), pp. 420–462.

Alexander, M. (2012) *The New Jim Crow: Mass Incarceration in the Age of Colorblindness*. New York: The New Press.

Amies, N. (2007) "The Demonized Face of G8 Protests," *Deutsche Welle*, July 6. Available at: https://www.dw.com/en/the-demonized-face-of-g8-protests/a-2578933.

Anderson, E. (2000) *Code of the Street: Decency, Violence, and the Moral Life of the Inner City*. New York: W.W. Norton & Company.

Anderson, E. (2012a) *The Cosmopolitan Canopy: Race and Civility in Everyday Life*. Reprint edition. New York: W.W. Norton & Company.

Anderson, E. (2012b) "The Iconic Ghetto," *Annals of the American Academy of Political and Social Science*, 642(1), pp. 8–24.

Anderson, E. (2013) "Emmett and Trayvon: How Racial Prejudice Has Changed in the Last 60 Years," *Huffington Post*, February 28. Available at: https://www. huffingtonpost.com/elijah-anderson/emmett-and-trayvon-how-racial-prejudice_b_ 2773439.html (Accessed August 1, 2018).

Anderson, E. (2014) "What Caused the Ferguson Riot Exists in So Many Other Cities, Too," *Washington Post*. Available at: https://www.washingtonpost.com/ posteverything/wp/2014/08/13/what-caused-the-ferguson-riot-exists-in-so-many-other-cities-too/ (Accessed August 1, 2018).

Anderson, E. (2015) "'The White Space'," *Sociology of Race and Ethnicity*, 1(1), pp. 10–21. doi: 10.1177/2332649214561306.

Anderson, E., Brighenti, A. M., and Bassetti, C. (2007) "From the Iconic Ghetto to the Cosmopolitan and Beyond. An Interview with Elijah Anderson," *Etnografia e Ricerca Qualitativa*, 2, pp. 303–309.

Anderson, K. (2002) "Anti-War Messages Dominate Protest," *BBC*, September 27. Available at: http://news.bbc.co.uk/2/hi/americas/2285745.stm (Accessed April 16, 2017).

Arzt, C., and Ullrich, P. (2016) "Versammlungsfreiheit versus polizeiliche Kontroll- und Überwachungspraxis," *Vorgänge. Zeitschrift für Bürgerrechte und Gesellschaftspolitik*, 55(1), pp. 46–60.

Associated Press (2014) "Police's Fatal Shooting of Black Teenager Draws Angry Crowd in St Louis Suburb," *The Guardian*, August 10. Available at: https://www. theguardian.com/world/2014/aug/10/police-fatal-shooting-black-teenager-angry-crowd-st-louis-suburb (Accessed August 15, 2018).

Athens, L. H. (1980) *Violent Criminal Acts and Actors: A Symbolic Interactionist Study*. Boston: Routledge & Kegan Paul.

Bates, K. G. (2015) "Is It an 'Uprising' or a 'Riot'? Depends on Who's Watching," *NPR*, April 30. Available at: https://www.npr.org/sections/codeswitch/2015/ 04/30/403303769/uprising-or-riot-depends-whos-watching (Accessed August 15, 2018).

Batson, C. D., Shaw, L. L., and Oleson, K. C. (1992) "Differentiating Affect, Mood and Emotion: Toward Functionally-based Conceptual Distinctions," in M. S. Clark (ed.), *Review of Personality and Social Psychology*, pp. 294–326. Newbury Park, CA: Sage.

BattleInSeattle (2008) *WTO 113099 HS9652*. Flickr—Photo Sharing! Available at: https://www.flickr.com/photos/26575571@N08/2672781650/ (Accessed February 18, 2018).

Bauer, J. (2011) *Schmerzgrenze: Vom Ursprung alltäglicher und globaler Gewalt*. Munich: Blessing.

BBC News (2013) "LA Trayvon Martin protests turn ugly," *BBC News*, July 16. Available at: https://www.bbc.co.uk/news/world-us-canada-23332602 (Accessed August 15, 2018).

BBC News (2014) *Ferguson protests: National Guard sent to Missouri unrest*. BBC News. Available at: https://www.youtube.com/watch?v=IeHBc3W4Raw (Accessed August 5, 2018).

Beikler, S., Hasselmann, J., and Tretbar, C. (2007) "Polizei: Wir wurden in Rostock verheizt," *Der Tagesspiegel Online*, April 6. Available at: http://www.tagesspiegel.de/zeitung/polizei-wir-wurden-in-rostock-verheizt/862284.html (Accessed August 14, 2017).

Bergesen, A., and Herman, M. (1998) "Immigration, Race, and Riot: The 1992 Los Angeles Uprising," *American Sociological Review*, 63(1), p. 39.

Bernard, H. R., et al. (1984) "The Problem of Informant Accuracy: The Validity of Retrospective Data," *Annual Review of Anthropology*, 13(1), pp. 495–517. doi: 10.1146/annurev.an.13.100184.002431.

Bernton, H., and Carter, M. (2012) "Violence arrives, dressed in black," *The Seattle Times*, January 5. Available at: http://www.seattletimes.com/seattle-news/violence-arrives-dressed-in-black/ (Accessed May 15, 2018).

Bertocchi, G., and Dimico, A. (2012) "The Racial Gap in Education and the Legacy of Slavery," *Journal of Comparative Economics*. (Slavery, Colonialism and Institutions Around the World), 40(4), pp. 581–595.

Bijitaq (2007) *WTO Protests: Seattle (2/3)*. Available at: http://www.youtube.com/watch?v=FHfKDgf7lp8&feature=youtube_gdata_player (Accessed April 12, 2011).

Birdwhistell, R. (1970) *Kinesics and Context: Essays on Body Motion Communication*. Philadelphia: University of Pennsylvania Press.

Black Lives Matter (2017) "#TalkAbout Trayvon: A Toolkit for White People," *Black Lives Matter*. Available at: https://blacklivesmatter.com/resource/talkabout-trayvon-a-toolkit-for-white-people/ (Accessed November 3, 2018).

Blatter, J. (2012) "Ontological and Epistemological Foundations of Causal-Process Tracing: Configurational Thinking and Timing," in *ICPR Joint Sessions*. Antwerp, pp. 1–33. Belgium: ICPR Joint Sessions.

Bliss (2009) *G-20*. Flickr—Photo Sharing! Available at: https://www.flickr.com/photos/przypadek/3953739935/ (Accessed April g, 2017).

Blumenthal, R. (1988) "A Deputy Chief, Criticized in Riot, Led Complaint Unit," *The New York Times*, August 16. Available at: http://www.nytimes.com/1988/08/16/nyregion/a-deputy-chief-criticized-in-riot-led-complaint-unit.html (Accessed May 10, 2018).

Blumer, H. (1986) *Symbolic Interactionism: Perspective and Method*. Berkeley: University of California Press.

Bobic, J., Pavicevic, L., and Gomzi, M. (2007) "Post Traumatic Stress Disorder in Armed Robbery Victims and Ex-prisoners of War," *Studia Psychologica*, 49(2), pp. 135–143.

Bourdieu, P., and Passeron, J.-C. (1973) *Grundlagen einer Theorie der symbolischen Gewalt—Kulturelle Reproduktion und soziale Reproduktion*. Frankfurt am Main: Suhrkamp.

Boyer, E. J. (1999) "Coroner Charges Police 'Overkill'," *Los Angeles Times*, July 26. Available at: http://articles.latimes.com/1999/jul/26/local/me-59719 (Accessed May 6, 2018).

Boykoff, J. (2006) "Framing Dissent: Mass-Media Coverage of the Global Justice Movement," *New Political Science*, 28(2), pp. 201–228.

Boyle, M. P., McLeod, D. M., and Armstrong, C. L. (2012) "Adherence to the Protest Paradigm: The Influence of Protest Goals and Tactics on News Coverage in U.S. and International Newspapers," *The International Journal of Press/Politics*, pp. 127–144. doi: 10.1177/1940161211433837.

Braga, A. A., and Schnell, C. (2013) "Evaluating Place-Based Policing Strategies Lessons Learned from the Smart Policing Initiative in Boston," *Police Quarterly*, 16(3), pp. 339–357.

Bramsen, I. (2018) "How Violence Happens (or Not): Situational Conditions of Violence and Nonviolence in Bahrain, Tunisia and Syria," *Psychology of Violence*, 8(3), pp. 305–315.

Brand, K.-W. (1991) "Kontinuität und Diskontinuität in den neuen sozialen Bewegungen," in R. Roth and D. Rucht. (eds.), *Neue soziale Bewegungen in der Bundesrepublik Deutschland*, pp. 40–53. Frankfurt am Main: Campus Verlag.

BrownBlaze (2014) *Ferguson Riot, Missouri, August 10 2014*. Available at: https://www. youtube.com/watch?v=EkACHGLugu8 (Accessed August 5, 2018).

Bundeszentrale für politische Bildung (2017) *Politisch motivierte Gewalt auf Demonstrationen*. Available at: http://www.bpb.de/politik/innenpolitik/innere-sicherheit/76644/politisch-motivierte-gewalt?p=all (Accessed May 5, 2016).

Burgis, T. (2016) *The Looting Machine: Warlords, Oligarchs, Corporations, Smugglers, and the Theft of Africa's Wealth*. New York: Public Affairs.

Busche, J. (2003) *Die 68er: Biographie einer Generation*. Berlin: Berlin Verlag.

Busse, P. (2004) "Pepper Sprayed Baby Sale—Activist's Settlement in Brutality Lawsuit Doesn't Settle the Matter," *Portland Mercury*, September 12. Available at: https:// www.portlandmercury.com/news/pepper-sprayed-baby-sale/Content?oid=32658 (Accessed October 27, 2018).

CBS (2009) *CBS Evening News with Roger Mudd: 200,000 at Washington Peace March*. Available at: http://www.youtube.com/watch?v=9KuvjRTQo2U&feature=youtube_ gdata_player (Accessed April 15, 2018).

CBS (2010) *CBS 60 mins—WTO Seattle Riots*. Available at: https://www.youtube.com/ watch?v=F6J25i2nhbU (Accessed May 10, 2018).

CBS News (2013) "MLK: A riot is the language of the unheard," August 25. Available at: https://www.cbsnews.com/news/mlk-a-riot-is-the-language-of-the-unheard/ (Accessed August 5, 2018).

Chamberlain, M. R. (2005) "Direct Action Protest Management," *Senior Leadership Program Research Papers—Florida Department of Law Enforcement*, 10. Available at: www.fdle.state.fl.us/Content/.../Chamberlain-mark-paper-pdf.aspx (Accessed June 15, 2018).

Charles, C. Z. (2003) "The Dynamics of Racial Residential Segregation," *Annual Review of Sociology*, 29, pp. 167–207.

Cheh, M. M. (2005) "Legislative Oversight of Police: Lessons Learned from an Investigation of Police Handling of Demonstrations in Washington, D.C., " *Journal of Legislation*, 32(GWU Law School Public Law Research Paper No. 176), pp. 1–32.

Chetty, R., et al. (2018) "Race and Economic Opportunity in the United States: An Intergenerational Perspective," *NBER Working Paper*, 24441.

Chicago Tribune (2015) "Federal Report Faults Police Actions During Ferguson Unrest," June 30. Available at: http://www.chicagotribune.com/news/nationworld/ct-ferguson-federal-report-20150630-story.html (Accessed August 5, 2018).

Chomsky, N. (2005) *Chomsky on Anarchism*. Edited by B. Pateman. Oakland, CA: AK Press.

Cicco, D. T. D. (2010) "The Public Nuisance Paradigm: Changes in Mass Media Coverage of Political Protest Since the 1960s," *Journalism & Mass Communication Quarterly*, 87(1), pp. 135–153.

Citizens' Panel on WTO Operations (2000) *Report to the Seattle City Council WTO Accountability Committee by the Citizens' Panel on WTO Operations*, pp. 1–82. Available at: http://www.seattle.gov/archive/wtocommittee/panel3_report.htm (Accessed February 5, 2018).

City Council's WTO Accountability Review Committee—Panel 3 (2000) *Final Report of Panel 3 of the WTO Accountability Review Committee*. Seattle, p. 27.

City of Miami Civilian Investigative Panel (2006) *Report on the Free Trade Area of the Americas Summit*. Miami, pp. 1–53. Available at: www.miamigov.com/cip/downloads/FTAAReport.pdf.

City of Seattle (2008) "Interactive Incident Map with Police Incident Timeline Description of Nov 30 1999 Seattle Protests." Available at: http://www.seattle.gov/archive/wtocommittee/maps/1130_800_829.htm (Accessed February 12, 2011).

Civilian Investigative Panel (2002) *A Developing CIP in the Aftermath of the Free Trade of the Americas Summit: A Status Report*, p. 207. Available at: www.ci.miami.fl.us/cip/Downloads/CIPStatusReport.pdf (Accessed March 15, 2018).

CNN (1999) *Reining in Protests—1999*. CNN. Available at: https://www.cnn.com/2012/09/07/us/gallery/speech-and-protest/index.html (Accessed October 30, 2018).

CNN (2007) *G8 Riots 2007 Rostock, Samstag 2 June, Live Records (Part 2)—CNN live report by Frederik Pleitgen*. Available at: http://www.youtube.com/watch?v=HnvOAHK2afA&feature=youtube_gdata_player (Accessed March 15, 2018).

CNN (2014) *Protest Over Killing of Teenager Turns to Looting*. Available at: https://www.youtube.com/watch?v=DT1kY9PZgEA (Accessed August 5, 2018).

Collins, P. H. (1986) "Learning from the Outsider Within: The Sociological Significance of Black Feminist Thought," *Social Problems—SOC PROBL*, 33. doi: 10.1525/sp.1986.33.6.03a00020.

Collins, P. H. (1993) "Toward a New Vision: Race, Class, and Gender as Categories of Analysis and Connection," *Race, Sex & Class*, 1(1), pp. 25–45.

Collins, P. H. (2008) *Black Feminist Thought: Knowledge, Consciousness, and the Politics of Empowerment*. 1 edition. New York: Routledge.

Collins, R. (1993) "Emotional Energy as the Common Denominator of Rational Action," *Rationality and Society*, 5(2), pp. 203–230.

Collins, R. (2005a) *Interaction Ritual Chains*. Princeton, NJ: Princeton University Press.

Collins, R. (2005b) "Review Forum: The Sociology of Almost Everything—Four Questions to Randall Collins About Interaction Ritual Chains," *Canadian Journal of Sociology Online*, pp. 1–11. Available at: https://core.ac.uk/download/pdf/49313436.pdf (Accessed December 10, 2018).

Collins, R. (2008) *Violence: A Micro-Sociological Theory*. Princeton (NJ): Princeton University Press.

Collins, R. (2009) "The Micro-Sociology of Violence," *The British Journal of Sociology*, 60(3), pp. 566–576.

Collins, R. (2012) "C-Escalation and D-Escalation: A Theory of the Time-Dynamics of Conflict," *American Sociological Review*, 77(1), pp. 1–20.

Collins, R. (2014) "Micro-Sociology of Mass Rampage Killings," *Revue de Synthèse*, pp. 1–16.

Collins, R. (2016a) "Can the War Between Cops and Blacks Be De-escalated?," *The Sociological Eye*, 13 July. Available at: http://sociological-eye.blogspot.com/2016/07/can-war-between-cops-and-blacks-be-de.html (Accessed August 15, 2016).

Collins, R. (2016b) "On Visual Methods and the Growth of Micro-Interactional Sociology: Interview to Professor Randall Collins (with Uliano Conti)," in U. Conti (ed.), *Lo spazio del visuale. Manuale sull'utilizzo dell'immagine nella ricerca sociale*, pp. 81–94. Rome: Armando Editore.

Collins, R. (2016c) "The Sociological Eye: What Has Micro-Sociology Accomplished?," April 17. Available at: http://sociological-eye.blogspot.com/2016/04/what-has-micro-sociology-accomplished.html (Accessed May 5, 2016).

Collins, R., Walby, K., and Spencer, D. (2010) "In Conversation with the American Sociological Association President: Randall Collins on Emotions, Violence, and Interactionist Sociology," *Canadian Review of Sociology/Revue canadienne de sociologie*, 47(1), pp. 93–101.

Corbin, J. M., and Strauss, A. (1990) "Grounded Theory Research: Procedures, Canons, and Evaluative Criteria," *Qualitative Sociology*, 13(1), pp. 3–21.

Council of the District of Columbia (2004) *Report on Investigation of the Metropolitan Police Department's Policy and Practice in Handling Demonstrations in the District of Columbia*. Available at: epic.org/privacy/surveillance/spotlight/1205/mpdrep5304.pdf (Accessed August 14, 2018).

Crapanzano, D. (2015) *Baltimore: April 25th, 2015*. Available at: https://www.youtube.com/watch?v=psTJL5Q0MjY (Accessed August 1, 2018).

Cratty, C. (2012) "Agencies Warn of Possible Anarchist Activity at Conventions," *CNN*, August 24. Available at: http://www.cnn.com/2012/08/22/politics/conventions-anarchists/index.html (Accessed May 15, 2017).

Crespo, A. (2006) *FTAA—Miami*. Center Lane Press. Available at: www.coldtype.net/Assets.06/Essays.06/0906.Miami.AlCrespo.pdf (Accessed February 15, 2018).

Daily Beast (2010) *Ed Koch on the Tompkins Square Park Police Riot of 1988*. Video. Available at: http://www.youtube.com/watch?v=nR_cbK7Gz1w&feature=youtube_gdata_player (Accessed May 9, 2017).

Das Erste (1981) "Panorama vom 14. April 1981." Available at: http://daserste.ndr.de/panorama/archiv/1981/panorama1579.html (Accessed April 17, 2018).

Davinca (2007) *The Answer My Friend Is Blowing in the Wind*. Available at: https://www.flickr.com/photos/davinca/534686760/ (Accessed October 7, 2015).

Della Porta, D. (1995) *Social Movements, Political Violence, and the State: A Comparative Analysis of Italy and Germany*. New York: Cambridge University Press.

Della Porta, D., Peterson, A., and Reiter, H. (eds.) (2006a) *The Policing of Transnational Protest (Advances in Criminology)*. Burlington, VT: Ashgate.

Della Porta, D., Peterson, A., and Reiter, H. (2006b) "The Policing of Transnational Protest: An Introduction," in D. Della Porta, A. Peterson, and H. Reiter (eds.), *The*

Policing of Transnational Protest (Advances in Criminology), pp. 1–12. Burlingtion, VT: Ashgate.

Della Porta, D., and Reiter, H. (1998a) "Introduction. The Policing of Protest in Western Democracies," in D. Della Porta and H. Reiter (eds.), *Policing Protest: The Control of Mass Demonstrations in Western Democracies*, pp. 1–34. Minneapolis: University of Minnesota Press.

Della Porta, D., and Reiter, H. (eds.) (1998b) *Policing Protest: The Control of Mass Demonstrations in Western Democracies*. Minneapolis: University of Minnesota Press.

Della Porta, D., and Reiter, H. (2006) "The Policing of Transnational Protest: A Conclusion," in D. Della Porta, A. Peterson, and H. Reiter (eds.), *The Policing of Transnational Protest (Advances in Criminology)*, pp. 175–190. Burlingtion, VT: Ashgate.

DeMian, H. (2014) *Ferguson, MO 08/10/2014*. Available at: https://www.youtube.com/watch?v=MVGoT4Xzwig (Accessed August 5, 2018).

Der Spiegel (1968) "Heißer Asphalt," *Der Spiegel*, May 20. Available at: http://www.spiegel.de/spiegel/print/d-46050031.html (Accessed August 5, 2018).

Der Spiegel (1981) "BROKDORF: Flexible Taktik," *Der Spiegel*, March 9. Available at: http://www.spiegel.de/spiegel/print/d-14317148.html (Accessed August 5, 2017).

DeRienzo, P. (2008) "Tompkins Square Riot Memories, New York 2008," *The Shadow*. (53). Available at: http://patterson.no-art.info/reviews/2008-08-01c_derienzo.html (Accessed August 6, 2018).

Deutschland Radio (2007) *Eine "einsatztechnische Dummheit."* Available at: http://www.ag-friedensforschung.de/themen/Globalisierung/g8-2007/gewalt3.html (Accessed May 5, 2018).

Diane Fossey Gorilla Fund International (2016) *Fossey Fund Develops Unique App for Studying Gorillas*. Available at: https://gorillafund.org/fossey-fund-develops-unique-app-for-studying-gorillas/ (Accessed September 30, 2016).

DiMaggio, P. (1997) "Culture and Cognition," *Annual Review of Sociology*, 23(1), pp. 263–287.

Dissent (2014) *Schwarzer Block im Rückblick | international mobilization against g8 summit 2007*. Available at: http://dissent-archive.ucrony.net/dissentnetwork/node/3671.html (Accessed October 2, 2018).

Douglas-Bowers, D. (2014) *Unmasking the Black Bloc: Who They Are, What They Do, How They Work*. Occupy.com. Available at: http://www.occupy.com/article/unmasking-black-bloc-who-they-are-what-they-do-how-they-work (Accessed May 10, 2015).

Drury, J., and Reicher, S. D. (1999) "The Intergroup Dynamics of Collective Empowerment: Substantiating the Social Identity Model of Crowd Behavior," *Group Processes & Intergroup Relations*, 2(4), pp. 381–402.

Drury, J., and Reicher, S. D. (2000) "Collective Action and Psychological Change: The Emergence of New Social Identities," *British Journal of Social Psychology*, 39(4), pp. 579–604.

Dupuis-Déri, F. (2013) *Who's Afraid of the Black Blocs? Anarchy in Action Around the World*. Toronto: Between the Lines.

Earl, J., and Soule, S. A. (2006) "Seeing Blue: A Police-Centered Explanation of Protest Policing," *Mobilization*, 11(2), pp. 145–164.

Eckert, R., and Willems, H. (2002) "Eskalation und Deeskalation sozialer Konflikte: Der Weg in die Gewalt," in W. Heitmeyer and J. Hagan (eds.), *Internationales Handbuch der Gewaltforschung*, pp. 1457–1479. Wiesbaden, Germany: Westdeutscher Verlag.

Eisenberger, N. I., and Lieberman, M. D. (2004) "Why Rejection Hurts: A Common Neural Alarm System for Physical and Social Pain," *Trends in Cognitive Sciences*, 8(7), pp. 294–300. doi: 10.1016/j.tics.2004.05.010.

Ekman, P. (2003) *Emotions Revealed: Recognizing Faces and Feelings to Improve Communication and Emotional Life*. New York: St. Martin's Griffin.

Ekman, P., Friesen, W. F., and Ellsworth, P. (1972) *Emotion in the Human Face*. New York: Pergamon.

Elfenbein, H. A., and Ambady, N. (2003) "Universals and Cultural Differences in Recognizing Emotions," *Current Directions in Psychological Science*, 12(5), pp. 159–164.

Equit, C., Groenemeyer, A., and Schmidt, H. (2016) *Situationen der Gewalt*. Belz. Available at: https://www.beltz.de/fachmedien/erziehungs_und_sozialwissenschaften/buecher/produkt_produktdetails/30427-situationen_der_gewalt.html (Accessed November 3, 2018).

Faulkner, K. A., Landsittel, D. P., and Hendricks, S. A. (2001) "Robbery Characteristics and Employee Injuries in Convenience Stores," *American Journal of Industrial Medicine*, 40(6), pp. 703–709.

Fels (2007) *G8-Gipfel 2007*. Fels—Für eine linke Strömung. Available at: http://fels.nadir.org/de/galerie/g8-gipfel-2007 (Accessed May 5, 2018).

Felson, M., and Boba, R. L. (2010) *Crime and Everyday Life*. Thousand Oaks, CA: SAGE.

Felson, R. B. (1984) "Patterns of Aggressive Social Interaction," in A. Mummendey (ed.) *Social Psychology of Aggression: From Individual Behavior to Social Interaction*, pp. 107–126. Berlin: Springer. doi: 10.1007/978-3-642-48919-8_7.

Felson, R. B, and Tedeschi, J. T. (1993) *Aggression and Violence: Social Interactionist Perspectives*. Washington, DC: American Psychological Association.

Felson, R., and Steadman, H. J. (1983) "Situational Factors in Disputes Leading to Criminal Violence," *Criminology*, 21(1), pp. 59–74.

Ferguson, R. B. (2013) "Pinker's List: Exaggerating Prehistoric War Mortality," in D. P. Fry (ed.), *War, Peace, and Human Nature: The Convergence of Evolutionary and Cultural Views*, pp. 112–131. New York: Oxford University Press.

Fernandez, L. A. (2005) "Policing Protest Spaces: Social Control in the Anti-Globalization Movement," *The Canadian Journal of Police & Security Services*, 3(4), pp. 241–249.

Feuerherd, B., and Fredericks, B. (2015) "Obama Calls Baltimore Rioters 'Criminals and Thugs'," *New York Post*, April 28. Available at: https://nypost.com/2015/04/28/obama-calls-baltimore-rioters-criminals-and-thugs/ (Accessed August 5, 2018).

Fillieule, O., and Jobard, F. (1998) "The Policing of Protest in France: Toward a Model of Protest Policing," in D. Della Porta and H. Reiter (eds.), *Policing Protest: The Control of Mass Demonstrations in Western Democracies*, pp. 70–90. Minneapolis: University of Minnesota Press.

Fiss, P., Marx, A., and Rihoux, B. (2014) "Getting QCA Right: Some Comments on Lucas and Szatrowski," *Sociological Methodology*, 44(1), pp. 95–100.

Fox 2 St. Louis (2014) *Looting in Ferguson*. Ferguson. Available at: https://www.youtube.com/watch?v=08rrstPisdw (Accessed October 28, 2018).

Fox 9 News (2008) *Anarchists Took Control of St. Paul During RNC Police Admit*. Available at: http://www.youtube.com/watch?v=gkZvtGCh5YA&feature=youtube_gdata_player (Accessed July 16, 2018).

Fox 10 Phoenix (2015) *Aerial Coverage of Baltimore Riots Following Freddie Gray Funeral*. Available at: https://www.youtube.com/watch?v=sCtKKU64e1M (Accessed August 1, 2018).

Fox 40 News (2012) *Robbers Attempt to Rob Store with AK47*. Available at: https://www.youtube.com/watch?v=BG-vEAGeMWM (Accessed October 28, 2018).

Fritz51202 (2010) *Filmaufnahmen über und aus Hamburg 1976–1977*. Available at: https://www.youtube.com/watch?v=B50X3dHFZWg (Accessed May 10, 2018).

Fujii, L. A. (2010) "Shades of Truth and Lies: Interpreting Testimonies of War and Violence," *Journal of Peace Research*, 47(2), pp. 231–241. doi: 10.1177/0022343309353097.

Fujii, L. A. (2011) *Killing Neighbors: Webs of Violence in Rwanda*. Ithaca, NY: Cornell University Press.

Fujii, L. A. (2012) "Research Ethics 101: Dilemmas and Responsibilities," *PS: Political Science & Politics*, 45(4), pp. 717–723. doi: 10.1017/S1049096512000819.

Fujii, L. A. (2013) "The Puzzle of Extra-Lethal Violence," *Perspectives on Politics*, 11(02), pp. 410–426.

Fyfe, N. R. (1991) "The Police, Space and Society: The Geography of Policing," *Progress in Human Geography*, 15(3), pp. 249–267.

G20 Peoples March (2009) *G20 Peoples March Bike Cops*. Available at: http://www.youtube.com/watch?v=_F38-VLuPFw&feature=youtube_gdata_player (Accessed March 4, 2018).

Gale, J.-A., and Coupe, T. (2005) "The Behavioural, Emotional and Psychological Effects of Street Robbery on Victims," *International Review of Victimology*, 12(1), pp. 1–22.

Galtung, J. (1969) "Violence, Peace, and Peace Research," *Journal of Peace Research*, 6(3), pp. 167–191.

Galtung, J. (1970) *Strukturelle Gewalt. Beiträge zur Friedens- und Konfliktforschung*. Reinbeck: Rowohlt.

Garfinkel, H. (2005) "A Conception of and Experiments with 'Trust' as a Condition of Concerted Stable Actions," in J. A. O'Brien (ed.), *The Production of Reality: Essays and Readings on Social Interaction*, pp. 370–380. Thousand Oaks, CA: Sage.

Gatehouse, G. (2013) "Kenya Military Names Westgate Mall Attack Suspects," *BBC News*, May 10. Available at: http://www.bbc.com/news/world-africa-24412315 (Accessed May 15, 2018).

German Police Union (2007) *G-8 Gipfel in Heiligendamm: Gewerkschaftliche Aufbereitung des Polizeieinsatzes*. Gewerkschaft der Polizei, p. 18. Available at: www.dfg-vk.de/dateien/gdp-abschlussberichtbfa_bupo_g8.pdf. (Accessed July 3, 2018).

Gerring, J. (2010) "Case Selection for Case-Study Analysis: Qualitative and Quantitative Techniques," in J. M. Box-Steffensmeier, H. E. Brady, and D. Collier (eds.), *The Oxford Handbook of Political Methodology*, pp. 645–684. New York: Oxford University Press.

Gerring, J., and Thomas, C. (2006) "Internal Validity: Process Tracing," in J. Gerring (ed.), *Case Study Research: Principles and Practices*, pp. 151–171. Cambridge, UK: Cambridge University Press.

Gilcher-Holtey, I. (2001) *Die 68er Bewegung: Deutschland, Westeuropa, USA*. Munich: C. H. Beck.

Gillham, P. F. (2011) "Securitizing America: Strategic Incapacitation and the Policing of Protest Since the 11 September 2001 Terrorist Attacks," *Sociology Compass*, 5(7), pp. 636–652.

Gillham, P. F., and Marx, G. T. (2000) "Complexity and Irony in Policing and Protesting: The World Trade Organization in Seattle," *Social Justice*, 27(2), pp. 212–236.

Gillham, P. F., and Marx, G. T. (2018) "Changes in the Policing of Civil Disorders Since the Kerner Report: The Police Response to Ferguson, August 2014, and Some Implications for the Twenty-First Century," *RSF*, 4(6), pp. 122–143. doi: 10.7758/RSF.2018.4.6.06.

Gillham, P. F., and Noakes, J. A. (2007) "More Than a March in a Circle: Transgressive Protests and the Limits of Negotiated Management," *Mobilization*, 12(4), pp. 341–357.

Giuffo, J. (2001) "Smoke Gets in Our Eyes," *Columbia Journalism Review*, 40(3), pp. 14–17.

Gladwell, M. (2015) "Thresholds of Violence: How School Shootings Spread," *The New Yorker*, October 19. Available at: http://www.newyorker.com/magazine/2015/10/19/thresholds-of-violence (Accessed May 5, 2016).

Glassner, B. (2010) *The Culture of Fear: Why Americans Are Afraid of the Wrong Things: Crime, Drugs, Minorities, Teen Moms, Killer Kids, Mutant Microbes, Plane Crashes, Road Rage, & So Much More*. New York: Basic Books.

Goertz, G., and Mahoney, J. (2005) "Two-Level Theories and Fuzzy-Set Analysis," *Sociological Methods & Research*, 33(4), pp. 497–538.

Goffman, A. (2014) *On the Run: Fugitive Life in an American City*. Chicago: University of Chicago Press.

Goffman, E. (2005) *Interaction Ritual: Essays in Face to Face Behavior*. New York: AldineTransaction.

Goodwin, J., and Jasper, J. M. (2006) "Emotions and Social Movements," in J. Stets and J. H. Turner (eds.), *Handbook of the Sociology of Emotions*, pp. 611–635. New York: Springer,

Gould, R. V. (2003) *Collision of Wills: How Ambiguity about Social Rank Breeds Conflict*. Chicago: University of Chicago Press.

Graham, D. A. (2015) "What Happened to Freddie Gray?," *The Atlantic*, April 22. Available at: https://www.theatlantic.com/politics/archive/2015/04/the-mysterious-death-of-freddie-gray/391119/ (Accessed August 15, 2018).

Graham, H. D., and Gurr, T. R. (1969) "Conclusion," in H. D. Graham and T. R. Gurr (eds.), *Violence in America: Historical and Comparative Perspectives*, pp. 788–822. New York: Signet Books.

Gramlich, J. (2018) "5 Facts About Crime in the U.S.," *Pew Research Center*, January 30. Available at: http://www.pewresearch.org/fact-tank/2018/01/30/5-facts-about-crime-in-the-u-s/ (Accessed November 2, 2018).

Grant, D. S. I., and Wallace, M. (1991) "Why Do Strikes Turn Violent?," *American Journal of Sociology*, 96(5), pp. 1117–1150.

Greenwald, R., and Jones, V. (2015) "What Do You Call White Rioters? Anything But Thugs," *Huffington Post*, June 16. Available at: https://www.huffingtonpost.com/robert-greenwald/what-do-you-call-white-rioters_b_7590362.html (Accessed August 5, 2018).

Greer, C., and McLaughlin, E. (2010) "We Predict a Riot?," *British Journal of Criminology*, 50, pp. 1041–1059.

Grefe, C., Greffrath, M., and Schumann, H. (2003) *attac. Was wollen die Globalisierungskritiker?* Berlin: Rowohlt.

Grossman, D., and Christensen, L. W. (2008) *On Combat, the Psychology and Physiology of Deadly Conflict in War and in Peace*. Mascoutah, IL: Warrior Science Publications.

Harding, M. (2009) "During G-20, Police Linked with Texting," *Pittsburgh Tribune-Review*, December 10. Available at: http://rnc08report.org/archive/1217.shtml (Accessed February 10, 2018).

Harvey, R. (2010) *Coming Back to Miami, Even If Your Voice Shakes*. Available at: http://voiceshakes.wordpress.com/2010/12/06/coming-back-to-miami/ (Accessed May 3, 2017).

Hatfield, E., et al. (2014) "New Perspectives on Emotional Contagion: A Review of Classic and Recent Research on Facial Mimicry and Contagion," *Interpersona: An International Journal on Personal Relationships*, 8, pp. 159–179.

Hatfield, E., Cacioppo, J. T., and Rapson, R. L. (1993) *Emotional Contagion Studies in Emotion and Social Interaction*. Cambridge, UK: Cambridge University Press.

Hatfield, E., Carpenter, M., and Rapson, R. L. (2014) "Collective Emotions: Perspectives from Psychology, Philosophy, and Sociology," in C. von Scheve and M. Salmella (eds.), *Collective Emotions: Perspectives from Psychology, Philosophy, and Sociology*, pp. 108–123. Oxford: Oxford University Press.

Hayden, T. (2003) *Miami Vice—Undercover Cops Acted as FTAA Protestors*. alternet. Available at: http://rense.com/general45/sfta.htm (Accessed February 15, 2013).

Hénaff, M. (2015) "Rätsel der Grausamkeit," *Lettre International*, 109 (Summer 2015), pp. 12–22.

Herron, D. (2003) "March 15, 2003, Protest Rally in San Francisco," *Politics and Sustainability*, 15 March. Available at: http://politics.7gen.com/2003/03/march-15-2003-protest-rally-in-san.html (Accessed 15 February 2013).

Hertz, N. (2001) *The Silent Takeover: Global Capitalism and the Death of Democracy*. New York: HarperCollins.

HiveMind (2008) *Aktionstag Migration*. Available at: http://flickrhivemind.net/blackmagic.cgi?id=575260099&url=http%3A%2F%2Fflickrhivemind.net%2FUser%2Fturbotorbs%2FInteresting%3Fsearch_type%3DUser%3Btextinput%3Dturbotorbs%3Bphoto_type%3D250%3Bmethod%3DGET%3Bnoform%3Dt%3Bsort%3DInterestingness%23pic575260099&user=&flickrurl=http://www.flickr.com/photos/8518760@N02/575260099 (Accessed August 12, 2016).

Hoebel, T. (2014) "Organisierte Plötzlichkeit: Eine prozesssoziologische Erklärung antisymmetrischer Gewaltsituationen / Organized Suddenness: An Explanation of Antisymmetric Situations of Violence in Terms of Social Process," *Zeitschrift für Soziologie*, 43(6), pp. 441–457.

Hogan, S. (2017) "St. Louis Officers Chant 'Whose Streets, Our Streets' While Arresting Protesters," *The Washington Post*, September 18. Available at: https://www.washingtonpost.com/news/morning-mix/wp/2017/09/18/st-louis-officers-chant-whose-streets-our-streets-while-arresting-protesters-against-police-killing/?utm_term=.5ee2fd1287f4 (Accessed August 5, 2018).

Hoggett, J., and Stott, C. (2010) "Crowd Psychology, Public Order Police Training and the Policing of Football Crowds," *Policing: An International Journal of Police Strategies & Management*, 33(2), pp. 218–235.

Höhl, S. (2009) "Südwest: Polizei und Kehl rüsten sich für den Nato-Gipfel," *Badische Zeitung*, March 21. Available at: http://www.badische-zeitung.de/suedwest-1/polizei-und-kehl-ruesten-sich-fuer-den-nato-gipfel--12912737.html (Accessed August 15, 2014).

Horowitz, D. L. (2001) *The Deadly Ethnic Riot*. Berkley and Los Anageles, CA: University of California Press.

Hylander, I., and Granström, K. (2010a) "Organizing for a Peaceful Crowd: An Example of a Football Match," *Forum Qualitative Sozialforschung / Forum: Qualitative Social Research*, 11(2). Available at: http://www.qualitative-research.net/index.php/fqs/article/view/1462 (Accessed August 15, 2018).

Hylander, I., and Granström, K. (2010b) "Preventing Crowd Violence," in J. Knutsson and T. Madensen (eds.), *Police Use of Active and Passive Mitigation Strategies*. Boulder, CO: Lynne Rienner.

IGuerilla (2007a) *Demonstration gegen den G8-Gipfel 2007 (8) Schwarzer Block Vermummt*. Flickr—Photo Sharing! Available at: https://www.flickr.com/photos/iguerilla/675669388/ (Accessed May 5, 2018).

IGuerilla (2007b) *Demonstration gegen den G8-Gipfel 2007 (23)*. Flickr—Photo Sharing! Available at: https://www.flickr.com/photos/iguerilla/2350044533/ (Accessed October 7, 2018).

Imbusch, P. (2003) "The Concept of Violence," in W. Heitmeyer and J. Hagan (eds.) *International Handbook of Violence Research*, pp. 13–39. Wiesbaden: Springer.

Imbusch, P. (2004) "'Mainstreamer' versus 'Innovateure' der Gewaltforschung: Eine kuriose Debatte," in W. Heitmeyer and H.-G. Soeffner (eds.), *Gewalt: Entwicklungen, Strukturen, Analyseprobleme*, pp. 125–148. Frankfurt am Main: Suhrkamp Verlag.

Independent Media Center (2011) *This Is What Democracy Looks Like (Seattle 1999 WTO)*. Available at: http://www.youtube.com/watch?v=yBUZH2vCD_k&feature=youtube_gdata_player (Accessed January 15, 2018).

Indymedia (2004) *The Miami Model—2003 FTAA Summit*. Available at: http://www.youtube.com/watch?v=u2QfHaFitMs (Accessed September 18, 2018).

Indymedia (2008) *The Miami Model Part 4/10*. Available at: http://www.youtube.com/watch?v=MZHMpuyAKYA&feature=youtube_gdata_player (Accessed October 3, 2010).

Inwood, J., Tyner, J. A., and Alderman, D. (2014) "Remembering the Real Violence in Ferguson," *Society & Space*, October 9. Available at: https://societyandspace.org/2014/09/10/remembering-the-real-violence-in-ferguson/ (Accessed October 30, 2018).

Jackson-Jacobs, C. (2013) "Constructing Physical Fights: An Interactionist Analysis of Violence Among Affluent, Suburban Youth," *Qualitative Sociology*, 36(1), pp. 23–52.

Jacobsen, A. (2001) "Die gesellschaftliche Wirklichkeit der Polizei: Eine empirische Untersuchung zur Rationalität polizeilichen Handelns." Available at: https://pub.uni-bielefeld.de/rc/2304180/2304183 (Accessed March 2, 2016).

Jamsven (2007) *G8—Polizei Taktik?* Available at: http://www.youtube.com/watch?v=bqI vShEZ4Po&feature=youtube_gdata_player (Accessed January 15, 2018).

Jasper, J. M. (2006) "Emotions and the Microfoundations of Politics: Rethinking Ends and Means," in S. Clarke, P. Hoggett, and S. Thompson (eds.), *Emotion, Politics and Society*, pp. 14–30. London: Palgrave Macmillan.

Jasper, J. M. (2009) "Cultural Approaches in the Sociology of Social Movements," in B. Klandermans and C. Roggeband (eds.), *Handbook of Social Movements Across Disciplines*, pp. 59–111. New York: Springer.

Jasper, J. M. (2014) *Protest: A Cultural Introduction to Social Movements*. Cambridge, UK: Polity Press.

Jasper, J. M. (2018) *The Emotions of Protest*. Chicago: University of Chicago Press.

Jimenez, S. (2008) *G-20 Pittsburgh*. Flickr—Photo Sharing! Available at: https://www.flickr.com/photos/jwjnational/3971787247/ (Accessed March 8, 2018).

Jordan, B., and Henderson, A. (1995) "Interaction Analysis: Foundations and Practice," *Journal of the Learning Sciences*, 4(1), pp. 39–103.

Jubilee Australia (2007) *Photo Gallery*. Available at: http://www.jubileeaustralia.org/photo-galleries.html (Accessed January 20, 2018).

Junge Welt (2007) *Polizei in Rostock beim G8 Gipfel*. Available at: https://www.jungewelt.de/loginFailed.php?ref=/artikel/72294.kritik-am-polizeigesetz.html, picture reprint at http://www.projektwerkstatt.de/index.php?domain_id=7&p=20434 (Accessed May 15, 2014).

Juris, J. S. (2005) "Violence Performed and Imagined Militant Action, the Black Bloc and the Mass Media in Genoa," *Critique of Anthropology*, 25(4), pp. 413–432.

Kaiser, S. (1999a) *WTO protests 10*. Flickr—Photo Sharing! Available at: https://www.flickr.com/photos/djbones/125523970/ (Accessed May 5, 2018).

Kaiser, S. (1999b) *WTO protests 20*. Available at: https://www.flickr.com/photos/djbones/125536480/ (Accessed January 16, 2018).

Kaiser, S. (1999c) *WTO protests 25*. Available at: https://www.flickr.com/photos/djbones/125534465/ (Accessed January 16, 2018).

Kalish, R., and Kimmel, M. (2010) "Suicide by Mass Murder: Masculinity, Aggrieved Entitlement, and Rampage School Shootings," *Health Sociology Review*, 19(4), pp. 451–464. doi: 10.5172/hesr.2010.19.4.451.

Katz, J. (1988) *Seductions of Crime: Moral and Sensual Attractions in Doing Evil*. New York: Basic Books.

Katz, J. (1991) "The Motivation of the Persistent Robber," *Crime and Justice: A Review of Research*, 14, pp. 277–306.

Keinan, G., Friedland, N., and Ben-Porath, Y. (1987) "Decision Making Under Stress: Scanning of Alternatives Under Physical Threat," *Acta Psychologica*, 64(3), pp. 219–228. doi: 10.1016/0001-6918(87)90008-4.

Kerner Commission (1968) "Report of the National Advisory Commission on Civil Disorders: Summary of Report." Available at: https://www.hsdl.org/?abstract&did= (Accessed October 28, 2018).

Kersten, J. (2012) "Polizei, Gewalt und Menschenwürde," *Systhema*, 3(26), pp. 288–297.

King, A. (2013) *The Combat Soldier: Infantry Tactics and Cohesion in the Twentieth and Twenty-first Centuries*. Oxford: Oxford University Press.

Kiro 7—Eyewitness News (2013) *Four Days in Seattle The 1999 WTO Riots plus news stories one week later*. Available at: https://www.youtube.com/watch?v=pFamvR9CpYw (Accessed October 15, 2018).

Klein, N. (2000) *No Logo*. New York: Picador.

Kleinert, U. (1984) *Gewaltfrei widerstehen. Brokdorf-Protokolle*. Hamburg: Rowohlt.

Klusemann, S. (2009) "Atrocities and Confrontational Tension," *Frontiers in Behavioral Neuroscience*, 3(42), pp. 1–10.

Klusemann, S. (2012) "Massacres as Process: A Micro-Sociological Theory of Internal Patterns of Mass Atrocities," *European Journal of Criminology*, 9(5), pp. 468–480. doi: 10.1177/1477370812450825.

Knoblauch, H., et al. (eds.) (2006) *Video Analysis: Methodology and Methods: Qualitative Audiovisual Data Analysis in Sociology*. Frankfurt am Main: Peter Lang.

Kraushaar, W. (1998) *Frankfurter Schule und Studentenbewegung. Von der Flaschenpost zum Molotowcocktail 1946 bis 1995. 3 Bände*. Hamburg: Rogner & Bernhard.

Krulwich, R., and Abumrad, J. (2015) "Outside Westgate." Available at: http://www.radiolab.org/story/outside-westgate/ (Accessed May 15, 2018).

Laitin, D. D. (2008) "Confronting Violence Face to Face," *Science*, 320(5872), pp. 51–52.

Langman, P. (2009) "Rampage School Shooters: A Typology," *Aggression and Violent Behavior*, 14(1), pp. 79–86.

Le Bon, G. (2010) *The Crowd: Study of the Popular Mind*. New York: Classic Books International.

Leary, M. R., et al. (2003) "Teasing, Rejection, and Violence: Case Studies of the School Shootings," *Aggressive Behavior*, 29(3), pp. 202–214. doi: 10.1002/ab.10061.

LeCompte, M. D., and Goetz, J. P. (1982) "Problems of Reliability and Validity in Ethnographic Research," *Review of Educational Research*, 52(1), pp. 31–60. doi: 10.3102/00346543052001031.

Leen, J. (1999) "The Vietnam Protests: When Worlds Collided," *Washington Post*, September 27. Available at: http://www.washingtonpost.com/wp-srv/local/2000/vietnam092799.htm (Accessed September 20, 2011).

Legewie, N. (2013) "An Introduction to Applied Data Analysis with Qualitative Comparative Analysis," *Forum Qualitative Sozialforschung / Forum: Qualitative Social Research*, 14(3).

Legewie, N. (2017) "Anchored Calibration: From Qualitative Data to Fuzzy Sets," *Forum Qualitative Sozialforschung / Forum: Qualitative Social Research*, 18(3). doi: 10.17169/fqs-18.3.2790.

Legewie, N., and Nassauer, A. (2018) "YouTube, Google, Facebook: 21st Century Online Video Research and Research Ethics," *Forum Qualitative Sozialforschung / Forum: Qualitative Social Research*, 19(3). doi: 10.17169/fqs-19.3.3130.

Léglise-Bataille, H. (2007) *June 2*. Flickr. Available at: https://www.flickr.com/photos/hughes_leglise/527069597/in/photostream/ (Accessed April 5, 2018).

Levine, M., Taylor, P. J., and Best, R. (2011) "Third Parties, Violence, and Conflict Resolution: The Role of Group Size and Collective Action in the Microregulation of Violence," *Psychological Science*, 22(3), pp. 406–412.

Lien, T., and Dave, P. (2016) "In a Cameras-Everywhere Culture, Science Fiction Becomes Reality," *Los Angeles Times*, November 4. Available at: http://www.latimes.com/business/la-fi-0411-cameras-everywhere-20150412-story.html (Accessed January 11, 2018).

Lindegaard, M. R., Bernasco, W., and Jacques, S. (2015) "Consequences of Expected and Observed Victim Resistance for Offender Violence During Robbery Events," *Journal of Research in Crime and Delinquency*, 52(1), pp. 32–61.

Ling, W. (2012) *Spring Offensive 1971—Mayday March on Washington*. Available at: http://www.youtube.com/watch?v=0dTEzIBcHfo&feature=youtube_gdata_player (Accessed August 20, 2018).

Lodhi, A. Q., and Tilly, C. (1973) "Urbanization, Crime, and Collective Violence in 19th-Century France," *American Journal of Sociology*, 79(2), pp. 296–318.

Lojowsky, M. (2009) "Seattle to Pittsburgh: A Look at North America's Global Justice Movement Ten Years Later via the G-20 in Pittsburgh," October 29. Available at: http://pittsburgh.indymedia.org/news/2009/10/31437.php (Accessed August 14, 2018).

Lopez, G. (2016) *What Does Race Have to Do with the Ferguson Protests?* Vox. Available at: https://www.vox.com/cards/mike-brown-protests-ferguson-missouri/ferguson-protests-police-racism (Accessed August 15, 2018).

Lucas, S. R., and Szatrowski, A. (2014) "Qualitative Comparative Analysis in Critical Perspective," *Sociological Methodology*, 44(1), pp. 1–79.

Luckenbill, D. F. (1980) "Patterns of Force in Robbery," *Deviant Behavior*, 1(3–4), pp. 361–378. doi: 10.1080/01639625.1980.9967533.

Luckenbill, D. F. (1981) "Generating Compliance: 'The Case of Robbery'," *Urban Life*, 10(1), pp. 1–25.

Luckmann, T. (2006) "Natural Problems of Naturalistic Video Data," in H. Knoblauch et al. (eds.), *Video Analysis: Methodology and Methods: Qualitative Audiovisual Data Analysis in Sociology*, pp. 29–35. Frankfurt am Main: Peter Lang.

Madensen, T. D., and Eck, J. E. (2008) "Violence in Bars: Exploring the Impact of Place Manager Decision-Making," *Crime Prevention and Community Safety*, 10(2), pp. 111–125. doi: 10.1057/cpcs.2008.2.

Madensen, T. D., and Knutsson, J. (eds.) (2011) *Preventing Crowd Violence*. Boulder, CO: Lynne Rienner Pub.

Mahler, J. (2014) "YouTube's Chief, Hitting a New 'Play' Button," *The New York Times*, December 20. Available at: http://www.nytimes.com/2014/12/21/business/youtubes-chief-hitting-a-new-play-button.html (Accessed November 7, 2018).

Martin, A. (2009) "Undercover with the Anarchist Mob: How the Mail Infiltrated the Group at Heart of the Violence," *Daily Mail*, February 4. Available at: http://www.dailymail.co.uk/news/article-1166549/Undercover-anarchist-mob-How-Mail-infiltrated-group-heart-violence.html (Accessed May 15, 2018).

Marx, A. (2006) "Towards More Robust Model Specification in QCA: Results from a Methodological Experiment." *Compasss Working Paper*, 43. http:\\www.compasss.org\wpseries\Marx2006.pdf (Accessed December 05, 2018).

Marx, G. T. (1998) "Afterword: Some Reflections on the Democratic Policing of Demonstrations," in D. Della Porta and H. Reiter (eds.), *Policing Protest: The Control of Mass Demonstrations in Western Democracies*, pp. 253–271. Minneapolis: University of Minnesota Press.

Marx, G. T. (2006) "Afterword: Some Reflections on the Democratic Policing of Demonstrations," in D. Della Porta, A. Peterson, and H. Reiter (eds.), *The Policing of Transnational Protest (Advances in Criminology)*, pp. 253–270. Burlingtion, VT: Ashgate.

Matthews, S., and Noor, M. (2018) *Black Lives Matter 4-Year Anniversary Report*. Black Lives Matter, pp. 1–33. Available at: https://blacklivesmatter.com/resource/4-year-anniversary-report/ (Accessed August 15, 2018).

Mayring, P. (2007) *Qualitative Inhaltsanalyse. Grundlagen und Techniken*. Basel, Switzerland: Beltz Verlag.

Mazur, A., et al. (1980) "Physiological Aspects of Communication Via Mutual Gaze," *American Journal of Sociology*, 86(1), pp. 50–74.

Mazur, A. (2009) "A Hormonal Interpretation of Collins's Micro-sociological Theory of Violence," *Journal for the Theory of Social Behaviour*, 39(4), pp. 434–447.

McAdam, D., Tarrow, S. G., and Tilly, C. (2001) *Dynamics of Contention*. Cambridge, UK: Cambridge University Press.

McCarthy, J. D., McPhail, C., and Smith, J. (1996) "Images of Protest: Dimensions of Selection Bias in Media Coverage of Washington Demonstrations, 1982 and 1991," *American Sociological Review*, 61(3), pp. 478–499.

McCleery, M. J. (2016) "Randall Collins' Forward Panic Pathway to Violence and the 1972 Bloody Sunday Killings in Northern Ireland," *British Journal of Politics and International Relations*.

McPhail, C. (1991) *The Myth of the Madding Crowd*. New York: Aldine Transaction.

McPhail, C., and McCarthy, J. D. (2005) "Protest Mobilization, Protest Repression, and Their Interaction," in C. Davenport, H. Johnston, and C. M. Mueller (eds.), *Repression and Mobilization*, pp. 3–33. Minneapolis: University of Minnesota Press.

McPhail, C., Schweingruber, D., and McCarthy, J. D. (1998) "Policing Protest in the United States: 1960–1995," in D. Della Porta and H. Reiter (eds.), *Policing Protest: The Control of Mass Demonstrations in Western Democracies*, pp. 49–69. Minneapolis: University of Minnesota Press.

Miami Police Department (2004) *FTAA After Action Review*, p. 54. Available at: http://www.docstoc.com/docs/89875998/FTAA-after-Action-Review (Accessed August 20, 2011).

Minkoff, D. (1995) *Organizing for Equality: The Evolution of Women's and Racial-Ethnic Organizations in America, 1955–1985*. New Brunswick, NJ: Rutgers University Press.

Minkoff, D. (1997) "The Sequencing of Social Movements," *American Sociological Review*, 62(5), pp. 779–799.

Mitteldeutsche Zeitung (2007) "Demo 'für globale Bewegungsfreiheit'," *Mitteldeutsche Zeitung Online*, April 6. Available at: https://www.mz-web.de/politik/g-8-gipfeltreffen-demo--fuer-globale-bewegungsfreiheit--8783292# (Accessed July 2, 2018).

Montgomery, D. (2000) "Protests End with Voluntary Arrests," *The Washington Post*, August 4. Available at: http://www.washingtonpost.com/archive/politics/2000/04/

18/protests-end-with-voluntary-arrests/0d629058-fc77-4547-9033-e1aacbd3c5b9/ (Accessed February 14, 2018).

Moran, M., and Waddington, D. (2016) "Back to the Future: Race and Riots in Ferguson, Missouri," in *Riots*, pp. 141–170. London: Palgrave Macmillan.

Mosselman, F., Weenink, D., and Lindegaard, M. R. (2018) "Weapons, Body Postures, and the Quest for Dominance in Robberies: A Qualitative Analysis of Video Footage," *Journal of Research in Crime and Delinquency*, 55(1), pp. 3–26.

MSNBC (2014) *Ferguson, MO: A Resident's Perspective*. MSNBC. Available at: https://www.youtube.com/watch?v=Kdo9C_GbdgI (Accessed August 5, 2018).

Mucchielli, D. L. (2009) "Autumn 2005: A Review of the Most Important Riot in the History of French Contemporary Society," *Journal of Ethnic and Migration Studies*, 35(5), pp. 731–751.

Nadir (1999) *0630WTO Winning*. Available at: https://nadir.org/nadir/initiativ/agp/images/global/2-seattle/0630wtowinning.jpg (Accessed February 22, 2018).

Nassauer, A. (2016) "Theoretische Überlegungen zur Entstehung von Gewalt in Protesten," *Berliner Journal für Soziologie*, 25, pp. 491–518.

Nassauer, A. (2018a) "A Peaceful Human Nature? Towards an Interdisciplinary Social Theory of Violence," in *American Sociological Association*, pp. 1–30. Philadelphia: American Sociological Association.

Nassauer, A. (2018b) "How Robberies Succeed or Fail: Analyzing Crime Caught on CCTV," *Journal of Research in Crime and Delinquency*, 55(1), pp.125–154.

Nassauer, A. (2018c). "Situational Dynamics and the Emergence of Violence in Protests," *Psychology of Violence*, 8(3), pp. 293–304.

Nassauer, A., and Legewie, N. (2018) "Video Data Analysis: A Methodological Frame for a Novel Research Trend," *Sociological Methods & Research*. Available at: https://doi.org/10.1177/0049124118769093 (Accessed December 05, 2018).

National Research Council (2004) *Fairness and Effectiveness in Policing: The Evidence*. Washington, DC: National Academies Press.

Nelson, M. (1999) *Image 51534325*. Getty Images. Available at: http://media.gettyimages.com/photos/demonstrator-smashes-the-window-of-a-starbucks-coffee-house-during-picture-id51534325 (Accessed February 20, 2018).

Nereim, V. (2009) "Closings Prevail as City Welcomes G-20 Summit," *Pittsburgh Post-Gazette*, September 21. Available at: https://www.myownplacehere.com/2009/09/closings-prevail-as-pitt-welcomes-g-20.html (Accessed May 15, 2018).

New York Times (1988) "Yes, a Police Riot," *The New York Times*, August 26. Available at: http://www.nytimes.com/1988/08/26/opinion/yes-a-police-riot.html (Accessed October 5, 2018).

New York Times (2012) "May 3, 1971—Mayday Tribe Holds Antiwar Demonstration," *The New York Times—The Learning Network Blog*, March 5. Available at: http://learning.blogs.nytimes.com/2012/05/03/may-3-1971-mayday-tribe-holds-anti-war-demonstration-in-washington/ (Accessed April 18, 2018).

New York Times (2014a) *Michael Brown's Body*. Available at: https://www.youtube.com/watch?v=fgk9ntN1Dp8 (Accessed August 5, 2018).

New York Times (2014b) *Standoff in Ferguson After Death of Michael Brown*. Available at: https://www.youtube.com/watch?v=J2wgGugTZg0 (Accessed August 5, 2018).

Newman, K. S., et al. (2005) *Rampage: The Social Roots of School Shootings*. New York: Basic Books.

Noakes, J. A., and Gillham, P. F. (2006) "Aspects of the 'New Penology' in the Police Response to Major Political Protests in the United States, 1999–2000," in D. Della Porta, A. Peterson, and H Reiter.(eds.), *The Policing of Transnational Protest (Advances in Criminology)*, pp. 97–117. Burlington, VT: Ashgate.

Noakes, J. A., Klocke, B. V., and Gillham, P. F. (2005) "Whose Streets? Police and Protester Struggles over Space in Washington, DC, 29–30 September 2001," *Policing and Society*, 15(3), pp. 235–254.

Norddeutscher Rundfunk (2011) "1981: Großdemo gegen AKW Brokdorf," *Norddeutscher Rundfunk*, May 31. Available at: http://www.ndr.de/geschichte/schauplaetze/brokdorfdemonstration101.html (Accessed August 19, 2018).

OECD (2015) *In It Together: Why Less Inequality Benefits All*. Paris: Organisation for Economic Co-operation and Development. Available at: http://www.oecd-ilibrary.org/content/book/9789264235120-en.

Offby1 (1999) *Broken Store Window*. Flickr—Photo Sharing! Available at: https://www.flickr.com/photos/offby1/346359748/ (Accessed February 10, 2018).

Ola, M. (2015) *Baltimore Freddy Grey Style Protests*. Available at: https://www.youtube.com/watch?v=Gi--ImW7gPE (Accessed August 1, 2018).

Olzak, S. (1989) "Labor Unrest, Immigration, and Ethnic Conflict in Urban America, 1880–1914," *American Journal of Sociology*, 94(6), pp. 1303–1333.

Owens, L., and Palmer, L. K. (2003) "Making the News: Anarchist Counter-Public Relations on the World Wide Web," *Critical Studies in Media Communication*, 20(4), pp. 335–361.

Oxford Dictionaries (2018) *English*. Oxford Dictionaries. Available at: https://en.oxforddictionaries.com/definition/riot (Accessed August 15, 2018).

Parry, G., Moyser, G., and Wagstaffe, M. (1987) "The Crowd and the Community: Context, Content and Aftermath," in G. Gaskell and R. Benewick (eds.), *The Crowd in Contemporary Britain*, pp. 212–254. London: Sage.

People's March Reaches Downtown Pittsburgh (2009) *People's March Reaches Downtown Pittsburgh*. Available at: http://www.youtube.com/watch?v=C7k5_1ZBjjw&feature=youtube_gdata_player (Accessed October 12, 2018).

Pérez-Peña, R. (2017) "Six Baltimore Officers Indicted in Death of Freddie Gray," *The New York Times*, December 21. Available at: https://www.nytimes.com/2015/05/22/us/six-baltimore-officers-indicted-in-death-of-freddie-gray.html (Accessed October 28, 2018).

Peterson, D., and Wrangham, R. (1997) *Demonic Males: Apes and the Origins of Human Violence*. Boston: Mariner Books.

Petrosino, A. J., Fellow, S., and Brensilber, D. (1997) "Convenient Victims—A Research Note," *Criminal Justice Policy Review*, 8(4), pp. 405–420. doi: 10.1177/088740349700800405.

Pfohl, M. (2007) "G8-Gipfel: "Es ging ums nackte Überleben'," *stern.de*, August 27. Available at: http://www.stern.de/politik/deutschland/g8-gipfel-es-ging-ums-nackte-ueberleben-596228.html (Accessed May 15, 2018).

PicAxe Productions (2000) *Breaking the Spell*. Available at: http://www.youtube.com/watch?v=HPXNuaTK1kM&list=PL036CAA765F313D6E (Accessed February 15, 2018).

Pilz (2007) *G8 Burning Car.* Flickriver. Available at: http://www.flickriver.com/photos/22053943@N07/2442752251/ (Accessed April 10, 1 2018).

Pinker, S. (2012) *The Better Angels of Our Nature: Why Violence Has Declined.* New York: Penguin Books.

Pitt, D. E. (1988) "Roots of Tompkins Sq. Clash Seen in Young and Inexperienced Officer Corps," *New York Times*, August 25. Available at: http://www.nytimes.com/1988/08/25/nyregion/roots-of-tompkins-sq-clash-seen-in-young-and-inexperienced-officer-corps.html?pagewanted=all&src=pm (Accessed August 12, 2018).

Purdum, T. S. (1988) "Findings on Tompkins Sq. Prompt 2 Police Supervisors to Lose Posts," *New York Times*, August 25. Available at: http://www.nytimes.com/1988/08/25/nyregion/findings-on-tompkins-sq-prompt-2-police-supervisors-to-lose-posts.html?pagewanted=all&src=pm (Accessed August 12, 2018).

Rabouin, D. (2014) "Ferguson Riots Underscore Lack of Modern Day Black Leadership," *International Business Times*, November 26. Available at: https://www.ibtimes.com/ferguson-riots-underscore-lack-modern-day-black-leadership-1729553 (Accessed August 5, 2018).

Radnor, A. (2014) "That's Me in the Picture: Jan Rose Kasmir at an Anti-Vietnam War Rally at the Pentagon, in 1967," *The Guardian*, November 7. Available at: https://www.theguardian.com/artanddesign/2014/nov/07/jan-rose-kasmir-anti-vietnam-rally-pentagon (Accessed September 2, 2018).

Rafail, P., Soule, S. A., and McCarthy, J. D. (2012) "Describing and Accounting for the Trends in US Protest Policing, 1960–1995," *Journal of Conflict Resolution*, 56(4), pp. 736–765.

Ragin, C. C. (1987) *The Comparative Method: Moving Beyond Qualitative and Quantitative Strategies.* Berkeley: University of California Press.

Ragin, C. C. (1994) *Constructing Social Research: The Unity and Diversity of Method.* Thousand Oaks, CA: Pine Forge Press.

Ragin, C. C. (2008) *Redesigning Social Inquiry: Fuzzy Sets and Beyond.* Chicago: University of Chicago Press.

Ragin, C. C. (2014) "Comment: Lucas and Szatrowski in Critical Perspective," *Sociological Methodology*, 44, pp. 80–94.

Ramelsberger, A. (2007) "Ausschreitungen in Rostock vor dem G-8-Gipfel: Polizei soll härter gegen Randalierer vorgehen," *sueddeutsche.de*, June 4. Available at: http://www.sueddeutsche.de/politik/ausschreitungen-in-rostock-vor-dem-g-gipfel-polizei-soll-haerter-gegen-randalierer-vorgehen-1.784342 (Accessed May 1, 2018).

Ransford, H. E. (1968) "Isolation, Powerlessness, and Violence: A Study of Attitudes and Participation in the Watts Riot," *American Journal of Sociology*, 73(5), pp. 581–591.

Reemtsma, J. P. (2008) *Vertrauen und Gewalt. Versuch über eine besondere Konstellation der Moderne.* Hamburg: Hamburger Edition.

Reicher, S. D. (1984) "The St. Pauls' Riot: An Explanation of the Limits of Crowd Action in Terms of a Social Identity Model," *European Journal of Social Psychology*, 14(1), pp. 1–21.

Reicher, S. D. (1996) "'The Battle of Westminster': Developing the Social Identity Model of Crowd Behaviour in Order to Explain the Initiation and Development of Collective Conflict," *European Journal of Social Psychology*, 26(1), pp. 115–134.

Reicher, S. D. (1997) "Social Identity and Social Change: Rethinking the Context of Social Psychology," in W. P. Robinson (ed.), *Social Groups and Identities: Developing the Legacy of Henri Tajfel*, pp. 317–336. London: Butterworth.

Reicher, S. D. (2001) "The Psychology of Crowd Dynamics," in M. A. Hogg and S. Tindale (eds.), *Blackwell Handbook of Social Psychology: Group Processes*, pp. 182–208. Oxford: John Wiley.

Reicher, S. D., et al. (2004) "An Integrated Approach to Crowd Psychology and Public Order Policing," *Policing: An International Journal of Police Strategies & Management*, 27(4), pp. 558–572.

Reicher, S. D., et al. (2007) "Knowledge-Based Public Order Policing: Principles and Practice," *Policing*, 1(4), pp. 403–415.

Revista (2009) "Der Gorleben-Treck 1979 kommt durch Hermannsburg und Celle," *Revista*, 42, pp. 20–23.

Rieff, D. (2007) "Battle over the Banlieues," *The New York Times*, April 14. Available at: https://www.nytimes.com/2007/04/15/world/europe/15iht-web-0415elections.5290550.html (Accessed August 15, 2018).

Rihoux, B. (2009) "Qualitative Comparative Analysis (QCA) and Related Techniques: Recent Advances and Challenges," in S. Pickel et al. (eds.), *Methoden der vergleichenden Politik- und Sozialwissenschaft: Neue Entwicklungen und Anwendungen*, pp. 365–386. Wiesbaden, Germany: Verlag für Sozialwissenschaften.

Rihoux, B., et al. (2013) "From Niche to Mainstream Method? A Comprehensive Mapping of QCA Applications in Journal Articles from 1984 to 2011," *Political Research Quarterly*, 66(1), pp. 175–184.

Rilling, J. K., et al. (2002) "A Neural Basis for Social Cooperation," *Neuron*, 35(2), pp. 395–405. doi: 10.1016/S0896-6273(02)00755-9.

RNC Review Commission (2009) *Report of the Republican National Convention Public Safety Planning and Implementation Review Commission*. Available at: https://www.stpaul.gov/DocumentCenter/Government/Marketing/Republican%20National%20Convention/RNC%20Commission%20Report%20&%20Executive%20Summary/FINALRNCCommissionReport.PDF (Accessed July 17, 2018).

Roelcke, E. (2007) "Eine 'einsatztechnische Dummheit'," *Deutschlandradio Kultur*, April 6. Available at: http://www.deutschlandradiokultur.de/eine-einsatztechnische-dummheit.945.de.html?dram:article_id=132531 (Accessed May 10, 2018).

Rogers, P. (2012) "Police, Peaceful Protesters: Beware the 'Black Bloc'," *NBC Chicago*, May 15. Available at: http://www.nbcchicago.com/news/local/chicago-nato-summit-protesters-black-bloc-151650715.html (Accessed May 15, 2018).

Rosie, M., and Gorringe, H. (2009) "The Anarchists' World Cup: Respectable Protest and Media Panics," *Social Movement Studies*, 8(1), pp. 35–53.

Rothstein, R. (2015) "From Ferguson to Baltimore: The Fruits of Government-Sponsored Segregation," *LSE Blog*, p. 5. Available at: http://eprints.lse.ac.uk/61952/1/blogs.lse.ac.uk-From%20Ferguson%20to%20BaltimorenbspThe%20Fruits%20of%20Government-Sponsored%20Segregation.pdf (Accessed August 2, 2018).

RT (2014a) *USA: Store Fronts Smashed as Looting Sets In During Ferguson Protest*. Available at: https://www.youtube.com/watch?v=rOwOh6oRCww (Accessed August 5, 2018).

RT (2014b) *"You Must Disperse Now!" Missouri Police Crack Down on Ferguson Protesters*. Available at: https://www.youtube.com/watch?v=SQkwrrMSyRE (Accessed August 5, 2018).

RTL Hessen (2008) *Studenten vs. Polizei*. Available at: http://ea-frankfurt.org/presseschau (Accessed May 16, 2013).

Rubinstein, J. (1973) *City Police*. New York: Ballantine Books.

Rummel, R. J. (1997) *Statistics of Democide: Genocide and Mass Murder since 1900*. Charlottesville: Center for National Security Law, School of Law, University of Virginia.

Ryan, C. (1999) *Prime Time Activism: Media Strategies for Grassroots Organizing*. Boston: South End Press.

Rydgren, J. (2007) "The Power of the Past: A Contribution to a Cognitive Sociology of Ethnic Conflict," *Sociological Theory*, 25(3), pp. 225–244.

Savkoeln (2009) *Anti-NATO-Demo, Kehl, 4.4.2009*. Available at: http://www.youtube. com/watch?v=1od3dFJiWxw&feature=youtube_gdata_player (Accessed August 15, 2018).

Sayoc, L. E. (1999) *WTO-Toy Soldiers*. Available at: https://www.flickr.com/photos/ 96826270@N00/363217634/ (Accessed October 29, 2018).

Scahill, J. (2003) *The Miami Model: Paramilitaries, Embedded Journalists and Illegal Protests. Think This Is Iraq? It's Your Country*. Common Dreams. Available at: http://www.commondreams.org/views/2003/11/25/miami-model-paramilitaries-embedded-journalists-and-illegal-protests-think-iraq-its (Accessed June 22, 2017).

von Scheve, C. (2012) "The Social Calibration of Emotion Expression: An Affective Basis of Micro-social Order," *Sociological Theory*, 30(1), pp. 1–14. doi: 10.1177/ 0735275112437163.

Schlieben, M. (2009) "Gipfel-Krawalle: Polizei befürchtet in Straßburg aggressive Proteste," *Die Zeit*, March 4. Available at: http://www.zeit.de/online/2009/15/gipfel-nato-strassburg-london (Accessed May 4, 2018).

Schneider, C. Q., and Rohlfing, I. (2013) "Combining QCA and Process Tracing in Set-Theoretic Multi-Method Research," *Sociological Methods & Research*, 42(4), pp. 559–597.

Schneider, C. Q., and Wagemann, C. (2007) *Qualitative Comparative Analysis (QCA) und Fuzzy Sets: Ein Lehrbuch für Anwender und Jene, die es Werden Wollen*. Opladen, Germany: Budrich.

Schneider, C. Q., and Wagemann, C. (2012) *Set-Theoretic Methods for the Social Sciences: A Guide to Qualitative Comparative Analysis*. Cambridge, UK: Cambridge University Press.

Schneider, J. (2014) "Ferguson: Riot or Rebellion?," *Huffingtion Post*, December 19. Available at: https://www.huffingtonpost.com/jack-schneider/ferguson-race-riots-rebellion_b_6354102.html (Accessed August 15, 2018).

Schröder, J. (2012) *Bericht über Brokdorf am 28.2.1981*. Available at: http://www.mao-projekt.de/BRD/NOR/S-H/Brokdorf_AKW_1981_Grundrechte.shtml (Accessed January 10, 2017).

Schweber, N. (2011) "Penn State Students Clash with Police After Paterno Announcement," *The New York Times*, November 10. Available at: https://www.nytimes.com/2011/11/

11/sports/ncaafootball/penn-state-students-in-clashes-after-joe-paterno-is-ousted. html (Accessed August 5, 2018).

Seattle Times (1999a) A Black-Clad Anarchist Smashes a Window at a Gap Store. *Seattle Times: WTO in Seattle 1999 Photo Gallery.* Available at: http://old.seattletimes.com/ special/wto/gallery/photo11.html (Accessed August 12, 2016).

Seattle Times (1999b) *Anti-WTO Protesters Use Bicycle Locks Around Their Necks to Chain Themselves Together to Block Access to the Convention Center. Seattle Times.* Available at: http://old.seattletimes.com/special/wto/gallery/photo8.html (Accessed June 12, 2016).

Shapira, H. (2016) "An Education in Violence: Teaching and Learning to Kill in America." Seattle: American Sociological Association—Annual Meeting. *Regular Session: Interpersonal Violence.*

Shott, S. (1979) "Emotion and Social Life: A Symbolic Interactionist Analysis," *American Journal of Sociology*, 84(6), pp. 1317–1334.

Shunpiker (1999) *It's a Dirty Job.* Available at: https://www.flickr.com/photos/shunpiker/ 136316121/ (Accessed January 16, 2018).

Siegel, A., and Victoroff, J. (2009) "Understanding Human Aggression: New Insights from Neuroscience," *International Journal of Law and Psychiatry*, 32(4), pp. 209– 215. doi: 10.1016/j.ijlp.2009.06.001.

Silverberg, J., and Gray, J. P. (eds.) (1992) *Aggression and Peacefulness in Humans and Other Primates.* 1 edition. New York: Oxford University Press.

Simpson, B., Willer, R., and Feinberg, M. (2018) "Does Violent Protest Backfire? Testing a Theory of Public Reactions to Activist Violence," *Socius*, 4, doi:10.1177/ 2378023118803189.

Simpson, I. (2011) "Students Protest Firing of College Coach Paterno," *Reuters*, November 10. Available at: https://www.reuters.com/article/us-usa-crime-coach-reaction/hundreds-of-penn-state-students-protest-paterno-firing-idUSTRE7A90WC20111110 (Accessed August 5, 2018).

Smith, R. S. (1995) "Giving Credit Where Credit Is Due: Dorothy Swaine Thomas and the 'Thomas Theorem'," *The American Sociologist*, 26(4), pp. 9–28.

Smydo, J. (2009) "City Schools to Close During G-20 Summit," *Pittsburgh Post-Gazette*, August 20. Available at: http://www.post-gazette.com/local/city/2009/08/20/City-schools-to-close-during-G-20-summit/stories/200908200370 (Accessed May 15, 2015).

Snow, D. A., and Moss, D. M. (2014) "Protest on the Fly: Toward a Theory of Spontaneity in the Dynamics of Protest and Social Movements," *American Sociological Review*, 79(6), pp. 1122–1143.

Solomon, B., and Levin, D. (directors) (2008) *Captured.* Blowback & Benvsdan Productions.

Sommer, F., Leuschner, V., and Scheithauer, H. (2014) "Bullying, Romantic Rejection, and Conflicts with Teachers: The Crucial Role of Social Dynamics in the Development of School Shootings—A Systematic Review," *International Journal of Developmental Science*, 8(1), pp. 3–24.

Soule, S. A., and Davenport, C. (2009) "Velvet Glove, Iron Fist, or Even Hand? Protest Policing in the United States, 1960–1990," *Mobilization*, 14(1), pp. 1–22.

Soule, S. A., and Earl, J. (2005) "A Movement Society Evaluated: Collective Protest in the United States, 1960–1986," *Mobilization*, 10(3), pp. 345–364.

Sousa, C., and Casanova, C. (2006) "Are Great Apes Aggressive? A Cross-Species Comparison," *Antropologia Portuguesa*, 22.

Stanford University (2009) "Dynamics of Collective Action Dataset." Available at: http://www.stanford.edu/group/collectiveaction/cgi-bin/drupal/ (Accessed April 15, 2018).

Starhawk (2002) *Webs of Power: Notes from the Global Uprising*. Gabriola Island, BC: New Society Publishers.

Starr, A., and Fernandez, L. A. (2009) "Legal Control and Resistance Post-Seattle," *Social Justice*, 36(1), pp. 41–60.

Steven, E., and Narr, W.-D. (2007) *Gewaltbereite Politik und der G8 Gipfel*. Edited by Komitee für Grundrechte und Demokratie. Einhausen, Germany: HBO Druck.

Stirland, S. L. (2008) "Video of Clashes Between St. Paul Police and RNC Protestors Bubble Up Online," *Wired*. Available at: http://www.wired.com/2008/09/footage-of-clas/ (Accessed May 16, 2018).

Stott, C., and Drury, J. (2000) "Crowds, Context and Identity: Dynamic Categorization Processes in the 'Poll Tax Riot'," *Human Relations*, 53(2), pp. 247–273.

Stott, C., and Reicher, S. (1998) "Crowd Action as Intergroup Process: Introducing the Police Perspective," *European Journal of Social Psychology*, 28(4), pp. 509–529.

Stowasser, H. (2007) *Anarchie! Idee—Geschichte—Perspektiven*. Hamburg: Edition Nautilus.

Süddeutsche Zeitung (2007) "Demo gegen G8—Bunt, bunter, nackt," *Süddeutsche.de*, May 6. Available at: http://www.sueddeutsche.de/politik/demo-gegen-g-bunt-bunter-nackt-1.309543-14 (Accessed January 15, 2016).

Sussman, R. W., and Marshack, J. (2010) "Are humans inherently killers?, " *Global Non-Killing Working Papers*, 1, pp. 7–28.

Sutterlüty, F. (2014) "The Hidden Morale of the 2005 French and 2011 English Riots," *Thesis Eleven*, 121(1), pp. 38–56.

Sutterlüty, F. (2017) "Fallstricke situationistischer Gewaltforschung," *WestEnd. Neue Zeitschrift für Sozialforschung*, 14(2), pp. 139–155.

Swidler, A. (1986) "Culture in Action: Symbols and Strategies," *American Sociological Review*, 51(2), pp. 273–286.

Swiola (2009) *Von Kehl nach Strasbourg: Wir sind friedlich, was seid ihr ?* Available at: http://www.youtube.com/watch?v=a-6PgWdJw4k&feature=youtube_gdata_player (Accessed August 20, 2017).

Tabibnia, G., Satpute, A. B., and Lieberman, M. D. (2008) "The Sunny Side of Fairness Preference for Fairness Activates Reward Circuitry (and Disregarding Unfairness Activates Self-Control Circuitry)," *Psychological Science*, 19(4), pp. 339–347. doi: 10.1111/j.1467-9280.2008.02091.x.

Taylor, K.-Y. (2014) *Rats, Riots and Revolution: Black Housing in the 1960s*. Chicago: Haymarket Books.

Taylor, K.-Y. (2016) *From #BlackLivesMatter to Black Liberation*. Chicago: Haymarket Books.

Telengard (2007) *Tompkins Square Park Riot*. Available at: http://www.youtube.com/watch?v=bunhcwSvil8&feature=youtube_gdata_player (Accessed May 18, 2018).

Terrill, W. (2003) "Police Use of Force and Suspect Resistance: The Micro Process of the Police-Suspect Encounter," *Police Quarterly*, 6(1), pp. 51–83.

Theweleit, K. (2015) *Das Lachen der Täter: Breivik u.a.: Psychogramm der Tötungslust. Unruhe bewahren*. St. Pölten, Austria: Residenz.

ThingLink (1967) *La jeune fille à la fleur de Marc Riboud (1967) by klaudia*. Available at: https://www.thinglink.com/scene/590894714060800000 (Accessed November 3, 2018).

Thomas, W. I., and Thomas, D. S. (1938) *The Child in America: Behavior Problems and Programs*. New York: A. A. Knopf.

Tilly, C., and Tarrow, S. G. (2006) *Contentious Politics*. Boulder, CO: Paradigm.

Time (2014) *Am I Next?' Ferguson's Protests Through the Eyes of a Teenager*. Available at: https://www.youtube.com/watch?v=KuqV1FwMws4 (Accessed August 5, 2018).

Transnational Institute (2007) *March G8 2 June, Rostock (114)*. Flickr—Photo Sharing! Available at: https://www.flickr.com/photos/tni/552227685/ (Accessed March 20, 2017).

Tresyk (1999) *Riot Police*. Available at: https://www.flickr.com/photos/tresy/4407549987/ (Accessed October 29, 2018).

Ullrich, P. (2017) "'Normalbürger' versus 'Krawalltouristen.' Polizeiliche Kategorisierung von Demonstrationen zwischen Recht und soziologischem Ermessen," in K. Liebl (ed.), *Empirische Polizeiforschung XX. Polizei und Minderheiten*, pp. 61–97. Frankfurt am Main: Verlag für Polizeiwissenschaft.

Unger, H. von, Narimani, P., and M'Bayo, R. (eds) (2014) *Forschungsethik in der qualitativen Forschung: Reflexivität, Perspektiven, Positionen*. Wiesbaden, Germany: Springer VS.

United Nations (1948) *Universal Declaration of Human Rights*. Paris: United Nations General Assembly, pp. 1–8. Available at: https://www.ohchr.org/EN/UDHR/Documents/UDHR_Translations/eng.pdf (Accessed May 15, 2018).

U.S. Department of Justice, COPS and IIR (2015) *After-Action Assessment of the Police Response to the August 2014 Demonstrations in Ferguson, Missouri*. Washington, DC: U. S. Department of Justice Office of Community Oriented Policing Services. Available at: https://ric-zai-inc.com/Publications/cops-p317-pub.pdf.

U.S. Marshals Service (2011) *History—U.S. Marshals and the Pentagon Riot of October 21, 1967*. Available at: http://www.usmarshals.gov/history/civilian/1967b.htm (Accessed May 4, 2017).

United States Department of Justice (2015) *Investigation of the Ferguson Police Department*. United States Department of Justice—Civil Rights Division. Available at: https://www.justice.gov/sites/default/files/opa/press-releases/attachments/2015/03/04/ferguson_police_department_report_1.pdf (Accessed August 5, 2018).

Universal Newsreel (2010) *Vietnam War—Pentagon Protest Newsreel*. Available at: http://www.youtube.com/watch?v=tV7CFB4yAdA&feature=youtube_gdata_player (Accessed April 16, 2017).

Useem, B. (1997) "The State and Collective Disorders: The Los Angeles Riot/Protest of April, 1992," *Social Forces*, 76(2), pp. 357–377.

Vaisey, S. (2014) "Comment: QCA Works—When Used with Care," *Sociological Methodology*, 44(1), pp. 108–112.

Vasi, I. B., and Macy, M. (2003) "The Mobilizer's Dilemma: Crisis, Empowerment, and Collective Action," *Social Forces*, 81(3), pp. 979–998.

Vetlesen, A. J. (2014) "Passions in Context—Atrocities. A Case of Suppressing Emotions or of Acting Them Out?," *Passions in Context: International Journal for the History and Theory of Emotions*, 1(2), pp. 35–66.

Vidal, J. (2014) "Virunga Film-Makers Ask Viewers to Join Campaign Against Oil Company SOCO," *The Guardian*, November 5. Available at: http://www.theguardian.com/environment/2014/nov/05/virunga-film-makers-ask-viewers-to-join-campaign-against-oil-company-soco (Accessed May 5, 2017).

Vogel, S. (2007) "Once More to the Pentagon," *The Washington Post*, March 16. Available at: http://www.washingtonpost.com/wp-dyn/content/article/2007/03/15/AR2007031502206.html (Accessed October 15, 2017).

Vrij, A., Hope, L., and Fisher, R. P. (2014) "Eliciting Reliable Information in Investigative Interviews," *Policy Insights from the Behavioral and Brain Sciences*, 1(1), pp. 129–136.

Waddington, P. A. J. (1991) *The Strong Arm of the Law: Armed and Public Order Policing*. New York: Oxford University Press.

Waddington, P. A. J. (1998) "Controlling Protest in Contemporary Historical and Comparative Perspective," in D. Della Porta and H. Reiter (eds.), *Policing Protest: The Control of Mass Demonstrations in Western Democracies*, pp. 117–40. Minneapolis: University of Minnesota Press.

Wahlström, M. (2011) "The Making of Protest and Protest Policing—Negotiation, Knowledge, Space, and Narrative," *Göteborg Studies in Sociology*, 47, pp. 7–81.

Wenner, K. S. (2002) "Major Rally, Minor Play," *American Journalism Review*, December. Available at: http://ajr.org/Article.asp?id=2698 (Accessed March 20, 2018).

Williams, M. (2013) "Trayvon Martin Protests Being Held in More Than 100 US Cities," *The Guardian*, July 20. Available at: https://www.theguardian.com/world/2013/jul/20/trayvon-martin-protests-us-cities (Accessed August 15, 2018).

Winter, L., and Kron, T. (2009) "Fuzzy Thinking in Sociology," in *Views on Fuzzy Sets and Systems from Different Perspectives*, pp. 301–320. Berlin: Springer. doi: 10.1007/978-3-540-93802-6_14.

Winter, M. (1998) "Police Philosophy and Protest Policing in the Federal Republic of Germany, 1960–1990," in D. della Porta and H. Reiter (eds.), *Policing Protest: The Control of Mass Demonstrations in Western Democracies*, pp. 188–213. Minneapolis: University of Minnesota Press.

Wissenschaftszentrum Berlin für Sozialforschung (2011) "PRODAT—Dokumentation und Analyse von Protestereignissen in der Bundesrepublik." Available at: http://www.wzb.eu/de/forschung/beendete-forschungsprogramme/zivilgesellschaft-und-politische-mobilisierung/projekte/prodat-dokument (Accessed April 15, 2018).

Wood, L. J. (2007) "Breaking the Wave: Repression, Identity, and Seattle Tactics," *Mobilization*, 12(4), pp. 377–388.

WorthWatching (2014) *Bassem Masri Gets His Phone Stolen While Livestreaming*. Available at: https://www.youtube.com/watch?v=sIiFkAaNgWw (Accessed August 1, 2018).

Wright, R., and Decker, S. H. (1997) *Armed Robbers in Action: Stickups and Street Culture*. Lebanon, NH: University Press New England.

WTO Accountability Review Committee (2000) *Report of the WTO Accountability Review Committee Seattle City Council*, p. 16. Available at: depts.washington.edu/wtohist/documents/arcfinal.pdf (Accessed January 15, 2018).

Zajko, M., and Béland, D. (2008) "Space and Protest Policing at International Summits," *Environment and Planning D: Society and Space*, 26(4), pp. 719–735.

ZDF Heute (1981) *ZDF Heute—Heinz Wrobel zu Brokdorf-Demonstrationen 28.2.1981 (Fragment).* Available at: http://www.youtube.com/watch?v=-sBnetod03k&feature=youtube_gdata_player (Accessed October 20, 2017).

Zeit Online (1970) "Terror kann keiner verhindern," *Zeit Online*. Available at: https://www.zeit.de/1970/20/terror-kann-keiner-verhindern (Accessed October 29, 2018).

INDEX

Note: Page references followed by a "*t*" indicate table; "*f*" indicate figure.

collective reinterpretations, 176
  mutual gaze and, 177
  out-group actions, 177–78
Collins, Randall, 23, 102, 172–73, 174–75
  on boredom, 121
  on culture, 180–81
  on duration of violence, 107–8
  on emotional dominance, 99–100
  on expectations, 180–81
  on forward panic, 111, 184–85
  on situational dynamics, 186, 197–98
  on tension and fear, 98
  on violence, 171–72
communication, 119, 151, 170
  failed robberies verbal and
    non-verbal, 162–63
  frequent and explicit intentions in, 123
  in-group peaceful intentions, 123
  at Kehl protest, 119–20
  at migrants' rights protest, 119–20
  peaceful protests and, 120
  police communication officers, 123–24
  police loudspeaker vans with LED
    panels, 124, 125
  police speaker trainings for, 120–21
  service announcements for, 120–21,
    123, 150–51
  technical equipment for, 123, 125
communication problems, among police
  at New York Tompkins Square
    Park, 46
  operational command and, 40
  at St. Paul RNC 2008, 46–48
communication problems, between
    protesters and police, 15, 87, 88, 90,
    94, 169, 170
  at Brokdorf protest, 88
  at Kehl protest, 90
  at Miami FTAA protest, 47–48, 88, 124
  mistrust and, 94
  at Rostock G8 protest, 88
  at Seattle WTO protest, 84
  spatial incursions, escalation signs
    and, 15, 94
  technical problems and, 87, 95
  violence and, 14f, 14–15

confrontational tension and fear, 63–64,
    98, 99–100, 143–44, 172, 173
constitutional right to protest, in public
    space, 51
context factors. *See* background factors
crime. *See also* armed store robberies
  culture and, 167–68
  key dynamics of micro-level, 166
crowd violence
  Le Bon theory on, 79–80
  from property damage, 79
cruelty and prolonged fear, 115–16
CS gas and tear gas use, 46–47, 52, 61,
    81–82, 85, 92–93, 99
  at Rostock G8 protest, 1, 4, 45
culturally expected routines, 12
culture, 10, 169. *See also* police
    culture
  armed robberies and, 179–80
  Collins on, 180–81
  crime and, 167–68
  emotion expressions across, 64
  expectations and, 179
  micro-situation and, 179–80
  of protest, violence and, 8–9, 12
  surprising outcomes and role of, 12
  of Western democracies, 104, 181

DAN. *See* direct action network
danger perception, 176
  loss-of-control path and, 67–68, 104
Della Porta, D., 195
demonstrations. *See also specific*
    demonstrations
  as contests over space, 51
  in new social movements, 20–21
  temporal danger zone of, 33
direct action network (DAN), Seattle
    WTO protest and, 82
disarming, as practical measure, 127
document data
  on armed robberies, 16–17
  on protests, 32
  on Rostock G8 protest, 67–68
  of Seattle WTO protest, 84–85
Drury, J., 178

management and, 125
planned police strategies and, 38
on proportionality principle, 39, 40
Rostock G8 protest and, 41
space and, 51–52
unit leaders leeway and, 39, 40
at Vietnam War Pentagon
  demonstration, 60–61
ordinance announcements,
  120–21, 150–51
out-group, 104, 177–78
  homogeneous group and, 178
outnumbered, in micro-situation,
  82–83, 102
out-of-proportion character, in forward
  panic, 111

parade-like atmosphere, 118–19
participant observation, in protest
  violence studies, 189, 209
Patterson, Clayton, 114–15
peaceful protests. *See* non-violent protests
physical contact, violence and, 53, 100–1
physical interpersonal violence. *See also*
  violence
  defined/means, 22, 197
  emotional dominance before, 103
  at Ferguson, 130, 137
  identification and analysis of, 23
  inhibition threshold and, 23
  micro-situation and, 106
  motivations and, 33
  against police, black bloc activists
    and, 36
  police and protesters direct, 22–23
  police shootings connection with, 134
  protest groups and, 19
  protest marches exceptions of, 24
  shouting or property damage
    fostering of, 23
  tension and fear before, 103
  during uprisings, 131
Pittsburgh G20 protest, 2009
  media on, 73
  police management at, 117–18
  video data on, 73, 118

violence expectations for, 72,
  74–75, 117–18
planned police strategies
  Kehl protest contradiction and, 38
  limited impact of, 38–39
  low-profile, tolerant, 14–15
  non-dominant, arrests increase
    and, 37–38
  non-implementation of, 38
  operational command and, 38
  police actions and, 37
  proportionality principle and, 39, 40
  at Rostock G8 protest, 39, 42
  tolerant, in new social
    movements, 20–21
  violence and tolerant, 41, 42
  in Western democracies, 183
police
  emotion expressions of, 55–56
  escalation signs recognition by, 76–77
  space importance to, 51–52
  tensions, from property damage, 78–79
  US situational control tactics of, 68–69
police actions
  police strategies and, 37
  surveillance focus of, 37
  tolerant in 1980s, 37
  Ward on New York Tompkins Square
    Park, 46
police culture, 12
  of control, 65, 67
  danger and loss of control, 67–68, 104
  police objectives and, 67
  police training and, 67
  rare loss of control and, 65
police dogs
  Berlin and, 150
  at Ferguson, 141
police mismanagement, 14*f*, 44, 169,
  170, 186–87
  at Ferguson, 137, 139
  loss-of-control path and, 58
  at New York Tompkins Square
    Park, 45, 59
  at Rostock G8 protest, 44
  at Seattle WTO protest, 83

police mismanagement (*Cont.*)
  spatial incursions and, 15, 58
  at St. Paul, 2008, 46
  tension increase and, 44
  at Vietnam War Pentagon, 60–62
  violence and, 14–15
police objectives, police culture and, 67
police-protester line break ups, 100
  face-to-face confrontation and, 101
  Kehl protest lack of, 100–1
  at Miami FTAA protest, 101
  at New York Tompkins Square
    Park, 101
  at Rostock G8 protest, 101
  solid lines and, 100
police:protester ratio, violence and, 82–83
police reactions
  from police serving state to police
    serving the citizens philosophy, 22
  policing professionalization and, 22
  protest groups and, 19
police riots, 16
  loss-of-control path and, 110–11
  at New York Tompkins Square Park, 45,
    59, 113
police shootings, 130–31, 170–71
  dissatisfaction and, 135
  physical interpersonal violence
    connections with, 134
  uprisings after, 131
  violent uprisings rarity and, 132
police sirens, as escalation sign, 76
police strategies, 200. *See also* tolerant
    police strategy
  agents provocateurs and, 42
  harsh or rigid, 14–15, 44, 62, 180–81
  at Kehl protest, 39
  non-implementation of, 38
  police actions and, 37
  police mismanagement and, 169
  violent outcomes and, 8–9, 10–12, 13, 37
police training, 183
  focus on control, 69
  loss of control and, 67
  management and, 125–26
  police culture and, 67

professionalism and, 68
  on use of force, 68
powerlessness
  emotional dynamics and, 64
  group homogeneity increase
    from, 63–64
  in loss-of-control path, to violence, 62
  at New York Tompkins Square Park, 62
  reinterpretations and, 63, 170
  at Rostock G8 protest, 64
  at Vietnam War Pentagon, 62
  of violent few, 26–27
practical measures, for violence, 17–18,
    24–25, 121
  clear communication, 123–25
  disarming and, 127
  escalation signs awareness and,
    126–27, 170
  police management, 125–26
  pre-emption of escalation signs
    perception, 127
  property damage consequences, 127–28
  temporal danger zone and, 128
  territorial boundaries respect, 126
pre-emptive strikes, 81
  DAN and, 82
process
  identification of, 209
  interactions and, 86, 193
  mechanism combinations and, 209
  QCA on, 209
  routines and, 17
  situational, 175–76, 186–87
  social interactions and, 63
professionalism, of police, 22, 183–84
  management and, 125–26
  police training and, 68
property damage, 78, 169, 170, 195
  of black bloc, 26, 29
  as claim-making, 29, 32
  crowd violence from, 79
  at Ferguson, 137, 143, 146
  at Frankfurt, 78–79
  media on violence of, 31, 81, 144–45
  police tensions raised from, 78–79
  practical measures and, 127–28, 170

escalation signs at, 77–78, 83
excessive violence at, 110
falling down at, 101
GJM and, 81–84
intensity of violence at, 105–6
loss-of-control path at, 84, 86
offense path at, 84–86
police mismanagement at, 83
property damage in, 26, 83–84
protesters outnumbering
    police, 82–83
self-fulfilling prophecy and, 74
temporal sequence of, 115
video and document data of, 84–85
violence expectations for, 74–75
self-fulfilling prophecy, 73, 74–75
Miami FTAA protest and, 74
Seattle WTO protest and, 74
service announcements, 120–21,
    123, 150–51
Shapira, H., 172–73
shouting, for end of violence, 108, 109
sit-ins, for social movements, 20, 195
of GJM, 21
in new social movement, 20–21
situational breakdowns
    in armed store robberies, 157
    beyond protest marches, 130–32
    beyond protest violence, 129
    in robbery, 16–17, 162–63, 166–67
    surprising outcomes and, 6, 17–18,
        129, 157, 170–71, 179, 187–88
    beyond violence, 154
situational dynamics, 24–25, 169
    Bramsen on Arab Spring, 185
    Collins on, 186, 197–98
    individual or group, 12–13
    motivations and, 7–8, 10–12
    for non-democratic countries
        violence, 174–75
    non-violent individual interactions
        and, 10
    of rampage shooters, 173
    routine breakdowns from, 32
    violence context factors
        compared to, 10

situational dynamics studies, in twenty-
    first century
    CCTV use, 190, 191
    interviews in, 189–90
    participant observation in, 189
    video data for, 191–92
    videos use in, 190
    Westgate Mall terrorist attack
        video, 190
    YouTube use, 190–91, 209–10
situational mechanisms, surprising social
    outcomes and, 171, 195
situational order, 173
situational processes, to violence,
    175–76, 186–87
situational unfoldings, 17–18, 34–35, 38–
    39, 41, 43, 122
situational violence researchers, 13
situational weakness, screaming and, 109
situations
    background factors compared to,
        10–12, 24–25
    motivations compared to, 175
    strategies overridden by, 12
social forums, GJM world, 21
social identity-interested crowd
    psychologists, 13
social movements, 183, 195. See also
    global justice movement; new social
    movements; student movements
    property damage and, 20
    sit-ins for, 20
    societal change through, 122
    transnational, 19
social outcomes, 17, 169, 187
social science theory, 175
solidary actions, 182
space. See also public space
    armed store robberies and, 160–61
    in failed robberies, 161
    negotiation for, 52
    police importance of, 51–52
    robbery and, 54
spatial incursions, 51, 170
    at America House, 53
    at Brokdorf protest, 52

invasion of, 65–66
low police profile and
  de-escalation, 126
management and, 126
parade-like atmosphere and, 118–19
at Pittsburgh G20 protest, 118
police and sanctioned route, 126
protest dynamics and, 56
Vietnam War Pentagon demonstration
  invasion of, 112
theoretical implications, 175
collective and individual
  reinterpretations, 176
emotions versus rationality, 175
expectations, culture and violence, 179
inhibition threshold for violence, 181
motivations versus situations, 175
Thomas, Dorothy Swaine, 79–80
Thomas, W. I., 79–80
tolerant police strategy
  arrests increase and, 37–38
  low-profile, 14–15
  in new social movements, 20–21
  in 1980s, 37
  at Vietnam War Pentagon, 61–62
  violence and, 41, 42
Tompkins Square Park. *See* New York
  Tompkins Square Park, 1988
triangulation, VDA and, 197

uncertainty, 15, 58, 87, 95, 96, 188
unfolding, of events, 39, 41, 42, 52, 71, 85
  of robbery, 160, 161–62, 163–65, 166
  situational, 17–18, 34–35, 38–39, 41,
    43, 122
  strategies and, 43, 159–60
United States (US)
  intensity of violence in, 106–7
  left protest group marches in, 19, 23–24
  new social movements in, 20–21
  peaceful protests percentage, 73
  physical violence rare in left protest
    marches, 23–24
  police forces decentralized in, 21–22
  police professionalism in, 68–69
  police situational control tactics in, 68–69

protesters violent actions data for, 24
protest marches 1960 to 2010 in, 9, 19,
  21, 195–96
protest marches routines and peace
  in, 24–25
student movements, 20
violence in uprisings after police
  shootings, 9–10
unit leaders leeway, operational command
  and, 39, 40
universal emotions, 64, 198–200, 201*t*,
  See also emotion expressions
uprisings, 211
  case selection for, 211
  data and analysis for, 212
  interactions, interpretations and
    emotional dynamics in, 16–17
  physical interpersonal violence
    during, 131
  police racial bias, 129
  after police shootings, 131
  police shootings and rarity of violent,
    132, 170–71
  protests differences from, 131
  protests similarities with, 130–31
  as routine breaks, 152
  severe background conditions of, 129
  system racism in, 129, 130–31, 132,
    133–34, 170–71
  VDA use in, 212
US. *See* United States
us-them boundaries, 44, 79–80, 122, 124,
  131, 137
  at Ferguson, 141–42, 149–50

vandalism. *See also* property damage
  anarchism and, 28
video data
  on armed robberies, 16–17, 213
  emotion expressions and, 191–92, 198
  on Kehl protest, 32–33
  on Pittsburgh G20 protest, 73, 118
  on protest marches, 9, 32
  on Rostock G8 protest, 67–68
  on Seattle WTO protest, 84–85
  triangulation and, 197

video data analysis (VDA), 191–92
  analytic procedure of, 211
  in protest violence studies, 196
  in robberies, 214
  in uprisings studies, 212
Vietnam War, 19–20, 65
  statistics on, 60
Vietnam War Pentagon demonstration,
    1967, 111
  forward panic and excessive violence
    in, 111–12
  loss-of-control path, 59
  McNamara and, 60
  numbers in, 60
  operational command at, 60–61
  police mismanagement at, 60–62
  powerless feeling at, 62
  spatial incursion at, 53, 61–62
  temporal sequence of, 112, 115
  territorial boundaries, 112
  tolerant police strategy at, 61–62
violence
  background factors of, 13
  collective behavior and, 79–80
  Collins on, 23, 107–8, 171–72
  communication problems and, 14–15, 87
  context factors compared to situational
    dynamics, 10
  defined, 22
  degree used, 16
  emotional dynamics and, 16, 33
  escalated force policing and, 37, 41
  escalation signs and, 14–15, 75–78
  fear of, 187
  human behavior avoidance of, 35
  human behavior nature of, 35
  inhibition threshold for, 122, 182–83
  interactions and paths to, 14f, 14–15, 43
  Kehl protest expected, 6
  media on property damage as, 31
  motivations for, 7
  perception of, 22–23
  physical contact and, 53, 100–1
  physical interpersonal violence as, 23
  police mismanagement and,
    14–15, 44–49

police:protester ratio and, 82–83
preventative measures for, 17–18, 24–25
property damage and, 14–15,
    22–23, 29–31
at Rostock G8 protest, 3, 4–5
situations end for, 107
spatial incursions and, 14–15, 54
structural, 22–23
tension and fear before, 13, 33, 41
tolerant police strategy and, 41, 42
violent few and outbreaks of, 32
violence, end of, 107
  Collins on duration, 107–8
  screaming and, 108–9
  shouting for, 108
violence, reasoning problems for
  motivations in peaceful marches
    and, 7–8
  situational dynamics and, 7–8
violence triggers, 99
  being outnumbered, 82–83, 102
  emotional dynamics and, 97
  falling down, 101
  police-protester line break ups, 100
  weak victim, 103
violent clashes
  avoiding, 149, 151, 170–71
  background factors during
    uprisings, 133
  black bloc activists rare, 79–80
  at Rostock G8 protest, 3, 4, 55
violent few, 13–14, 27
  agents provocateurs as, 43
  as media scapegoats, 31
  motivations of, 28
  physical violence root cause, 31
  powerless feeling of, 26–27
  violence outbreaks and, 32

Washington DC, 1967. *See* Vietnam War
    Pentagon demonstration, 1967
Washington DC IMF protest, 2000,
    98–99, 178
Washington Peace March, 1971, 74–75
water cannon trucks, 4, 45, 56–57, 76–77,
    92–93, 95–96, 127, 150

weak victim, as violence trigger, 103
emotional dominance and, 103–4
at Rostock G8 protest, 103
screaming and, 109
Western democracies, 27
anarchists and black bloc, 26
culture of, 104, 181
Della Porta on non-violent protest
events in, 195
escalated force policing,
in 1960s, 37
police strategies in, 183
protest marches in, 6–7

Westgate Mall, in Nairobi, Kenya terrorist
attack, 190
World Bank, GJM target of, 21
World Trade Organization (WTO). *See
also* Seattle WTO protest, 1999
GJM target of, 21, 81–84

YouTube videos
on armed robberies, 191, 213
on Rostock G8 protest and
Ferguson, 9, 191
situational dynamics studies use of,
190–91, 209–10